History Films, Women, and Freud's Uncanny

T0334675

University of Texas Press   Austin

HISTORY FILMS, WOMEN, AND FREUD'S UNCANNY

Susan E. Linville

Library of Congress Cataloging-in-Publication Data

Linville, Susan E. (Susan Elizabeth), 1949–
    History films, women, and Freud's uncanny / Susan E. Linville.—
1st ed.
        p.   cm.
Includes filmography.
Includes bibliographical references and index.
    ISBN 0-292-70260-4 (cloth : alk. paper) — ISBN 0-292-70269-8
(pbk. : alk. paper)
    1. Women in motion pictures.   2. Sex role in motion pictures.
3. Historical films—United States—History and criticism.   4. Psychoanalysis and motion pictures.   I. Title.
    PN1995.9.W6L56   2004
    791.43′658—dc22
                                                    2003025191

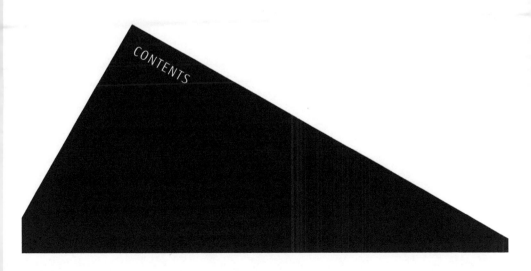

CONTENTS

Much of the research for this book was made possible by a Faculty Fellowship provided by the University of Colorado at Denver, and I want to thank the institution for its support. I also wish to thank the UCD English Department for providing course release time, and Brad Mudge, the department's resourceful chair, for finding creative ways to promote faculty research and for offering sage advice on an early version of the book. Other members of the department were generous with their time and intelligence, as well, and they have my gratitude for their insights into everything from Beetle Bailey to Shakespeare. (I alone am responsible, however, for dubious uses I may have made of the bard.) In particular, Elihu Pearlman, Jake York, and Joanne Addison were generous with ideas related to my project, while Pompa Banerjee, Nancy Ciccone, and Gillian Silverman provided close scrutiny of the manuscript and astute feedback at various stages of its development. Among the present and former students who inspired me, Paola "Alex" Arvizu, Tony Garcia, Sheigla Hartman, Mila Labudovic, and Matt Wigdahl deserve special mention. My dear colleague and husband, Kent Casper, offered the most support of all, in every conceivable way, and our collaboration has been the most rewarding of my life.

Beyond UCD, I owe a considerable debt to Diane Waldman for her intellectual generosity and expert advice. My gratitude also goes to the University of Texas Press, and especially Jim Burr, for their continuing commitment to my work, and to the two anonymous readers for the press, whose input made an appreciable difference in the quality of the finished product. Additionally, I would like to thank Bill Johnston, a POW during World War II, whose memories of the Battle of the Bulge helped me understand the importance of *A Midnight Clear*.

Two chapters of this book appeared elsewhere in different form. An

ACKNOWLEDGMENTS

earlier version of Chapter 4 was first published in *Cinema Journal* 39, no. 2 (2000), and a version of Chapter 3 first appeared in *Women's Studies: An Interdisciplinary Journal* 31, no. 1 (January-February 2002) and is reproduced by permission of Taylor & Francis, Inc., http://www.routledge-ny.com. I gratefully acknowledge these sources. Film stills from *The Street* (Stern-Film), *Courage Under Fire* (Twentieth Century Fox), and *Nixon* (Hollywood Pictures) are reproduced here courtesy of the Museum of Modern Art/Film Stills Archive, New York. Additional credits appear in the filmography. Finally, *Christina's World* is reproduced by permission of MOMA, Scala, and Art Resource, New York; *Whistler's Mother* is reproduced by permission of Erich Lessing and Art Resource, New York.

History Films, Women, and Freud's Uncanny

Missing History

Near the beginning of William Shakespeare's play *The Tempest,* Prospero instructs his daughter Miranda for the first time about his past and, in passing, about her own. She has been watching a harrowing sea storm and shipwreck, a physically harmless piece of magic that Prospero has created to rectify history, but one so overwhelming that Miranda is quick with sympathy for its human victims. The tempest and Prospero's inquiries about what Miranda remembers of her early childhood, what "house or person," prompt the young woman to ask two questions, queries which Carol Gilligan astutely paraphrases as "Why all the suffering?" and "Where are the women?" [1] Prospero's reply reflects his interest in justifying his present actions as remedies for past injustices—"what's past is prologue," as his traitorous brother Antonio will later say—but as Gilligan notes, Prospero's account fails to do justice to Miranda's curiosity, memory, and desire. In the course of the play, Miranda herself learns to forget her own initial questions, and her education about her father's past forms the groundwork of her forgetting. Her future marriage (and, extradiegetically, that of ill-fated Princess Elizabeth, daughter of James I) is celebrated in another illusion staged by Prospero, a wedding masque that dramatizes Miranda's regenerative role through fertility imagery of the goddess Ceres while stressing her function as the ligature binding feuding political factions. Yet the marriage that Prospero arranges, though it recaptures and consolidates political power and identity, comes at the expense of Miranda's grasp of a history that encompasses women, their sense of home, and their ties to each other.

In a similar fashion, the narration of U.S. history through cinematic illusion was a paramount interest of Hollywood moviemakers in the closing

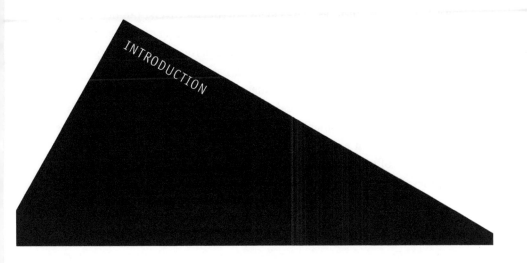

INTRODUCTION

decade of the twentieth century, as evidenced by their production of numerous films concerning World War II, the American presidency, and other history-based topics. Yet rarely did these films find compelling answers to the questions "Where are the women?" and "Why all the suffering?" Film scholars in turn focused their attention on Hollywood's drawing on history for its subject matter, and they generated original, highly illuminating studies on the topic, including Robert A. Rosenstone's *Visions of the Past: The Challenge of Film to Our Idea of History* (1995), Vivian Sobchack's anthology *The Persistence of History: Cinema, Television, and the Modern Event* (1996), Robert Burgoyne's *Film Nation: Hollywood Looks at U.S. History* (1997), and Marcia Landy's anthology *The Historical Film: History and Memory in Media* (2000), as well as influential work by Fredric Jameson, Hayden White, and others. Moreover, pioneering feminist film scholars, such as Susan Jeffords and Lucy Fischer, made critical inroads in demonstrating the disproportionate burden of blame women and the feminine have borne in film narratives that seek both to reflect and deflect masculine trauma in the wake of war.[2] Yet where women's history is concerned, a spectrum of critical issues remains underexamined, underacknowledged, and underexplored.

By taking Miranda's questions as a central focus, this book aims to address some of these gaps. More precisely, I propose to examine a series of significant cinematic depictions of twentieth-century American history—films from the 1990s whose subjects range from World War II, to the cold war, to contemporary techno-warfare and globalization—in order to chart the narrative and aesthetic means by which they both evoke and elide perspectives on the changing place of women. As will become apparent, I am especially interested in exploring the uncanny as a complex psychological and aesthetic mode that both subtly and overtly informs the gender portrayals these films create, as well as in identifying the diverse political visions the uncanny can serve. These range from the forgetting of women's multifaceted historical trajectory—and especially the role of the women's movement—in the name of a nostalgic ideal of nation, to the radical erosion of the very gender identities on which that retrograde ideal depends.

To be sure, although I contend that Hollywood cinema often replays a pattern of erasure of women's place in history that is at least as old as *The Tempest*, it is worth emphasizing that, according to Jameson, Hollywood history films of recent decades do not confine the erasure to women's history; they extend it to history per se. That is, in his words, the genre of the historical film "with its surface sheen of a period fashion reality [offers] a formal compensation for the enfeeblement of historicity in our own time, and as it were a glossy fetish in the service of that unsatisfied craving."[3] Although this insight is provocative, Jameson's development of it overlooks significant gendered dynamics within a larger process.

One of these is gender's function as the "glossy fetish" par excellence through which history is jettisoned—for example, in films that honor, elevate, and celebrate iconic versions of women (as symbols of a nation, as mothers, and as first ladies) within narrative trajectories that deracinate and derealize them as historical entities. A second and related dynamic, previously mentioned, is the creation of historical erasure within the aesthetic mode of the uncanny or unhomey, a mode that resembles the process of fetishization insofar as it relies on repression and forgetting for its effects, yet that also activates the dread, anxiety, and identity destructuration that a meeting with the repressed can arouse. In this context, uncanny moments often reduce women to eerie dolls and abject monsters, beings stirring repressed memories of both womb and tomb. As I also intend to demonstrate, however, the uncanny can alternatively serve as a springboard to unconventional cultural critique and to the engendering of less masculinist depictions of the past.

In a further, related dynamic, the evasion of women's history is implicated in the management of other social groups and social histories in recent films, a dynamic that, again, eerily echoes elements from *The Tempest*, with its reliance on Miranda as a conduit for justifying a patrilineal, heterosexual, Eurocentric hierarchy. That is, films about the past glimpse at histories of cultural groups for whom the ambiguously gendered Ariel, the powerful Algerian "witch" Sycorax, and her feared son Caliban can be seen as stand-ins, yet often shape and wield them in the name of protecting a politicized ideal of womanhood.[4] An additional important example is the gender-specific means by which profit-motivated, image-generating corporations provide women—like the fetishized Rachel in the cult film *Blade Runner* (1982)—with implanted memories that allow them limited power and self-representation; memories often designed, as in Rachel's case, in a way that supplants women's actual histories and belies the larger reality of their "home." Finally, in a dynamic related to all of these, there is the pattern in which women form structuring narrative absences, in the manner of the "fallen" woman Hero in *Much Ado about Nothing*. That is, a woman is metaphorically buried alive, and then ultimately returned, redeemed, or resurrected, her narrative absence having structured the resolutions of men's conflicts over power, identity, and hierarchy, the very conflicts that, as often as not, made her "death" necessary in the first place.

While such broad generalizations as these forecast some of my key concerns, they also beg for further exemplification and explanation, and perhaps no films better illustrate the patterns in question here than the classics of the 1950s, specifically *Singin' in the Rain* (Gene Kelly and Stanley Donen, 1952), *The Searchers* (John Ford, 1956), and *Vertigo* (Alfred Hitchcock, 1958). The latter two, along with two films from the decade on which my study focuses—the ostensibly more equitable 1990s—provide especially revealing examples in the context of the present study and will serve as entry points to my larger subject.[5] The 1990s films I shall consider here are the much-debated, wildly popular *Forrest Gump* (Robert Zemeckis, 1994) and the politically provocative *Bulworth* (Warren Beatty, 1998).

Lacking the patina of gender and ethnic equality that characterizes much Hollywood cinema of the 1990s, *The Searchers* and *Vertigo* provide models that are the more telling because of their relatively more transparent evocation and elision of women's history as a means of managing a range of intractable problems from the past. Generically disparate, these two films nonetheless share concerns with traumatic history and conflicted identity boundaries, centrally symbolized in female characters. Set in post–Civil War Texas, 1868–1873, *The Searchers* narrates a quest to recover Debbie Edwards (Natalie Wood), the niece of embittered ex-Confederate soldier Ethan Edwards (John Wayne), by Ethan and Martin Pawley (Jeffrey Hunter), her adoptive brother. Debbie's captor, a Comanche chief named Scar (Henry Brandon in "racial drag"), bears responsibility for the killing of her family and the rape of her mother, whom Ethan loved and desired; when Debbie comes of age, Scar takes her as a wife. Sexually and racially "contaminated" in Ethan's eyes, her identity becomes the subject of fierce conflict between him and Marty, with her life and possible reintegration into the "Texican" community of her childhood hanging in the balance. The battle over who Debbie *is* is played out in the sublime and sacred Native American landscape of Monument Valley, and is also powerfully embedded in images of archways, cave openings, and rock cleavages, uncanny formations that visually rhyme the earth as mother, the sexualized female body, and the film's various thresholds of "home," from the settler's homestead to the native's teepee.

Within this symbolically charged world, Debbie functions as the displaced and recovered, fractured then healed, symbol of the uncanny home that makes Ethan as hero possible. And through Ethan's quest for and recovery of Debbie, the film evokes and seeks to contain not only the bloody history of conquest and civil war that gave birth to the nation in the nineteenth century, but also anxieties about race, gender, and miscegenation born of the 1950s, fears exacerbated by *Brown vs. Board of Education of Topeka* (1954) and the school desegregation it mandated.[6] To achieve symbolic mastery of this legacy, however, the film conspicuously sacrifices Debbie's own desire and coherence. That is, although Debbie initially refuses rescue and insists that her home is with the Comanches, barely escaping Ethan's bullets in the process, in the film's climax she readily agrees to leave with Marty when he sneaks into her teepee, and after Ethan's dramatic recognition of her and change of heart, is spared and taken "home." Brian Henderson rightly contends, "The text itself rides roughshod over Debbie by making her change her mind . . . a conspicuously unmotivated act in a film that elsewhere supplies too many motives."[7]

If Debbie's captivity story lacks crucial motivation, strikingly, the film itself calls attention *not* to this absence but to the missing causality in a secondary story, that of her counterpart "Look" (Native American Beulah Archuletta), the ample-bodied Comanche wife whom Marty unwittingly acquires while doing trade with her family. After some terrible humor at her expense, Ethan and Marty impel Look to go find Scar; when the men eventually catch up with her, she has been killed by U.S. soldiers on an apparent terrorist raid. Her death prompts Marty's poignant questions about her destiny and desires, whether she sought to warn Scar's people or to find Debbie for him. As he calls attention both to her innocence and to the lack of satisfactory answers, the scene reveals her body lying in a teepee, its entrance a significant iteration of the threshold motif. In this moment, *The Searchers* comes as close to a direct confrontation with U.S. destruction of the Native American population and culture as it ever dares.

Yet in her story, too, there are crucial displacements, shaped by the fact that *looking* and *looking back* are defining prerogatives for Ethan—sources of unspeakable sexual knowledge and obsessive self-motivation. Hard on the heels of this scene centered on Look, the sight of traumatized white women and girls, recovered from the Comanches by the army, prompts Ethan's famous look back in horror, an act that epitomizes the motivation for his quest even as it enforces the film's shift in focus from Look as victim to the Euro-Americans. In keeping with this symbolic logic, Look is not just a casualty of Ethan's quest; like Lot's wife, she is punished for looking back, but in this case, looking back at the white man's behest. Moreover, she becomes both a sacrificial object of Ethan's obsessive retrospection and a woman whose death substitutes for Debbie's, in yet another displacement that makes Ethan as hero possible.

Janet Walker forcefully argues that traumatic Westerns such as *The Searchers* "represent the massacre of American Indians *as* the massacre of settlers" and thereby "represent indirectly a historical reality they cannot really justify: the conquest of Native Americans and the appropriation of their land."[8] My reading of the functions of Look and Debbie identifies the critical role of Native and Euro-American female characters in effecting these problematic transpositions. Reinforcing this view is the broader historical resonance of the film's deployment of Look and Debbie as symbols. A large Native American woman, similar in build to Look, served as a European and Euro-American symbol of America as early as the sixteenth century. She was sometimes known as L'Amérique or the Indian Princess and was often portrayed wearing a feathered headdress and perched on an alligator-like reptile. A precursor of Lady Liberty, the Indian Princess became slimmer and increasingly Europeanized by the time of the American Revolution, and in the course of the nineteenth century (and well before Disney's Princess Pocahontas), she evolved a persona with the look of a beauty queen.[9] By the time of *The Searchers*, she is movie star Natalie Wood, costumed as a squaw who anachronistically wears lipstick.

Like *The Searchers*, *Vertigo* too reveals how Hollywood historiography has depicted and situated female characters in ways that simultaneously call up and conceal broader constellations of historically determined problems, especially those that emerge from the nation's complex ethnic, racial, and economic legacy. It reveals, as well, how such historiography tends to evoke and disguise these problems through a heroine constructed to fit a hero-centered narrative. At times, the process is not one of reducing a complex set of identity differences to the difference of gender, but rather a practice of voiding women's identity of its complex historical, ethnic, and class specificity and thereby effecting other forms of evocation and erasure as well. In fact, *Vertigo*, as a product of the era nostalgically viewed as America's "golden age," offers an especially illuminating instance of this practice.

A fictional overlay on a fictional overlay, the film centers on the deception of Scottie (James Stewart), a former detective who is duped into thinking he is protecting the beautiful blonde Madeleine, ostensible descendant and double of the mad Carlotta Valdez, from insanity and suicide. Although the film represents the ancestral Carlotta as a "real," aristocratic-looking person and part of local San Francisco history, she is in fact a fictionalized double of the historical wife of Maximilian (1832–1867), archduke of Austria, a man installed as emperor of Mexico in 1864 under the mistaken belief that he had been elected, and later, despite his wife's vigorous and wide-reaching efforts to prevent it, executed when he refused to abdicate. As a result of his execution and her grief over his death, this Carlota (so spelled) spent the remaining sixty years of her life living in a chateau in her home country of Belgium in a state of madness.

The complex intersection of Mexican, European, Native American, and U.S. history that the film's construction of "Madeleine" draws on need not be fully recounted here, but the "bleaching" of identity that the film and its protagonist execute deserves commentary, since it reflects how history is deracinated through the person of the woman on the border. The historical fact that Carlota was the daughter of Belgium's Leopold I in effect legitimizes the film's creation of a blonde Spanish woman—congruent with Hitchcock's and 1950s North American fantasy ideals—even though the film's Carlotta Valdez lived in a California that, though part of Mexico, was home to few actual descendants of the Spaniards. Judy (Kim Novak), the woman hired to play Madeleine, must herself be transformed into the era's and director's northern European blonde ideal, and that ideal, like the film's Carlotta, symbolically exists on multiple borders. These include the boundaries between respectability and illegitimacy, nobility and destitution, the U.S. and Mexico, an interchangeable past and present—but especially between reality and illusion, sanity and delusion, the living and the dead.

The setting and aesthetic look of the film, which draw on the protosurrealist work of Giorgio de Chirico, reinforces this sense, and as Helen Gardner notes, de Chirico's work takes inspiration from the historical past, infusing its locales with "a mood of intense and mysterious melancholy . . . a foreboding sense of departure and of *a time long past yet always present*" (emphasis added).[10] Hitchcock replaces the squares, arcades, and palaces of Roman and Renaissance Italy seen in de Chirico's early work, and the towers of his *Tower Series,* with shots of the Golden Gate Bridge, the Palace of the Legion of Honor, the mission at San Juan Batista and other settings, relying on framings, points of view, and embellishments to make the film's visual architecture uncannily resemble de Chirico's. Hitchcock's handling of mise-en-scène evokes, spatializes, and reconfigures the layers of Spanish,

Mexican, and Anglo history in a manner that complements Judy/Madeleine/Carlotta's function, and together these elements represent the past that haunts the film's tragic "all-American" protagonist. The history to which they allude becomes the mirror of his haunted, fragmented, modernist inner self. If history is what haunts us—and is therefore "what hurts," in Jameson's famous formulation—then perhaps we should speak of two histories here. One is Scottie's psychological history, the basis of the film's manifest content—to play on Freud's ideas of manifest and latent dream content—and the other is the social, ethnic, and gender history that informs the film's latent content and its "political unconscious" (in Jameson's words); that is, the "colorful" past before it was reduced to Madeleine's platinum blonde swirl and pale gray suit. Thus, just as *The Searchers* transforms Debbie into a fetishized substitute for history, *Vertigo* homogenizes the past through the fetish of Madeleine, and both women serve reductively subsumptive functions.

More recently, in a 1990s film that is ostensibly more "about" history, Jenny (Robin Wright), Forrest Gump's childhood sweetheart in the film that bears his name, serves both as a resonant symbol of a key facet of women's history—the kind of abuse and suffering that helped motivate the second-wave feminist movement of the 1960s and 1970s—and, simultaneously, as an example of how Hollywood cinema conjures up then empties out women's history in order to serve socioeconomic ends not at all women's own.[11] In a visually striking scene set in the 1970s, Jenny and Forrest (Tom Hanks), the film's simpleminded, picaresque hero, return to the small farmhouse in Alabama where her "white trash" father had physically and sexually abused her as a small child. Releasing years of pent up rage about what she endured at his hands—and at the hands of most of the men in her adult life as well—she throws first her sandals and then all the stones she can find at the empty house, shattering its windows, and finally collapses in a heap in front of the dreaded "home" that she never fully managed to escape, despite her engagement with what the film presents as counterculture rebellion, including protest against the Vietnam War. Through a juxtaposition of the emotionally crippled Jenny with the house, the sequence evokes *Christina's World* (figure I.1), Andrew Wyeth's 1948 painting of Christina Olson, a woman who was physically crippled from the time of her childhood on.

It thereby heightens the pathos of Jenny's unfulfilled dreams by raising them to the more general level of a resonant symbol of a longing for and si-

Fig. I.1. Andrew Wyeth (b. 1917) © copyright. *Christina's World,* 1948, tempera on gessoed panel, 32¼" x 47¾", Museum of Modern Art, New York.

multaneous exclusion from "home"—a move that mirrors Terrence Malick's citation of the painting in *Days of Heaven* (1978) as well. Although Jenny, unlike Christina, faces the viewer, the film's quotation of Wyeth is nonetheless reinforced by Jenny's pose, her slender limbs, and her childhood closeness with the formerly leg brace–bound Gump, whom she often urged to run to safety.[12] It is also reinforced by the shot's ambiguous blend of loss and longing and its complication of attitudes toward America's so-called golden age, ambiguity counterpointed in the original by Wyeth's infusion of his realist style with a feeling of abstract expressionist introspection and a sense of home as a place that is always already unhomey, inherently its own eerie opposite.[13] A few scenes later, Jenny is tied to an even more recognizable, historically resonant American symbol: she and an image of the Statue of Liberty—associated here with the celebration of the American bicentennial in 1976—are juxtaposed when it appears on a television in Forrest's home, and Jenny holds her hand up in a pose that echoes, with a difference, the raised arm of Liberty.

Yet, even though the film visually generalizes Jenny's situation, it fails to acknowledge the ways in which women's history in the 1960s and 1970s is centrally about collective efforts to solve the problems that her antinostalgic story instantiates. The film's only direct allusion to the women's movement comes when an African-American woman reporter asks Forrest, now a celebrity runner, why he is spending his days traversing the nation. Is he running for world peace or for women's rights? she queries. Although he provides no real answer—"I just felt like running," he claims—the film's visuals do when the sequence cuts to a shot of him running in a logo tee shirt on which both "Nike" and its ubiquitous swoosh are emblazoned, the ostensible tokens of Jenny, since his Nike running shoes were her gift to him. In the logic of images that jumps from *Christina's World* to the Statue of Liberty to Nike—all tied to Jenny—the film advances Nike as the unabashedly commercial culmination point; in context, the preeminent symbol of freedom and a synonym of the American nation, borne by Forrest as he crisscrosses the country's beautiful vistas—Monument Valley among them—moving to a film score of exuberantly rhythmic rock music, while Jenny herself catches news of him on yet another television, as she waits tables in a restaurant.

At the level of character motivation, Forrest's running has been spurred by Jenny's departure from his home; she had sought refuge there from the excesses and disillusionment of the disco scene, but then felt compelled to move on, leaving behind the gift of Nikes (a product he happily endorses as "the best gift anyone could get in the wide world"). Nonetheless, the central motivation for the symbolism is unmistakable. What here almost literally boots out women's history generally, and even upstages Jenny's personal story as Forrest's soul mate, is a consumer emblem in a virtual television infomercial. More precisely, what both displaces women's history and serves as a synonym for American freedom is a multinational corporation with a notorious history of paying slave wages to its employees—overwhelmingly women—working in sweatshops located in Vietnam, Indonesia, and China.[14] (Cynthia Enloe's comments about the militarization of shoes heightens the irony here: "A pair of sneakers is militarized to the extent that the women who are sewing those sneakers [in China, Indonesia, or Vietnam] have their wages kept low because major brand corporations and their factory contractors hire former military men as their managers, call on local militarized security forces to suppress workers' organizing, or ally with governments who define the absence of women workers' independent organizing as necessary for 'national security.'")[15] Finally, in *Forrest Gump*, "Nike," a female-gendered symbol of victory in ancient Greece, no longer bears any trace of its own history either.

To appreciate the depth of the irony of the configuration of questions and images that this sequence contains, it is useful to go back to the historical record and specifically to the position paper circulated at the event that was the inaugural public act of second-wave feminist protest, the "No More Miss America" demonstration held in August 1968. Contrary to caricatures of late-1960s feminism, this paper is neither theoretically unsophisticated nor essentializing, but is instead a complex, nonreductionist assessment of the intersections of sexism, racism, consumer culture, and militarism.[16] It sharply criticizes not only the pageant's objectification of women but also the lack of racial and ethnic diversity among its winners, including its lack of "a *true* Miss America—an American Indian." Further, the position paper indicts the routine use of Miss America as a "walking commercial for the Pageant's sponsors," who plugs their products on television and promotional tours, and it censures the ways in which she was used to promote U.S. involvement in the Vietnam War, where, as the "highlight of her reign," she was sent "to pep-talk our husbands, fathers, sons and boyfriends into dying and killing with a better spirit. She personifies the 'unstained patriotic American womanhood our boys are fighting for.'"[17] In sum, the position paper's larger vision offers a framework that could elucidate the connections among the film's African-American woman reporter, the Vietnamese woman who might have made the running shoes Hanks wears, and Jenny herself. That is to say, it offers exactly what *Forrest Gump* does not, a telling critical perspective on the *intersecting* historical problems affecting women during the era traversed by the film. Nike's mid-1990's ad campaign, based on images of women's empowerment, makes the ironies noted here all the more acute.

If Chicano and Mexican-American histories are simultaneously evoked and erased through an aestheticized blonde ideal in Hitchcock's film, and the history of the women's movement is both conjured up and concealed in *Forrest Gump,* African-American women's history is alluded to and elided through an ideal of young, black, womanly beauty in Beatty's *Bulworth.* Nina (Halle Berry), the woman in question, exists as an amalgamation of those qualities that serve the needs of theme, plot, and character instead of as a coherently conceived dramatis persona, and in this regard she resembles Debbie in *The Searchers,* Jenny in *Forrest Gump,* and women characters in numerous historically based films.[18] Specifically, Nina combines roles as (1) a hip-hop woman; (2) an assassin's assistant, hired to help kill U.S. Senator Bulworth (Beatty) by a stereotyped Italian crime figure, who is being paid by none other than the despairing Bulworth himself; (3) an exquisitely attractive, very much younger love interest for Bulworth, a man who is unaware that she is trying to set him up and who develops second thoughts about dying; (4) an articulate Marxist political savant whose mother was a Black Panther; and finally, (5) a family-identified daughter and sister, who agrees to set Bulworth up so that she can pay off her brother's debt to a local gang leader and thereby save his life.

It is possible to see this portrait as an improvement over the consignment of African-American women and girls to what Jacquie Jones calls the "accusatory space" of the black ghetto film—an emphatically sidelined position that serves as a reproach to young black females for the troubled lives of young black males. "Somehow," Jones explains, "these girls seemed to me to exist in the space of the accused. After all, according to the news of the early eighties, it was those teenage, female-headed households that produced those boys."[19] Yet, if Nina's diverse traits and less marginal position, along with Berry's fine performance, potentially make for a more complex and less stereotypical portrait, the film itself fails to connect all the character dots. Nina articulates an astute political analysis of a host of problems besetting contemporary African Americans, but only in a single scene is she given this strong political voice, and it is a scene that centers on a conversation with Bulworth in the romantically lit backseat of a limo.

Nostalgically reflecting on a time when young black people knew who Huey Newton was, Bulworth asks her, "Why do you think there are no more black leaders?" Nina's response makes it clear that she knows not only who Huey Newton was but also the impact of the assassination of black leaders on American politics. As she develops her answer, she also explains how, in contemporary America, issues of race and class merge, how the increasing globalization of capital has moved jobs away from U.S. urban centers into the third world, undermining the urban black political base, and how consumerism militates against the self-sacrifice that social progress requires. Further, she spotlights how the present-day increase in media monopolies curtails cultural opportunities and limits the expression of alternative visions.[20] The film would have us believe, however, that at the time its events take place—the 1996 elections—well-publicized debates about the culturally specific forms of sexism in the Black Panther Party, in gangster rap, in ghetto-based films, and in the idea of the 1995 Million Man March would register not so much as a blip on Nina's highly informed political consciousness, or that she would revere the name of Huey Newton and the memory of her own Black Panther mother but fail even to mention women such as Angela Davis, Elaine Brown, or bell hooks. The scene thus affords a variant on the kind of forgetting of women's historical interconnections that is played out in Miranda's history lesson in *The Tempest*'s second scene. By the end of her speech, Nina has become not so much the voice of the black community or a credible female emblem of black nationalism, as a kind of ventriloquist's doll, reciting the white filmmaker's male-centered view of black history in America.

If Nina's voice nevertheless provides lessons in history and politics for Bulworth, who for once is nearly silent (but later appropriates Nina's lesson in a media appearance), it is she herself who is finally reduced to near silence by the film's end. At this point, Bulworth wants her to follow him out of her family's ghetto home and into the media spotlight. She does, and the two kiss seconds before he is assassinated by the interest group (insurance) that his new political stance has most pointedly offended. In the moment before the assassination, the romance plot comes dangerously close to reducing Nina not only to a silent love interest, but, in effect, to something like the prone position that Stokely Carmichael notoriously said was the only one open to women in the Black Panther Party. Specifically, Nina reassures the racially insecure sixty-year-old Bulworth by saying "you're my nigger" just before their last kiss. She thereby confirms his "black" masculinity, creating a dissonant echo of the kind of confirmation that some Black Panther leaders, motivated by a specific history of castrations, emasculation, and lynchings, had demanded of black women; along with it (in the revealing vocabulary of the film's preamble), Nina confirms Bulworth's distinctive ability as a politician able to get the populace "aroused."[21] In this way, Nina is defined more by the requirements of Beatty's politics and plot—and by Bulworth's black-phallus-envy-driven developmental trajectory—than by internal coherence or by black women's historical experience vis-à-vis white men in America.[22] (Bulworth's assassination further doubles him with black men; in this case, with the martyrs whom he has admired and sought partly to emulate.)

The requirements of Beatty's plot and politics are also reflected by his desire to make Bulworth into an often comic but ultimately perceptive white version of a homey or homeboy, a part with a dress code he adopts while he is in Nina's neighborhood, where he also plays a kind of Shakespearean fool. To be sure, there has probably never been a more unhomey homey than Beatty. Yet his odd presence and behavior underscore the *unheimlich* (unhomey) aspects of Nina's neighborhood as home, and to the film's credit, it conveys this point in some telling effects. Nina's extended family lives in a house that is warmly lit and comfortable on the inside but surrounded by dangers that also make it seem like a prison. Strangely enough, those dangers take the shape of little African-American boys of five or six, children who, along with slightly older boys, "soldier" surreal, steely blue nighttime streets, packing guns and dealing drugs in a virtual third-world setting. The boys are so young that, when they threaten Bulworth, he can easily buy them off with ice cream cones, a humorous move that converts them back to children and ironically spares him from Nina's bullets as well.

For her part, Nina brings Bulworth to her home to set him up for the hit. When one of her family members, not knowing her aim, admonishes her not to become involved with this white man and to remember the destructive consequences of a similar involvement for her mother, Nina protests that she has something else in mind, and at this point, she still does. But the narrative also recalls an old pattern of African-American women offering sexual appeasement to white men in order to protect their families from harm. Safiya Bukhari-Alston's historical perspective illuminates this issue. Focusing on the ways in which the legacy of slavery shapes ideas of gender, she explains, "Since [Black men] had been stripped of their manhood in every way but the ability to 'pleasure' women and make babies, the sexual act soon became the measure by which the Black man measured his manhood. The Black women worked right alongside the Black man in the field and she worked in the Master's house. The Black man could not defend or protect his family, while in most cases the Black woman was the one who defended or protected the family from the slavemaster's wrath by any means necessary." [23] The film, then, glimpses historically and racially specific forms of literal unhominess, rooted in the black slave woman's role in the master's home and the white man's place in hers, yet it also romances away that legacy's relationship to the surreal, third-world quality of contemporary ghetto life.

What the four examples just examined share, in addition to a pattern of displacing women's history, are diverse, historically specific forms of uncanniness. That is, all four films envision versions of the home—and by extension, particular images of the nation—as an unheimlich (strange, weird, or disquieting) place whose strangeness stems from past events that the narratives aim to master. Moreover, each seeks mastery precisely through a complex, equivocal, reductive symbolization of women. In each case, women become identified with sites of conflict—from the thresholds of the Western homestead, teepee, and landscape in *The Searchers,* to Judy/Madeleine/Carlotta's various haunts in *Vertigo,* and from the abandoned farmhouse of Jenny's childhood, remembered as the dreaded site of abuse in *Forrest Gump,* to Nina's neighborhood in *Bulworth,* a place turned inside out, in her view, by the globalization of capital but also made strange by the presence of Bulworth himself. And in each case, it is the process of *not* telling women's histories that makes possible women's deployment in these narratives as symbolic answers, identified with these sites, to the needs of narrative and hence national identity. Yet just as women's lack of distinct histories and their resulting fragmentary status are preconditions for their iconic functions in "solving" problems of identity rooted in the past, so, too, are they part and parcel of women's obverse roles, as signs of identity's mutability, incoherence, and uncanniness. In short, besides being intended to help solidify ideas of home and nation, women in history films can serve as synonyms for a legacy of division, displacement, and ambivalence.

If this formulation of the unhomey seems a closed loop, a further shift in historical perspective can lead to a view of how these same sites crystallize the intractable, often overlooked unhominess of the home for women, whose place traditionalists claim that it should be. As will become evident, the trajectory of the theory of the uncanny, from its origins in Freud, through feminist revisions of the 1970s and 1980s, and on to more recent cultural studies reworkings, is one in which a problematic concept has been recuperated, fostering alternative understandings of narrative and aesthetics along with powerful critiques of standard narrative practices. At stake is an expansion of Freud's original concepts of the unheimlich into an extremely valuable framework for conceptualizing the historical and symbolic positioning of women in film. In the chapters ahead, I shall explore the concept of the historical unheimlich in greater detail and use it to bring various problems of film and history into focus. My goal here, however, is to introduce basic tenets of theories of the uncanny and to provide a brief overview of their development during the last century.

Theories of the Unheimlich

Although Ernst Jentsch published a medicopsychological study of the uncanny in 1906, Sigmund Freud's extraordinary 1919 essay, "The 'Uncanny'," which cites Jentsch's work, represents the canonical opening volley in debates about the concept as an aesthetic category and a psychological phenomenon. Defining the uncanny as "that class of the terrifying which leads back to something long known to us, once very familiar," Freud posits the unheimlich as a universal intrapsychic experience (albeit one to which he feels himself virtually immune), a phenomenon rooted in repressed memory, as well as an aesthetic category designating figurations opposite to "what is beautiful, attractive and sublime."[24] Further, Freud famously explains that "*heimlich* is a word the meaning of which develops towards an ambivalence, until it finally coincides with its opposite, *unheimlich*."[25] Thus the word *heimlich* itself conveys an ambiguous sense of home, configuring it as a site that is cozy and comfortable yet also secret, covered, best left unseen, and therefore threatening and strange. If *canny* and *uncanny*, as English counterparts to *heimlich* and *unheimlich*, do not precisely convey these same home-centered meanings, they nonetheless point toward a similar ambivalence and synonymity in their meanings of *clever* and *too clever*. That is, like the words *heimlich* and *unheimlich*, they jointly enact the potentially frightening interchangeability, doubling, and lack of clear boundaries that they denote. Although such uncertainty is potentially terrifying in life, as Freud indicates, in art and literature, aestheticization can render such ambivalence *enjoyably* terrifying and can also mask it altogether, in effect rendering it un-uncanny.

Further, the word *canny* possesses a denotative meaning that harmonizes with Freud's theory of the origin of all unheimlich experience. Specifically, in Scottish a "canny wife" is a midwife and the "canny moment" is the moment of birth.[26] Although not noted by Freud, these meanings point toward what he identifies as the unheimlich's first source: "the entrance to the former *heim* [home] of all human beings, to the place where everyone dwelt once upon a time and in the beginning."[27] For Freud, this biological past is the prelude to all experience of the uncanny, including that generated by aesthetic motifs such as doubles, dolls, and automata; a severed head or limb; psychological experiences such as déjà vu; and the fears of being buried alive or castrated. All bespeak anxieties about identity boundaries, including the division between past and present, living and dead, and self and (m)other, although Freud considers none of these motifs in light of the potential unhominess of the home for the women who live there.

Beginning in the 1970s, however, feminist scholars including Hélène Cixous, Julia Kristeva, Tania Modleski, and Lucy Fischer, challenged, expanded, and revised Freud's ideas to fill in this gap, thereby illuminating the social and psychological positioning of women in creative and theoretical works concerned with the unheimlich. Drawing on Kristeva, Fischer's work, for example, investigates the double in films about sisters and, in the process, reiterates "the real and benevolent possibility of the female body for doubling" in pregnancy, a benevolence that contrasts with masculine projections of women as dual creatures, encompassing womb and tomb or mother and whore.[28] Fischer also uses the concept of the *doppelgänger* to shed light on German filmmaker Margarethe von Trotta's woman-centered *Sisters*, a film that productively reflects on Germany's suppression of Nazi history.[29] For her part, Cixous criticizes Freud's analysis of his primary literary example of the uncanny, E. T. A. Hoffmann's tale "The Sand-Man," because it effaces Clara and minimizes Olimpia, the story's two principal female characters, in order to focus on Nathaniel, the male. Cixous faults Freud, as well, for trying to tame the uncanny by underestimating its radical potential for destabilizing the borders of identity, including his own.[30] She thereby points the way toward the use of the aesthetics of the uncanny to intervene in conventionally gendered narratives, including historical ones.

Freud's theory of the uncanny also serves as the jumping off point for Modleski's feminist investigation of *Vertigo*, with its theme of radically destabilized identity parameters—in this case, those of gender in particular. She reads Judy/Madeleine/Carlotta as Scottie's troubling double, a woman who surprisingly takes him back to his own home and self. In Modleski's words, "It is as if [Scottie] were continually confronted with the fact that woman's uncanny otherness has some relation to himself, that he resembles her in ways intolerable to contemplate—intolerable because this resemblance throws into question his own fullness of being."[31] Thus feminist scholarship exposed anxious masculine suppression and projection of destabilizing uncanniness within the self; it also focused attention on the benevolent dimensions of female duality.

In this same context, pathfinding feminist scholars also investigated the unheimlich in literary and film genres addressed to women, especially the female Gothic, with its stories about women who are literally terrorized in their own homes.[32] In particular, Modleski's work recognizes that "Gothic novels for women continually exploit the sensation of the uncanny as it was defined by Freud to a far greater extent than any other type of mass fiction," and she theorizes that the basis of the genre's appeal to women lies in the separation anxiety that daughters experience in relation to their mothers.[33]

Examining the woman's film of the 1940s, Mary Ann Doane focuses on the uncanny in relation to dynamics specific to cinema, with the less-bounded experience of subjectivity it provides, relative to that of novels, and on film's distinctly spacialized and specularized uncanny dimensions.[34] And, identifying the source of ideological tensions within Fritz Lang's *Secret Beyond the Door* (1948), Diane Waldman stresses the historical pressures that marked the period immediately after World War II—especially the push to move women out of the paid workforce and into the traditional, presumably more socially stabilizing home—and how these pressures shaped an architecture of uncanniness in the gothic romance film.[35]

Indeed, with the advent of cultural studies and the new historicism in the 1980s, theorists increasingly reworked Freud's theory to historicize uncanniness within the frameworks of the ethnic, racial, and sexual dynamics of particular nations, cultures, and histories, and especially in relation to postcolonialism, migratory labor, and globalization. In *Strangers to Ourselves,* Kristeva focuses on the foreignness of migrant workers within the modern metropolitan nation and on the correspondence between these strangers without and the uncanny strangers that exist within the psyches of native citizens, a correlation that can lead, in her view, to one of two trajectories. The first is a path of paranoia and destruction, as the boundaries between imagination and reality dissolve and the dreadful imaginary is mistaken for material reality; the second is a hopeful path of productive confrontation with the inner unknown as the basis for identification with the unfamiliar foreigner and hence for sociality. Revealingly, Kristeva also observes that "a foreigner seldom arouses the terrifying anguish provoked by death [or] the female sex."[36] Yet, powerfully illuminating as her analysis is, it never fully examines the implications of this assertion for the foreigner who happens to be female.

A related lapse appears in Jameson's suggestive investigation of magic realism. Jameson enlists Freud's concept of the uncanny in order to account for resistant effects of magic realist aesthetics in third-world and especially Latin American cinema. He contrasts the deep layering of history in magic realist texts with the Hollywood history film's reliance on an idealized, nostalgic, superficial vision of America in the 1940s and 1950s as its key historic reference point—in effect, the fetishized replacement for history identified in my earlier quotation from Jameson. In the context of magic realism, he productively matches Freud's ideas about the aesthetics of the uncanny with the historical depth and resonance generated by magic realist films. The lapse arises from the inferences that he draws based on his conclusion that Freud's choice of "The Sand-Man" as his exemplary text was unduly constraining. Jameson argues that "what is to be retained from Freud's canonical demonstration . . . is the way in which narrative elements can be intensified and marked from within by an absent cause undetectable empirically but read off the sheerest formal properties."[37] Thus, for example, third-world filmmakers have transformed the technical imperfections in the kind of film stock that their limited budgets allow into a deliberately crafted, resistant aesthetics, a counterstatement to Hollywood's technical perfection and to the advanced capitalist values such perfection connotes. Yet, given the striking importance of powerful, often subversive women figures in a wide variety of magic realist literary and film texts—an importance far greater than that found in the Hollywood paradigm—and given Hollywood's own methods for managing the historical uncanny, Jameson's theory gives short shrift to Hoffmann's tale, with its female human characters and its *unheimlich* female automaton, Olimpia.

For Homi Bhabha, however, the idea of Olimpia serves as a springboard to another extension and recontextualization of Freud's idea of the uncanny. Bhabha's interest centers on the cultural uncanny; that is, on the interstitial social spaces and historical asynchronicities—the doubled-up spaces and times—that adumbrate the colonialist-imperialist history embedded in contemporary politics, literature, and culture. From Bhabha's perspective, the aesthetics best suited for configuring the historical past reveals it as always already intruding on and intermingling with the present, thereby creating in-between spaces and interwoven temporalities in which innovation, interruption, and exposé occur. In this context, Toni Morrison's work serves as a primary example. Her novel *Beloved* (1987) effectively rewrites the un-*heimlich* in a distinct African-American register, one informed by her cognizance of a legacy of slavery that invaded, displaced, colonized, and deprivatized the home. As Bhabha writes, her work reveals the process by which "the recesses of domestic space become sites for history's most intricate invasions. In that displacement, the borders between home and world become confused, and uncannily, the private and the public become part of each other, forcing upon us a vision that is as divided as it is disorienting."[38]

Bhabha also draws on feminist theory to hint at the uncanny's deconstructionist potential. Defining the "unhomey moment" as one that "relates the traumatic ambivalences of personal, psychic history to the wider disjunctions of political existence," Bhabha argues that feminism makes "visible the forgetting of the 'unhomely' moment in civil society." It thereby reveals "the patriarchal, gendered nature of civil society and disturbs the symmetry of private and public which is now shadowed, or uncannily doubled, by the difference of genders which does not neatly map onto the private and the public, but becomes disturbingly supplementary to them." The result is a redrawing of "domestic space as the space of the normalizing, pastoralizing, and individuating techniques of modern power and police: the personal-*is*-the political; the world-*in*-the home." [39] In a related vein, he reinterprets Hoffmann's "Sand-Man" as a particularly "canny" illustration of how colonized subjects are expected to perform in order to gain cultural membership. Like the young women in Hoffmann's tale who are pressed by their suitors to prove their difference from the beautiful doll-like Olimpia by imperfectly performing identifiably human acts and gestures, colonized subjects must generate slightly imperfect reiterations of culturally accredited formulas and conventions if they are to establish their credentials as human. [40]

Despite Bhabha's attention to Morrison and to feminism, Maureen Molloy, in an important essay on recent New Zealand cinema, criticizes his study, along with Freud's essay and Kristeva's *Strangers to Ourselves,* for missing the centrality of the figure of woman in their concepts of the uncanny. Molloy's critique speaks to oversights in some other scholarship as well:

> "Woman" is the specter that haunts [their] essays, appearing in tantalizing but evanescent references. All three scholars allude to, but none develops, the significance of "woman" in relation to the uncanny . . . Of the three theorists, Bhabha makes the most of the feminine ghost who is at the center of the haunting uncanny of cultural domination. He is, however, oblique in his analysis, using "the figure of woman" to signify the private "home" of the culturally oppressed . . . However, what he misses in metaphorizing "the figure of woman" is woman, as female, caught not only within a cultural and racialized oppression but caught within it as a woman. [41]

Thus Molloy returns the focus not only to woman as symbol but to the experiential world of women per se. She thereby underscores not only *woman*'s ambiguous positioning at or as the nation's hearth and home and yet as peripheral to the civil state, but also *women*'s corresponding ambivalence toward home and nation. For women, home and nation are always something more, and less, than homey.

At the same time, Molloy never loses sight of historical shifts in the dynamics that generate complex and troubling symbolic equivalencies among the feminine, the home, national identity, and the unheimlich. She highlights, in particular, the ways in which the increasing destabilization and fragmentation of national identities, under the pressures of postcolonialism and globalization, renewed the production of nationally resonant figurations of female uncanniness in the 1990s, a phenomenon she explores in relation to three New Zealand films from that decade, including *The Piano* (Jane Campion, 1993) and *Once Were Warriors* (Lee Tamahori, 1994). The third of these, *Heavenly Creatures* (Peter Jackson, 1994), is a film whose uncanny imagery conjures up a private female world and a historical act of matricide—famously committed by two teenage girls in the 1950s—in what Molloy reads as a kind of allegory of the nation, bespeaking the ruptures and ambivalences in New Zealand's sense of national identity in the 1990s. Molloy thus connects an ostensibly private, if historically based narrative with a public narrative of nation and national history in ways that acknowledge the larger ramifications of a seemingly eccentric or anomalous tale as well as its power as a revenant. Molloy summarizes the place of the uncanny as follows: "The uncanny, with its implications of doubling, merging, and return of the repressed, is the expression and the effect of the feminine. The lack of boundaries, surety, and the return of the archaic make it also a powerful expression of the postcolonial nation." [42]

Addressing U.S. cinema, Molloy illustrates her theory by pointing to the correspondence between *Blade Runner* and "The Sand-Man," and between Rachel and Olimpia, foregrounding gender in the process. [43] The linking of the cult film to the tale is evocative and also points beyond Molloy's argument toward further historical shifts. Whereas Olimpia is pure mechanism (a "dry" machine), the far more human but extremely fetishized Rachel is a replicant (a "wet" machine, "colloidal"), a contrast that reflects both the increasing importance of technologies that magnify gender distinctions in a wide variety of contexts and the radical diminution of difference between the human and nonhuman in recent science fiction and science fact, as in, for example, the concepts of the cyborg, android, and replicant. [44] Moreover, as a living doll, Rachel possesses implanted memories, epitomized in the film by a constructed family snapshot of her and her mother sitting on the steps of the porch of their home. This image both links her back to Shakespeare's Miranda, whose memories her spectacle-producing father simultaneously supplants and implants, and ahead to twenty-first-century audiences, whose prosthetic memories[45]—derived from film, video, and television viewing, digitally enhanced family albums, and packaged travel and theme park experiences—Rachel's photo doubles. In fact, the brief suggestion of movement within a play of light and shadow that marks the final seconds in which Rachel's snapshot appears on screen directly ties it to the viewer's cinematic experience, and Rachel's mistaken belief that the snapshot is proof of her humanity thus reflects on the viewer's beliefs and humanity as well—especially so, given the highly reiterative nature of cult film experience. Thus the uncanny doll and the celluloid double point toward evolving technologies of reproduction and their ambiguously human effects.

Additionally, it has become not only the doll that disturbs as "she" magnifies the borderlines of identity, but also, symbolically, *Dolly*, the history-making cloned Scottish sheep, and the real capacity for biological doubling that science now possesses. The uncanny, in short, currently exists on a distinct and heightened historical plane, given these scientific and science fiction developments, which complement the destabilization of identities that globalization, postcolonialist dynamics, and population and labor shifts have ushered in. Even films that do not directly engage these scientific developments may reflect them obliquely or rely on them as frames of reference and reception. At the same time, the gender and name of "Dolly," or "little doll," also suggest a clear perpetuation of patterns of the uncanny from the past, and both traditional and shifting reiterations of the uncanny are important contexts for comprehending the films that this book explores in the chapters ahead.

Before I turn to the project of outlining those chapters, however, some further comments on the historical embeddedness of the concept of the uncanny are in order. The previous discussion demonstrates the inseparability of aesthetic and psychological theories from historical pressures and political values. The fact that Freud himself wrote his treatise in the shadow of the First World War points as well to the importance of historical context to a theory, such as his, that defines itself in universal rather than historically or politically specific terms. This context also offers clues about the relevance of his theory to the war film genre—perhaps the major form of U.S. history film at the end of the twentieth and the beginning of the twenty-first centuries—a genre conventionally associated with the sublime. Factoring in the history of the uncanny as an aesthetic category, one closely related to the sublime and the beautiful, also provides a springboard to theorizing a more equivocal gendering of the aesthetics of the uncanny, not just as the problematic synonym of the feminine that Molloy describes, but as a destabilizing third term that productively deconstructs the binarisms of male-female and sublime-beautiful, and can thereby erode nostalgically masculinist versions of the past.

Aesthetics, Gender, and Genre: A Historical Perspective

In Hollywood cinema, an aesthetics of the sublime has conventionally defined key male-centered genres, and in particular the Western, with its vast, majestic, overwhelming landscape, and, as I have noted, the war film, with its immense scale of battle and sacrifice. Conversely, an aesthetics of the beautiful has been conventionally aligned with the sociality, domesticity, and intimacy of female-centered genres such as romantic comedy and domestic melodrama, although aesthetic beauty is by no means limited to this role.[46] This aesthetic division of the sublime and the beautiful, which has roots contemporaneous with the founding of America, emerges in the eighteenth-century theories of Edmund Burke and Immanuel Kant, thinkers who helped to establish the stereotyped gender values of these categories in the last half of that century. For both Burke and Kant, the masculine sublime contrasts with the feminine beautiful, and the arguments and assumptions of both point toward the inseparability of aesthetic form from political dynamics and historical forces.

An example of the gendering of aesthetics especially pertinent to the war film is Kant's discussion of warriors and sublimity. Kant urges that certain military personnel, if they wage war with respect for citizens' rights, are aesthetically superior entities, sublime opposites to the "effeminate" types who spring up during long periods of peace:

> For what is that which is, even to the savage, an object of the greatest admiration? It is a man who shrinks from nothing, who fears nothing, and therefore does not yield to danger, but rather goes to face

it vigorously with the most complete deliberation. Even in the most highly civilized state this peculiar veneration for the soldier remains, though only under the condition that he exhibit all the virtues of peace, gentleness, compassion, and even a becoming care for his own person; because even by these it is recognized that his mind is unsubdued by danger. Hence whatever disputes there may be about the superiority of the respect which is to be accorded them, in the comparison of a statesman and a general, the aesthetical judgment decides for the latter. War itself, if it is carried on with order and with a sacred respect for the rights of citizens, has something sublime in it, and makes the disposition of the people who carry it on thus only the more sublime, the more numerous are the dangers to which they are exposed and in respect of which they behave with courage. On the other hand, a long peace generally brings about a predominant commercial spirit and, along with it, low selfishness, cowardice, and effeminacy, and debases the disposition of the people.[47]

A few years later, in the course of the French Revolution, Kant was to affirm a universalist pacifist stance (*Perpetual Peace* [1795]), but his idea here that peace and effeminacy form opposites to sublime war and warriors looks back to a position articulated earlier by Burke.[48] As W. J. T. Mitchell explains, "Burke's most notorious derivation of political values from the mechanics of sensation is his linking of sublimity and beauty with stereotypes of gender. Sublimity, with its foundation in pain, terror, vigorous exertion, and power, is the masculine aesthetic mode. Beauty, by contrast, is located in qualities such as littleness, smoothness, and delicacy that mechanically induce a sense of pleasure and affectionate superiority . . . ."[49]

For Burke, not only gender but also national identity (and as I will later discuss, race) came to derive political valence from aesthetic perception. In the wake of the French Revolution, Burke took pains to distinguish between the purportedly false French sublime, and what he saw as the gender-destabilizing feminine or transvestite character of its violence, and the true English one, which he perceived as moderate, masculine, and mediated—

that is, something one experiences at a safe distance, and paradigmatically, a phenomenon in nature.[50] Shedding light on this idea of feminine French violence, Patrice Leconte's film *La Veuve de Saint Pierre* (2000) reminds us that the guillotine was nicknamed *la veuve* or *widow*. Moreover, according to Regina Janes, the explicitly erotic contemporary representations of the French Revolution's instrument of death as "a gaping, single-toothed vagina dentata" underscored the "parallels between female anatomy and guillotine geometry and set up a tense oscillation between desire and destruction."[51] Thus, for Burke's theories, the French Revolution—clearly a watermark sublime image of armed political struggle—created a serious discrepancy, since he both preferred the sublime as an aesthetic mode and condemned this particular political embodiment of it—in fact, dissociated the event from true sublimity.

More recently, the issue of the sublime in history became an important focus in the work of Hayden White, who criticizes Burke's *Reflections on the Revolution in France* as illustrative of a misguided movement to "exorcize the notion of the sublime from any apprehension of the historical process."[52] To White, Burke's position and his preference for a "sort of delightful horror" reveal the "domestication of history effected by the suppression of the historical sublime," a move that renders history too familiar, comfortable, safe, and comprehensible.[53] On the contrary, White argues, history, and the cataclysmic events of the twentieth century in particular, should be represented as a succession of sublimely terrible developments that are irreconcilable with the sort of realist, romance-inflected narrative exemplified by the nineteenth-century novel.[54] The unfathomable irrationality and sublimity of history must be laid bare, in White's view, so that witnesses, driven by a utopian yearning for change, are spurred to act out politically significant choices. Thus White sees the fragmentation of modernist and postmodernist narrative as better suited for representing twentieth-century history than conventional "domesticated" narratives. Although White's analysis is compelling and significant, and his concept of "domestication" pertinent to 1990s films, that concept, with its implicit associations not only of "taming" but also of femininity and falsification, nonetheless perpetuates a problematic tradition of gender hierarchies in aesthetic categories. It also neglects to consider any potential role or value for the conventional association of the feminine and the beautiful with peace.

The same era that created what is now called the Romantic sublime, theorized in Burke's and Kant's work, also produced exemplary uncanny texts and prototheoretical work on the relatively elusive idea of the uncanny. Hoffmann's "The Sand-Man" (1816), with its beautiful yet terrifying doll-like automaton, Olimpia, exemplifies the former, and Heinrich von Kleist's remarkable treatise "On the Puppet Theater" (1810) illustrates the latter. Unlike the sublime and the beautiful, however, the uncanny became a significant category of aesthetic and cultural analysis only in the twentieth century when Freud published "The 'Uncanny'" in 1919, as I have already noted. With the horrors of World War I as its backdrop, Freud's essay fuses evocations of death, trauma, beauty, domesticity, and epistemological uncertainty.

As Freud explains, the uncanny gives aesthetic expression to anxieties about a range of distinctions, including those between child and mother, self and other, the living and the dead, human and machine, imagination and reality, and mind and body. Although Freud never expressly discusses war, and initially even postpones considering the subject of death because, as he says, of its gruesomeness, his essay's relevance to these topics is powerfully apparent. He notes that because the "uncanny is in reality nothing new or foreign but something familiar and old-established in the mind that has been estranged only by the process of repression," it can be a source of morbid anxiety, regardless of whether the uncanny thing originally triggered dread. Nonetheless, he adds, "many people experience the feeling [of uncanniness] in the highest degree in relation to death and dead bodies," a phenomenon clearly intensified in wartime and necessarily aestheticized in its fictional representations.[55]

Warfare is linked to the uncanny in additional ways as well. During war, identity boundaries are typically rigidified, for example, through propaganda that reduces the enemy to inhuman automata. Indeed, extending this idea of rigidification to an extreme was the eighteenth-century Prussian ideal of state governance on a military model, an ideal which later spread through Germany and finally became all-pervasive and normative during the Nazi years. As Michel Foucault observes, war and the militarization of society were conceived to function as sources, in effect, of a general automatization: "Historians of ideas usually attribute the dream of a perfect society to the philosophers and jurists of the eighteenth century; but there was also a military dream of society; its fundamental reference was not to the state of nature but to the meticulously subordinated cogs of a machine, not to the primal social contract but to permanent coercions, not to fundamental rights but to indefinitely progressive forms of training, not to the general will but to automatic docility."[56] (Not coincidentally, eighteenth-century Europe also witnessed the acme of the popularity of automata.) Thus the militarized society and the enemy as automata heighten an uncanny self-other doubling that tests the boundaries of difference. At the same time, war also tests identity boundaries through experiences of physical and psychological trauma that throw the limits of the self into doubt and that result in compulsive, mechanical behavior.

Significantly, Freud's catalog of uncanny images moves from those that evoke precisely such trauma to the vision of our original "home" in the womb:

> Dismembered limbs, a severed head, a hand cut off at the wrist, feet which dance by themselves— all these have something peculiarly uncanny about them, especially when, as in the last instance, they prove able to move of themselves in addition. As we already know, this kind of uncanniness springs from its association with the castration-complex. To many people the idea of being buried alive while appearing to be dead is the most uncanny thing of all. And yet psycho-analysis has taught us that this terrifying phantasy is only a transformation of another phantasy which had originally nothing terrifying about it at all, but was filled with a certain lustful pleasure— the phantasy, I mean, of intra-uterine existence.[57]

Elaborating on this last insight a few pages later, Freud offers what he terms a "beautiful confirmation" of his theory in the saying *Liebe ist Heimweh* (love is homesickness): "Whenever a man dreams of a place or a country and says to himself, still in the dream, 'this place is familiar to me, I have been there before,' we may interpret the place as being his mother's genitals or her body."[58] The uncanny is thus a double of nostalgia (from the Greek for "return home" and "pain").[59]

Paradoxically, then, the German word *heimlich* (homey, domestic, domesticated) can mean its opposite, *unheimlich* (uncanny; literally *unhomey*), and thus contains a darker double of itself—the double being a defining element of the uncanny. Paradoxically, too, the fear of castration provoked by images of severed hands and limbs finds its roots, in Freud's view, in our oneness with our first home, the mother's body. And paradoxically, the origin of the larger deadly terror produced by the uncanny is the memory of the domestic and maternal and even of "a certain lustful pleasure," a certain "home-sickness." A further implication colors these insights but goes repressed and unstated: namely, that the idealized maternal provides a means of evoking and evading the reality of death that war horribly magnifies, and of conjuring up yet concealing an intensified psychic conflation of womb and tomb as doubles in their power to define the limits of human existence.

This submerged connection between wartime and the maternal is further reinforced in one of Freud's references to the recent war, in a passage on the overaccentuation of psychical reality, a passage that is sandwiched between his paragraphs on the maternal uncanny. Here, too, the relationship of combat to the uncanny remains implicit yet unmistakable. Indeed, the segment offers an especially revealing glimpse into how Freud's repression of the recent war shades his thought:

> In the midst of the isolation of war-time a number of the English *Strand Magazine* fell into my hands; and, amongst other not very interesting matter, I read a story about a young married couple, who move into a furnished flat in which there is a curiously shaped table with carvings of crocodiles on it. Towards evening they begin to smell an intolerable and very typical odour that pervades the whole flat; things begin to get in their way and trip them up in the darkness; they seem to see a vague form gliding up the stairs—in short, we are given to understand that the presence of the table causes ghostly crocodiles to haunt the place, or that the wooden monsters come to life in the dark, or something of that sort. It was a thoroughly silly story, but the uncanny feeling it produced was quite remarkable.[60]

This anecdote itself is remarkable for a number of reasons, including Freud's earlier claim that it had been some time since he had "experienced or heard of anything which has given him an uncanny impression,"[61] as well as his lack of express analysis of the story's highly suggestive details—

the young married couple, the typical evening-time odor, and the accompanying crocodiles, animals known for their terrifyingly toothy maws. These elements function together to hint at a particular kind of imaginary fear, namely, the dread of the vagina dentata. In light of Freud's remembered wish to escape "the isolation of war-time" through such "silly" literature, there seems to be a double symbolism at work. To put it punningly, in the contexts of the story itself and of the historical pressures of the war, the crocodile stands as a primitive symbol that conflates the terrible "maw of war," devouring the youth of Europe, and the "ma of war," the castration anxiety–producing mother, who symbolizes both womb and tomb according to a familiar formulation, both the source of the soldier's "homesickness" and emblem of the war's terrible toll in human life. (The connection between the terrors of trench warfare and the forms of desire that drive classic 1930s horror films—at least as these are posited by the fictionalized biography of James Whale, *Gods and Monsters* [Bill Condon, 1998]—furthers this association between war and uncanniness. So, too, does the driving influence of unheimlich homes on post–World War II soldier-cowboys such as Jeb in *Pursued* [Raoul Walsh, 1947] and Ethan in *The Searchers*.)

Beyond pointing toward an important if half-buried linkage of war, women, and the uncanny, Freud's reflections also offer evidence of an erosion and slippage of aesthetic categories, the blurring of boundaries that is itself a mark of the uncanny, the wish to cover over the discomforting uncanny with a "beautiful confirmation" of viability. Indeed, insofar as the aesthetics of the beautiful and the unheimlich overlap, and insofar as the aesthetics of the sublime and the uncanny share a focus on terror, the uncanny has the potential to subvert distinctions based on aesthetics and gender posited by earlier theories of the sublime and the beautiful.[62] In terms of the triad of aesthetic categories that I have presented, then, the uncanny has the power to function as the deconstructionist's third term. That is, while the uncanny ostensibly stands outside of the binarisms aligned with the sublime and the beautiful—male-female, immensity-smallness, strength-weakness, terror-pleasure, wartime-peacetime, Anglo-Saxon–French, and so on—it exists between them and functions to reveal how, in Derrida's words, "each allegedly 'simple' term is marked by the trace of another term."[63] The uncanny thus traces, for example, how terror resides in (being born of) woman—an idea that famously subtends the bloody struggles undertaken by Shakespeare's Macbeth.[64]

The question then becomes, what implications do these aesthetic considerations hold for gender and genre issues of the World War II combat film (especially in the expressly commemorative forms in which it emerged at the end of the twentieth century), in films that depict cold-war history, and in films that rewrite more contemporary techno-warfare? If, as Robin Blaetz maintains, the combat film has tended to "manage" femininity and especially maternity (and hence death, I would add) by submitting them to male mastery, to what extent is this sense of control both furthered and called into question in late-twentieth-century cinema by the destabilizing aesthetic forces of the uncanny?[65] That is, how has the uncanny both served nostalgic, masculinist agendas and mobilized feminist-friendly cultural critique? And if reimagining the past has very often entailed negating the history and impact of the women's movement by reducing women to mothers and icons of the nation, in what ways has the uncanny helped to revive remembrance of the historical differences that women's ideas and actions could make?

Chapter Overview

The pages that follow seek answers to these questions through their investigation of 1990s films in the Hollywood narrative model, although the last chapter, which considers two films by independent filmmaker John Sayles, treats work that also provocatively departs from that paradigm. The films engage U.S. history from World War II to the present, including the complex legacies of the cold war and the techno-war in the Persian Gulf. A recurring focus within this cinema is the calculated military or political use of symbolic women for public-relations purposes, and my study also traces what happens when female characters move from the largely symbolic position they occupy in the World War II combat films to a more central position in a Gulf War film (anticipatory of Jessica Lynch's status in 2003), as well as the effects of this shift on the critiques of image manipulations that are developed. Only one of the films in my study centrally concerns actual historical personages, Oliver Stone's *Nixon* (1995), but all of them fictionalize and aestheticize historical events, and are in varying degrees shaped by an aesthetics of the uncanny—a mode that can reduce women to dolls and monsters, yet can also serve as a means of unconventional cultural critique and of engendering less masculinized inscriptions of the past.

Chapter One focuses primarily on masculine identities inscribed in World War II combat films. I examine three combat films; among them, Keith Gordon's *Midnight Clear* (1991) is the one most defined by an uncanny aesthetics, as it expressly conjoins home and battlefield in order to generate tellingly unconventional configurations of combat masculinity and an unequivocally antiwar critique. The other two films, *Saving Private Ryan* (Steven Spielberg, 1998) and *The Thin Red Line* (Terrence Malick, 1998), are both better known and more conventionally conceived in relation to aesthetic sublimity and beauty. Nonetheless, they too make innovative and revealing use of uncanny aesthetic configurations to reimagine received ideas about warfare, moral accountability, gender, and generational difference. On the other hand, equivocal inscriptions of the maternal— shifting, for example, between the mother as revered bearer of soldiers and troubling public-relations symbol, or between idealized life force and terrible "ma(w) of death"—provide highly problematic moments across these films. Insofar as these works reduce symbolic women to womb and tomb, they provide predictably inadequate answers to Gilligan's questions, where are the women and why all the suffering?

Chapter Two focuses on first ladies, and specifically Pat Nixon—wife of World War II veteran and consummate cold warrior Richard Nixon—as she is recreated in Oliver Stone's film *Nixon*. I read Stone's construction of her against the popular image of Plastic Pat and, more generally, against America's historical ambivalence toward its first ladies, ambiguously situated public figures who share the White House and serve the contradictory function of symbolizing both the nation and the private, familial realm. Stone's film generates an iconic portrait of Pat that in some measure contradicts the popular view of her as an uncanny doll or a rigid robot, an image defining her instead as an idealized truth figure. It thereby situates her as an opposite to Nixon's mother, Hannah, whom Stone vilifies as the maternal symbol of a long history of Protestant repression. An array of uncanny images reflect back on her deficient mothering and forecast Nixon's haunted adult personality, revealing him as plagued by neuroses that undermine his public success and private happiness. Stone's Nixon, for example, hallucinates that his wife and mother are one and the same, thereby fetishizing both as he displaces the familiar wife into the repressed "mother" of his familiar but estranged past. Yet, it is not only Stone's Nixon who effectively mistakes these women for the uncanny stranger within; at times, the film itself also conflates Hannah and Pat, reinscribing both in fetishistic terms and reinforcing the ambivalence that defines the maternal as uncanny.

Concerning repressed history, the film underplays Nixon's insistence on a Stepford wife public image for Pat, whose warmth and humor he stifled, as well as a pattern of profound mistrust of women that marked his entire political career. This facet of the cold warrior's leeriness is revealed not only by the historical Nixon's color-coded conflation of femininity and Communism (for example, his labeling of the non-Communist Helen Gahagan Douglas as the "pink lady"), but also by his unconscious creation of a painful pun on his wife's name. Drawing a metaphor from poker, the game he profited from while serving in the Pacific during World War II, Nixon claimed that America "cannot stand pat" in its war against Communism, a revealing, symptomatic conflation. Similarly, *Nixon* underexposes the unselfconscious blend of racism and sexism that existed within his administration. It thereby forms a vantage point that essentially exculpates Nixon, painting him as a leader whose potential for greatness was tragically sabotaged by his mother and the cold piety of her childrearing. Perhaps most importantly, the film never discloses the extent to which the historical record refutes the media construction of an uncanny Pat. Specifically, that record reveals that, in sharp contrast to her husband, Pat Nixon was at ease with people of various nationalities, races, ethnicities, and disabilities— that is, with those whom Kristeva calls the uncanny "strangers without." The record also verifies her success as a goodwill ambassador to third-world nations, the kind of countries that her husband, along with Henry Kissinger, made the mistake of deeming peripheral to U.S. foreign policy and thus felt free to treat badly, with tragic long-term consequences.

Chapter Three begins by tracing the history of gender and ethnic integration in the U.S. military after the Vietnam War, along with that of 1990s sexual scandals in the American armed forces, and the persistent fetishization of masculine-coded combat technology, in order to provide a context for reading *Courage Under Fire* (1996), Edward Zwick's film about the Gulf War and its aftermath. I consider this film not only a compelling depiction of the stakes and destructiveness of sexual harassment within the military, but also a confirmation of the abilities of women soldiers in combat zones and an exposé of some of the political mechanisms by which U.S. history gets lost. First among them is the public-relations machinery of the government and military that cares more about selling expedient images than presenting historically accurate information. Thus, for example, the film shows a White House public-relations man intent not on the truth but on the capital he gains by giving the public a perfectly packaged woman hero of the Gulf War, posthumously honored with a congressional medal—an echo, with an important difference, of the military's ambiguous use of a symbolic woman for public-relations purposes in *Saving Private Ryan*.

Yet, even though Zwick's film revealingly remembers woman-centered history and directly confronts some of the manipulation and censoring to which it is subject, *Courage Under Fire* also positions the woman hero in a way that both calls up and obscures other pertinent histories. These include the so-called collateral damage of the war (often dead and injured Iraqi women and children) and the North American patriarchal legacy that segregates black men from white women—the white woman soldier's death in the film being not only the subject of an investigation by an African-American officer but also the apparent prerequisite for the close bond he ends up feeling toward her. Also obscured is the historical fight for control over oil and the so-called Muslim Orient as a means to a born-again American masculinity. Last but not least, the film's missing history includes the subjectivity of the central woman character herself. Because she has been killed by a fellow soldier and hence is seen only through flashbacks, serving as the narrative springboard for the memories of various male characters, viewers are never positioned to identify directly with her and her own experiences of the war.

As I argue, the uncanny pervades *Courage Under Fire*. It surfaces in the evocations of the Vietnam War film genre through reiterated images of napalm and repeated sounds of whirring helicopter blades, generic elements patterned like recurrent nightmares. It erupts in the haunted, guilty dreams, flashbacks, and "buried alive" feelings experienced by its protagonist, an African-American officer who served in the Vietnam and Gulf Wars and who, during the latter war, was responsible for the death of a white friend amidst the confusion of battle. The uncanny also appears in the southern, plantation-style home to which this black hero, ironically enough, goes to beg for forgiveness from that white friend's parents, and it is manifest in the film's echoes of the Watergate scandal, with its incriminating evidence on secret tapes. More generally, it reverberates across this film to a range of films from 1990 onward, including *The Hunt for Red October* (John McTiernan, 1990), *Braveheart* (Mel Gibson, 1995), and *Gladiator* (Ridley Scott, 2000), that use the death of a woman as a narrative and political springboard to a new or renovated political order, symbolic systems that are also highly reflective of contemporary U.S. identity. Above all, it breaks through in the film's maternal imagery, encompassing not only a tank that serves as womb and tomb for the protagonist's friend but also the film's ambivalent construction of the woman soldier and its resonant citation of Saddam Hussein's infamous phrase, "the mother of all battles."

The final chapter pairs John Sayles's *Lone Star* (1996) and *Limbo* (1999), companion films set, respectively, in Texas and Alaska, states that help define the southern and northern boundaries of the continental U.S. The chapter contextualizes these films in relation to the reiterative, uncanny motifs, characters, and stories that Molloy analyzes in her study of recent New Zealand cinema, including the recurring figure of the daughter-storyteller as a significant symbol in the narrative of nation. Like the New Zealand films, *Lone Star* and *Limbo* reflect directly and indirectly on the symbolic status of females in relation to the contemporary destabilization of national identity boundaries by a variety of social, economic, and historical pressures. In Sayles's two films, paramount among these pressures are competing ideas about the past and the interests it should serve, about how multiethnic, multinational border history defines community, and about the past as a resource for economic exploitation, in the form, for example, of the highly commercialized, environmentally irresponsible theme park tourism that hallmarks contemporary globalization.

Unlike the New Zealand films (at least as Molloy reads them), and unlike many of the films discussed elsewhere in this book, Sayles's work creates female characters whose functions are instrumental in recovering and reimagining repressed history, especially socially symbolic personal history, and in debunking nostalgic notions of nation, as well as in complicating the symbolism that equates woman and nation. Moreover, his films achieve these effects without overlooking the cultural oppression that affects women and girls specifically as *females*. Further, although both *Lone Star* and *Limbo* center on middle-aged male protagonists, they move female characters to the center of their stories in surprising, revelatory ways and simultaneously challenge established patterns of Hollywood aesthetics and narrative, including narrative closure, to reveal the "past-present" that continuously defines the complex temporality of lived social existence in America. In this context, *Lone Star*'s innovative use of Latin American–affiliated magic realist aesthetics to depict the dynamics of the past-present is especially noteworthy. Finally, this chapter recognizes that Sayles does not abandon the idea of the nation as an unheimlich home, but instead relates that national uncanny to women's experiences and, in the process, imaginatively transforms it into a provocation for considering alternative visions of the future to those that look nostalgically back to the kind of nuclear families and couple formations that purportedly defined America's "golden age."

In an epilogue I reflect on some of the filmic and historical ramifications of September 11, 2001. In particular, I consider the television documentary *9/11* (2002), with its doubling of Hollywood combat film conventions, and I explore documented evidence of women's resistance to the seemingly ubiquitous U.S. rhetoric of the war on terror that followed the attacks on September 11. In thus moving broadly from Prospero and Caliban to the contemporary West and the Taliban, I emphasize the ways in which Miranda's queries, "Where are the women?" and "Why all the suffering?" appear to be as essential now as ever.

Beginning in the early 1990s, fiftieth-anniversary celebrations of the major events of World War II served to inaugurate a wider series of commemorative acts that would encompass the release of Hollywood films, the broadcast of television miniseries, the publication of best-selling books, and, belatedly, the bestowal of congressional medals honoring Navajo code talkers, men whose communications, undecipherable by the Japanese, turned the tide of decisive battles in the Pacific. Celebrating a dying generation of national war heroes was hardly new to U.S. history. Indeed, such rituals of remembrance extend back to the nation's origins, with the public counting and celebration of surviving soldiers of the Revolutionary War during that generation's waning years. A distinctive element for the veterans of World War II, however, was the unprecedented role that film commanded, both in representing the historical conflict and in motivating further public gestures of collective homage and remembrance. Thus, for example, Tom Hanks, the star of *Saving Private Ryan,* drew on the power of his film image to serve as a highly effective promoter of a National World War II Memorial in Washington, D.C., a project that nonetheless drew considerable criticism for its aesthetic design (reminiscent of a nineteenth-century mausoleum) and its vista-obstructing location (between the Lincoln Memorial and the Washington Monument).

At the same time, the role of film itself as a memorial to the war was by no means free of controversy. In particular, some veterans and commentators rejected *The Thin Red Line* (Terrence Malick, 1998), claiming that it betrayed American World War II veterans by showing Japanese soldiers as victims of GI cruelty and by reducing accepted differences between the World War II combat film and the Vietnam War film—differences some cultural commentators deemed essential to a renewed sense of national identity.

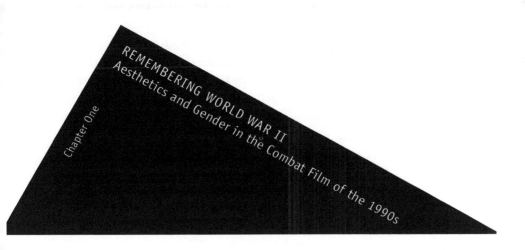

Chapter One

REMEMBERING WORLD WAR II
Aesthetics and Gender in the Combat Film of the 1990s

Some critics also saw the aesthetic beauty of this film as jarringly out of place.[1] Despite the generally very positive reception of *Saving Private Ryan*, it, too, sparked controversy. For example, in talk shows and other popular venues, some commentators challenged the screen masculinity of Hanks, citing the fact that he had cross-dressed in the ABC sitcom *Bosom Buddies* (1980–1982), played a gay lawyer felled by AIDS in *Philadelphia* (Jonathan Demme, 1993), and been the lead in romantic comedies such as Nora Ephron's *Sleepless in Seattle* (1993).[2] Was this Everyman actor "man enough" to embody the 1940s-style epic masculinity of Spielberg's combat hero?

Ironically, in *Sleepless in Seattle*, Hanks's Sam Baldwin asserts his masculinity precisely by expressing a genre preference for war movies like *The Dirty Dozen* (Robert Aldrich, 1967) over the kind of "beautiful romance" typified by the tearjerker, *An Affair to Remember* (Leo McCarey, 1957)—a not completely convincing moment in Hanks's performance, to be sure.[3] Yet, Sam's express taste in movies notwithstanding, this father-widower, haunted by the memory of his dead wife, serves as the wholesome 1990s counterpart to Cary Grant's handsome playboy, Nickie Ferrante, of that same 1957 film, which *Sleepless* remakes and replays when Sam finally meets Annie Reed (Meg Ryan) atop the Empire State Building, and they form a couple at film's end. Given the undercutting caption affixed to a film still of Meg Ryan in one review of *Courage Under Fire* (1996)—"WHEN SALLY MET G.I. JOE"[4]—there is an odd symmetry in these judgments about the war-film casting of Hanks and Ryan, views that are predicated on the alignment of certain stars, gender roles, and genres, based on the history that each carries.

With these controversies in mind, my objective in the present chapter is to explore the ways in which the World War II combat films of the 1990s shape the remembrance of gender identities as they simultaneously revisit and revise established generic and aesthetic standards. Like other Hollywood history films, the World War II combat film engages in a citation and displacement of events from both the period it portrays and the one in which it was produced, as well as from eras between and beyond these. It thereby illustrates a principle described by Hayden White: "Every narrative, however seemingly full, is constructed on the basis of a set of events that might have been included but were left out; this is as true of imaginary narratives as it is of realistic ones. And this consideration permits us to ask what kind of notion of reality authorizes construction of a narrative account of reality in which continuity rather than discontinuity governs the articulation of discourse."[5]

The notion of reality in question in the present context is one that absents women's particular history and derealizes female characters, while simultaneously deploying these characters to manage some of the intractable content that the combat genre bears. Thus, most conspicuously, the genre relies on female characters as structuring absences, love objects who motivate and enable the warrior to fight, as they validate his heterosexuality within the homosocial world of combat. It also depends upon the paradoxical depiction of female characters who serve doubly as the maternal bearers of soldier sons and as harbingers of the intractable fact of death in battle. Thus, for example, the fecund mother whose soldier sons have died becomes the immediate reason and symbolic cause that necessitates further mortal sacrifice in *Saving Private Ryan.*

No less importantly, the aesthetic dimensions that mark 1990s combat films always carry metahistorical implications; that is, beyond depicting particular historical moments—centrally, a "good war"—they also imply how history *ought* to be envisioned, narrated, and valued, and what kinds of felt responses it should provoke. Thus, they participate in a value-laden aesthetic tradition that considerably precedes the cinema's own brief history, one defined in part by its conceptualizations of the sublime, the beautiful, and the uncanny. I have traced the evolution of these three aesthetic modes in relation to gender and genre in the introduction. As I noted there, the sublime stirs feelings of terror through awful grandeur, and it is an aesthetic mode associated in American culture with male-centered narratives, including the overwhelming landscapes of John Ford's Westerns and war stories. The following passage from Tim O'Brien's Vietnam War–based work *The Things They Carried* provides a concise example of its paradoxical, painful allure: "It can be argued . . . that war is grotesque. But . . . for all its horror, you can't help but gape at the awful majesty of combat . . . It fills the eye. It commands you. You hate it, yes, but your eyes do not."[6] A quintessential example on film is blacklisted American director Cy Endfield's *Zulu* (British, 1964), which depicts the attempts of 140 Welsh infantrymen in the British Army to defend their mission from attack by 4,000 implacable Zulu warriors. Shot in Technirama (2.35:1) and based on a historical event from 1879, *Zulu* is also a striking illustration of how technology, racial conflict, and battle intersect in shaping a troubling politics of the sublime.

Although writing on the concept of the sublime extends back to Longinus, Edmund Burke's definitions afford more recent compass points, including his preferred focus on the sublime as a natural phenomenon rather than a historical or sociological one. For Burke, sublime aesthetics entail the delight that natural horror, experienced at a safe distance, has the power to arouse. Twentieth-century critics identify numerous problems in Burke's model, including his stereotyped gendering of sublimity as masculine and beauty as feminine, as well as the political constraints he places on the concept, which amount to an incipient desublimation of the historical sublime.

As previously noted, Hayden White, in particular, disparages these latter constraints and the tamed, consoling, "beautified," "domesticated" aestheticization of history to which they gave rise. Such aestheticization, White warns, "permits the historian to see some beauty, if not good, in everything human and to assume an Olympian calm in the face of any current social situation, however terrifying it may appear to anyone who lacks historical perspective."[7] In opposing Burke, White aligns himself with Schiller, who anticipates Nietzsche in exclaiming, "Away then with falsely construed forebearance [sic] and vapidly effeminate taste which cast a veil over the solemn face of necessity and, in order to curry favor with the senses, *counterfeit* a harmony between good fortune and good behavior of which not a trace is to be found in the actual world . . . We are aided [in the attainment of this point of view] by the terrifying spectacle of change which destroys everything and creates it anew, and destroys it again."[8]

To White's way of thinking, a focus on the raw brutality of events, on their horrific, radically disjunctive, *non*transcendent sublimity, becomes the most conscionable paradigm for conceptualizing and conveying history—especially twentieth-century history—since it alone has the power to generate a Freudian reaction formation, an overwhelming sense of revulsion that would drive a collective desire for profound, utopian social transformation. The notion of the sublime that White underwrites not only opposes the nineteenth-century bourgeois ideas of realism, ideas that subtend "domesticated" novels and historical accounts alike, but also twentieth-century films that inherit and extend their narrative conventions, aesthetics, and political visions. An example of such a work is Ken Burns's celebrated documentary *The Civil War* (1990), with its central vision of the nation as a family coming to terms with a terrible tragedy. In this context, Shelby Foote and other experts describe the unbearable chaos of the war and its gruesome statistics, including a thirty percent casualty rate in some battles, while Burns's visuals and plaintive, sensual score construct a consoling story, one revealed in beautiful landscape imagery and voice-overs that read, for example, from the diary account of a young son who yearns to see his mother.

Yet, if White's position is radical in its preference for a depiction of historical cataclysm as a virtual brand of terrorism, wholly unauthorized by transcendent value, its gender alliances are not, for, as I previously explained, they implicitly and problematically bifurcate aesthetics according to very conventional gender dualisms. Moreover, they overlook both the retrograde and radically deconstructive potentials of unheimlich aesthetics, which, by definition, root the unhomey horror within an ambiguous domestic realm. A flawed but suggestive example of this potential is Roman Polanski's 1971 adaptation of Shakespeare's most uncanny tragedy, *Macbeth*, an adaptation that depicts brutality unredeemed by beauty, pointedly links the warrior's being "of woman born" with his mortality, and reverberates with horrific and holocaustal events of the twentieth-century that Polanski himself witnessed. The present chapter explores this potential through other films and in greater depth as it analyzes the relationships of the aesthetic models of the sublime, the beautiful, and the uncanny to gender in the following: *Saving Private Ryan*, with its blending of convention and innovation in creating an aesthetics of sublime terror; *The Thin Red Line*, with its haunting and controversial aesthetics of the beautiful; and the less known but highly illuminating *Midnight Clear* (1991), with its overt gender bending and pervasive aesthetics of the uncanny. All three of these films exhibit a dominant aesthetic mode, yet each also relies on the interaction of aesthetic modes to depict gender identities in the combat genre. Simultaneously, the destabilizing uncanny, shadowed between the sublime and the beautiful, complicates each film's configurations of gender and its vision of twentieth-century warfare.

Spielberg's Sublime in *Saving Private Ryan*

If, as theorists argue, the sublime is founded on terror, pain, power, and exhausting exertion, then the grim, graphic, twenty-seven-minute-long assault on the viewer's senses that prefaces the rescue narrative of *Saving Private Ryan* is sublime. Indeed, through this inaugural combat sequence, Spielberg effectively reinvents the sublime of the World War II combat film by deploying the mechanisms of computer graphic imaging (CGI), digital sound, and forensic makeup to represent the Allied landing at Normandy on June 6, 1944, specifically the American landing at Omaha Beach. Heightening the terrifying visceral impact is Spielberg's refusal, at least initially, to make narrative or cinematic sense of the event, which is so deliberately fragmented—spatially, temporally, acoustically, and for that matter, corporally—as to defy the kind of comprehensive overview that affords the viewer a protective shield, the feeling of safe distance Burke preferred. Indeed, mirroring White's theories, the segment's disjointed editing counterpoints fragmented visuals and the dismemberment of human form and character, as when it confronts the viewer with images of a man picking up his severed arm and carrying it off. Time's inexorability also finds sublime expression. In contrast to Sam Peckinpah, who famously slows time to wrench incongruous beauty from violence, Spielberg shows in real, merciless time a soldier's helmet intercepting a bullet, the soldier quickly removing the helmet to marvel at his luck, and in the same instant, the soldier being shot squarely in his now bare forehead. Further, this focus on individual experience is the more harrowing because it frames what is clearly a mere representational fragment, a small slice of a cataclysm beyond anything the imagination can comprehend.

Collectively, these elements not only convey a tour de force of technologically generated sublimity but also enhance the stature of Tom Hank's Captain Miller, the leader of the group that seeks out Ryan. Physically mature, muscular, and emotionally seasoned, the idealized Miller is capable and courageous—a match for Kant's theory of sublime masculinity in the warrior and for 1940s war-film heroes as well. He can joke in the face of this horrific onslaught, and is revealed later in the film to be a married man and high-school teacher with "all the virtues of peace, gentleness, [and] compassion" that define the Kantian ideal. Although he exhibits doubts and the vulnerability of a trembling hand, his soldierly fitness is confirmed in a throwaway line that dovetails with genre convention. Against the backdrop of the landing's many horrific shots of blood-tinted salt water, Sergeant Horvath (Tom Sizemore) jokes that Miller's mother would disapprove of his current dire situation; Miller's easy response: "I thought *you* were my mother." The exchange glances back to *The Big Red One* (Samuel Fuller, 1980), wherein related imagery comically matches the trauma of battle with the trauma of birth, and the soldierly competence of the sergeant (Lee Marvin) is proven through mastery of both.[9]

The home-front sequence that follows the landing motivates the film's rescue mission and counterpoints the sublimity of battle with the desublimated beauty of the home front, which is both biologically maternal and steeped in Americana. Centered on an Iowa farm woman about to receive notification that three of her four sons have been killed in separate engagements, all within a week of one another, the sequence begins with Army Chief of Staff General George C. Marshall's pledge to save the life of the remaining son. The mother appears in a framing that echoes the threshold tableaux of *The Searchers*—an enormously influential film for Spielberg.[10] Yet, whereas Ford positions his pioneers on the porches and doorways beyond which lies the sublime and dwarfing grandeur of the American West and the terror that white settlers associate with its racially other native inhabitants, Spielberg positions the mother in a framing that retains no trace of the threat inherent in that earlier spectacle. Instead, the tranquility of the land frames Mrs. Ryan, who is shown in a shot with her back turned to the camera, anticipating an unspeakable loss.

The sequence in which this mother appears is given an emotional and revealing description by Richard T. Jameson, as follows:

> It just might be that the most shattering sequence of *Saving Private Ryan* takes place as far from Europe's battlefields as you can get. . . . Spielberg has never directed a more iconographically precise scene: the farmhouse on the hill, the fields and barn, the roll of the land and the curve of the road on which, momentarily, a car will appear. Each frame— and these are *frames,* distillations of hearth, home, country, security such as exist somewhere in the national unconscious— intensified the awful anticipation as Mrs. Margaret Ryan (Amanda Boxer), drying dishes at her kitchen window, becomes aware that her life is about to change forever. She walks to her door, opens it, steps onto the porch, sees her minister and a man in uniform getting out of the car, sways, and sits abruptly on the porch flooring before she can fall. *Saving Private Ryan* is scrupulous about both the grandeur and the wastefulness of its central mission, a mission that will place many lives in jeopardy so

that one life, that of the remaining Ryan son, might perhaps be spared. But really, this sequence renders the ambivalence moot at best. For that woman, anything; anything at all.[11]

Thus, insofar as *nostalgia* derives from the Greek *nostos* (to return home) and *algia* (a painful condition), the scene is consummately nostalgic in its layered yearnings for womb, mother, home, rural heartland, and America—the beautiful (mother) marshaled as an aesthetic counterweight to, and simultaneously justification for, the grim battle abroad. The film memorializes maternal reproduction as an American ideal—indeed, as America *herself*—in the person of a mother whose iconic status remains unencumbered by character detail.

Just as this icon of America as maternal motivates the saving of young Ryan—to be sure, in part for public-relations purposes—that undertaking in turn affords further moments in which the mother or wife and her beauty are honored through soldierly memory. Specifically, the film foregrounds maternal sacrifice through the recollections of the medic in Miller's squad, a youth whose thoughts of his mother give rise to expressions of longing and regret. Related emotions also define Captain Miller, who reflects, "Sometimes I wonder if I've changed so much my wife is even going to recognize me," a sentiment that resonates anew in his later death scene. Moreover, as A. Susan Owen observes, in words that stress aesthetic beauty, "As befits a conventional democratic hero, Miller figures his (absent) wife as the idealized image of peace, content and sensual pleasure. He likes to watch her prune the rose bushes. It is easy to imagine Mrs. Miller as a national treasure."[12]

Not only do the thoughts of wives and mothers back home define these soldiers, however, but also the men's incorporation of conventionally feminine traits, an incorporation that, not coincidentally, also defined 1990s media representations of the Gulf War. Again to quote Owen: "Although biological women recede into the margins of this war story, the feminine is prominently inscribed in and on the male characters," and as evidence Owen points to Miller's genial, self-revelatory techniques for conflict resolution and his refusal to participate both in the killing of hostages and in sexist banter, qualities that are enforced by Tom Hank's identities in other movies mentioned above.[13] In her influential work, Susan Jeffords identifies this kind of reformulated masculinity with post–Vietnam War narratives:

"The apparent breaking of gender boundaries that occurs when men [occupy female positions] is simultaneously a spectacle to distract from the reaffirmation of gender boundaries and a controlling of gender movement through the reinstitution of rational violence. In this way, the apparent occupation of the feminine position by the masculine is not seen as a challenge to constructions of gender but instead as an appropriation of them. As Zoe Sofia phrases it, 'masculinist production depend[s] upon the prior cannibalization of women, and the emulation of female qualities.'" [14]

From this perspective, then, *Saving Private Ryan* creates Miller as a masculine ideal that incorporates conventionally feminine traits—that is, it anachronistically aligns 1940s male behavior with women's-movement ideals of masculine behavior—and thereby retrospectively erases a significant motivation for the movement's very existence. Or, in Owen's words, "historical characterizations like John Miller can function to discredit the urgency of feminist critiques of past and present American gender practices, or to imply that contemporary feminist critique is obsolete," [15] a potential reinforced in the film by the absence of corresponding depictions of women in the contemporary munitions labor force, personified in the 1940s by the capable, muscular Rosie the Riveter, or for that matter in farm labor, apart from Mrs. Ryan's household chores. Owen even goes as far as to argue that the feminization of Miller extends to his inscription, in his dying speech, as a figure of feminized democracy, as he urges Ryan to earn this sacrifice.

However that may be, it seems undeniable that the film's feminization of Miller gives a new dimension and relevancy to White's argument. [16] That is, White's concern with the evasion of history through the desublimation or domestication of narrative can here be related to the creation of a historical narrative centered on an anachronistically "domesticated" male who "occupies" women's identities and thereby effaces significant ruptures in American history. These include post–Vietnam anxieties, evidenced in film depictions of that war, that the women's movement sabotaged American manhood to the point that it was no longer battle-worthy. Thus, like the film's desublimated evocation of *The Searchers*—a Western evoked without reference to its complex racial legacy—the domestication of the most idealized of the film's soldiers effaces a complex, divisive past.

Yet, significantly, another aesthetic dynamic, the unheimlich, also shapes the film's narrative, complicating the gender dynamics considered to this point, and it does so nearly from the outset. Most simply, at a technological level, uncanny elements underpin the sublime of the Normandy landing sequence, for what turns this sequence into a cinematic landmark and gives it an unprecedented visceral impact is in part its multiplication and magnification of the kinds of effects that made lowbrow, insistently home-centered, 1990s teen horror flicks horrific—the CGI-generated uncanny aesthetics of blood and dismemberment and of doubt about the line between the living and the dead; in short, a technologically updated version of the aesthetic mode that Freud ultimately ties to the fantasy of intrauterine existence. Thus, in an important sense, the uncanny inheres in this battlefield sublime.[17]

It does so far more, and far more complexly and provocatively, in the film's final battle, waged over the bridge at Ramelle, and especially in a disturbing scene within this sequence that centers on the slender, bright, bumbling translator Corporal Upham (Jeremy Davies), a young clerk and outsider figure pressed into combat duties for which he is totally unprepared. The scene in question is a disquietingly intimate one, played out with a few individuals in the interior of a blasted-out building. Here, a fireplace, drapes, and other homey details of what was once a second-story residence form a kind of primal mise-en-scène for the disturbingly sexualized, excruciating, hand-to-hand struggle of Mellish (Adam Goldberg), a Jewish GI in Miller's squad, and a German SS soldier, as Upham sits helplessly frozen and traumatized at the (liminal) midpoint of the stairs below.[18] Never having been "reborn" through battle or prepared for combat beyond basic training, the boyish Upham is too petrified to deliver aid or ammo to Mellish, who consequently dies when the German, uttering intimate admonishments, pierces his heart with Mellish's own bayonet. Whereas Upham had earlier proven himself capable of translating beautiful love lyrics sung by Edith Piaf and of sympathetically reaching out in French to a frightened little girl, and in German to a terrified enemy soldier taken captive, here Upham is a culpably passive witness and, in his inability to reach out to Mellish, an opposite to the more masterful and "masculine" Miller, as well as to the *über*-masculine SS soldier.[19]

Tellingly, Spielberg has said that he identifies with Upham, and his assertion tips us off, I believe, to the film's positioning of its viewers, men and women alike.[20] Situated as Upham's doubles, viewers are perforce impotent, virtually motionless witnesses, capable at most of fantasies of heroic intervention, and like him, a majority of them have never lived through anything remotely like what they are witnessing, and thus cannot know with any certainty that their response would be more honorable than his. Indeed, the spectator positioning at the moment of Upham's terror is related to one in *Schindler's List* (1993), wherein Spielberg, borrowing a horror film technique, plunges the audience into the dark precisely as the lights go out on a group of Jewish concentration camp inmates, women and girls who may or may not be immediately exterminated. Being situated to identify with the passive, wretched Upham, however, is also something quite different from being situated to identify with the terror of innocent female victims of the German concentration camps; for whereas the latter provokes a raw appreciation of the Jewish plight, the former implicates the audience and enforces an antinarcissistic identification with agonizing liminality.

If, as Burke theorizes, the sublime is individual and painful, the effect Spielberg generates in this scene is devastatingly so. At the same time, the symbolic scope of the moment, wherein German and Jew are locked in mortal combat, points toward the Holocaust, a crucial context that is evoked as well by the presence of the SS insignia on the German soldier's lapel, revealed most clearly after Mellish is killed. Affiliating this German with the elite Nazi military unit that served as Hitler's bodyguard, ran the extermination camps, and dedicated itself to the implementation of the so-called Final Solution, the SS insignia magnifies the resonance of the scene's horrifyingly intimate, eroticized, unheimlich experience. And it is the interweaving of the uncannily intimate and domestic moment with the cataclysmic dynamics of fascism, the global war, and the Holocaust that grants this scene its terrible sublimity, just as it is the image of the small girl in the red coat in *Schindler's List* that is that film's most haunting image.

If Upham's failure implicates the spectator as passive, helpless, and guilty, it also painfully mirrors the ways in which he or she perhaps has not "earned" the sacrifice of people like Mellish and Miller, who is finally killed by the Wehrmacht (regular army) soldier whose life he had earlier spared. Indeed, Upham's pivotal dilemma forms a more discomforting illustration of the questions raised by the modern-day frame story of veteran Ryan, who agonizes in the military cemetery in Normandy about whether he has "earned" the sacrifices that saved him, as Miller, with his dying words, admonished him to do. Although, like Upham, young Ryan is at one point in the film's final battle utterly traumatized and incapacitated, and though he, like Upham, is one of the few men who survives the battle—a battle that Miller's squad joins because of him—the film never positions the audience to identify closely with the young private's trauma. In part, this is because the film shows his breakdown—he is in close shot, grasping his knees, and emitting a silent scream—from the aural and visual vantage point of Miller, who is temporarily stunned and deafened by artillery fire. Further, the critical scene with Upham is also more engaging than the issue of whether the rescue mission to save Ryan makes sense; that is, it is crafted in a way that involves viewers more punitively and painfully than the question about whether Mrs. Ryan's Niobe-like sacrifice is rightly rewarded by risking the lives of Miller's squad.

If Spielberg's reliance on this kind of aesthetic and moral dynamic serves him well, he is arguably less well served by the ways in which his film's narrative seems ultimately to convert and solidify Upham's identity by aligning him with amoral violence and lawless killing, behavior that the movie treats equivocally. It does so through its deployment of the Wehrmacht soldier who kills Miller and who was earlier captured by Miller's squad when they took out a German radar installation at Miller's insistence. The skirmish costs the life of the squad's beloved, maternally identified medic and results in his comrades' resentment toward Miller and their eagerness to retaliate against the German prisoner by killing him on the spot. Upham's command of the German language and concomitant ability to see the enemy's humanity, coupled with his sense of ethics, motivate his lonely resistance to the others. Finally heeding Upham, Miller elects to release the POW on his own recognizance and manages to avert a mutiny only by revealing, at long last, his much speculated-on stateside identity—he was a teacher of English composition—in dialogue that demonstrates his "feminine" ability to diffuse aggression through domestic discourse. Of course, Miller's and Upham's choices come back, uncannily, to haunt them, with deadly consequences for Miller. The direct result of witnessing Miller's death is Upham's conversion to violence against the German, who strongly resembles Mellish's killer. When the German attempts to surrender a second time, Upham promptly shoots him.

Frank Tomasulo contextualizes and forcefully indicts this anti–Geneva Convention trajectory of the film's narrative, along with its fusion of American cynicism, sentimentality, and flag-waving patriotism. By appearing to sanction the murder of surrendering enemy soldiers and prisoners of war—which the film apparently does, not only in Upham's case but in other contexts as well—it can be seen as vindicating what Tomasulo wittily calls the "empire of the gun," a U.S. identity and modus operandi that the film identifies with America's "glorious past," partly as justification for

America's subsequent cold war history and its "future unilateral military invasions, incursions, and interventions" of the 1990s and beyond.[21] Thus, the surgically precise, "clean" kills of the southern fundamentalist sharpshooter, Private Jackson (Barry Pepper), might be seen as an implicit validation of the "surgically precise" strikes in "holy" wars against Iraq. (As I will argue in the epilogue, subsequent combat films about more recent, more controversial military interventions were increasingly assimilated to evolving World War II film conventions as well.)

In the same vein, Tomasulo aptly criticizes the film's failure to represent America's allies and the segregated African-American units that participated in the D-Day invasion (a fault shared by *A Midnight Clear* in its omission of African-American soldiers from the Battle of the Bulge).[22] He takes exception as well to *Saving Private Ryan's* reduction of the German enemy to automata, the killing of which can be easily justified. And, indeed, in the climactic battle scene images of parallel German soldiers with weapons trained at the American enemy recall the automatized Prussian military ideal, and even the most developed of the German characters, the soldier whom Upham first defends and later kills, can be seen as split into two *unheimlich* halves. One half is the captive who tries to prove his humanity and "good guy" credentials to the Americans by doubling them and reeling off a grab bag of familiar U.S. pop culture references— "Fancy, schmancy," "Steamboat Willie," "Betty Boop—what a dish," "Betty Grable—nice gams."[23] The other half is portrayed as an efficient, inhuman killing machine who deliberately shoots Miller and bears a striking physical resemblance to the SS soldier who kills Mellish, making these Germans difficult to differentiate *doppelgängers*. Here, uncanny elements support dubious historiography.

Although Tomasulo's critique is astute and compelling, there is also considerable friction between the film's strategies of narrative justification and containment and its relatively less formulaic sublime and uncanny dimensions. This friction recalls the tension between the chaotic, terrorizing historical sublime and the conventional narrative of nation that Robert Burgoyne perceptively charts in Oliver Stone's *JFK* (1991).[24] The result for *Saving Private Ryan* is a greater degree of complexity than Tomasulo's reading allows. The graphic realism of the film's Omaha Beach sequence still prompts viewers to question the kind of policies and politics that drive nations to reduce their young to cannon fodder, even if it motivates a trajectory of vengeance. As Owen puts it, "The crux of this cultural struggle to remember the past lies in the contradictions of Spielberg's realism: The full measure of sacrifice requires a full measure of horror. The full measure of horror destabilizes ideological claims to 'just war.'"[25] And, to focus more squarely on Upham, while one could argue that he serves as a mechanism for disavowing a certain kind of feminized masculinity (the obverse of Miller's), the film hardly presents his "masculinization" and conversion to lawless killing as redemptive. In fact, Upham's earlier moral courage in the face of fierce opposition from Miller's squad, along with the other marks of youth and civilized understanding that he bears, can be seen as casualties of the war, losses worthy of mourning in his development toward conventional 1940s manhood. And if Miller's "feminization" glosses over feminist history, then Upham's "masculinization" functions more complexly, neither to cancel out his cowardice nor to invalidate his civility, but rather to point out the absurdity of the developmental trajectory that culminates in his murder of the German.

Focusing on the interpretive challenges that Upham embodies, Marouf Hasian, Jr., offers still another view: "When we see Upham, we don't just think of World War II, we think of a perspective—a hesitance to believe in any 'Good War.' Upham's detached interest in the war distances him from the others in the platoon, and when he tries to convince them that they should not be shooting prisoners, his notions of transcendent morality seemed to be idiosyncratic and naive."[26] Yet, again, Upham's belief in the just treatment of prisoners is odd evidence of a detached disbelief in the possibility of any "good war." And in this same vein, even if Miller's death is the direct result of his release of the German as a POW—a POW who rejoins the battle since there is no American unit to turn him over to or to recapture him—viewers may well feel that Miller's failure to make that ethical choice would have compromised his heroic stature and contradicted the higher "feminized" humanity that defines his part. To be sure, in other scenes Miller fails to comment on violations of military codes by other American soldiers, but he does not cross the line with them. Thus, the film's arguably problematic blend of expediency and nostalgia does not cancel out its provocations to complex self-reflection about the act of commemoration. And its depictions of gender—complicated by its mix of aesthetic modes and political reference points and by its implication of the viewer through the figure of Upham—are not ultimately as reductive as they initially may seem.

Beauty and Madness in Malick's *The Thin Red Line*

As its critics noted, the importance of visual beauty to Malick's *The Thin Red Line* is utterly unmistakable, and so, too, is that of the sublime, albeit Malick's sublime is far more nature-centered and metaphysically charged than Spielberg's.[27] Malick's camera trains with equal concentration on the delicate finesse of lace or leaves as on the looming hills and ancient trees of the story's Guadalcanal setting; equally on an interior influenced by Vermeer as on nature's abiding grandeur or war's terror. In his particular kind of emphasis on the beautiful and the sublime, Malick preserves a good deal from the 1962 James Jones novel on which his film is based, but Malick's version also differs from the novel in significant and revealing ways, a surprising number of which concern the uses of the uncanny. Partly for that reason, the novel offers keys to understanding the aesthetic dynamics of the film, and it therefore forms the point of departure for my discussion of Malick's work.

Like the film, the novel is both epic in scope and often sublime in its aesthetic force, and like the film, it interweaves numerous individual reflections from the soldiers of Charlie Company, infantrymen charged with retaking Guadalcanal atoll from the Japanese in 1942–1943. Moreover, just as the film relies on an unconventional narrative structure through its placement of battle scenes and its fragmentation of the storyline, the novel develops a self-conscious resistance to the kinds of narrative coherence and patterns of meaning that, according to White, inhibit politically responsible representations of twentieth-century history. The novel even articulates a kind of aesthetic self-justification in this regard. Specifically, Jones's Private John Bell, a former engineer officer now serving in the infantry, reflects on the falsifying tendencies of war films and novels and dismisses them precisely for their insistence on making false sense of the meaningless:

> If this was a movie, this would be the end of the show and something would be decided. In a movie or a novel they would dramatize and build to a climax of the attack. When the attack came in the film or novel, it would be satisfying. It would decide something. It would have a semblance of meaning and a semblance of emotion. And immediately after, it would be over.

> The audience could go home and think about the sem-
> blance of the meaning and the semblance of the emo-
> tion. Even if the hero got killed, it would still make
> sense. Art, Bell decided, creative art— was shit.[28]

Bell's consciousness often conveys an exceptionally self-aware preoccupation with the psychological processes that many of Jones's characters experience as they are deprived of certainty about how they will hold up, perform, or define themselves in combat; and as the above passage suggests,
Bell's is a kind of privileged voice in the novel, not only psychologically but
also where the political dimensions of aesthetics are concerned. Given to reflections on the dissonance between beauty and war, he frequently associates the beauty and tranquility of the tropical setting with his wife, Marty, a
kind of life force and a woman for whom he feels great desire. Hence, after
news spreads through Charlie Company of the discovery of an instance of
extreme enemy brutality—E Company has found a man from G Company
beheaded, his genitals severed and stuffed in his mouth—Bell focuses on
and escapes into the incongruous luminous loveliness of the tropical setting: "The evening itself that night, in cynical contrast to the news, was very
lovely. . . . a lovely striated tropic sunset to look at in the western sky. It was
a time to think of peacefulness and women." [29]

The novel, however, also complicates this sense of oppositeness between
beauty, nature, peace, life, and women, on the one hand, and the terror of
war and death on the other—and in images charged with a nightmarish uncanniness. Indeed, Bell's experiences of and reflections on uncanny visions
go a long way toward spelling out the implications of the novel's title—the
thin red line that, according to an old Midwestern saying, divides the sane
from the mad (and beyond the saying, also intersects with other divides,
such as race and gender, as will become apparent). When Bell first witnesses
the remains of a soldier killed in infantry combat, he hallucinates that he
is the dead man's double and that his own wife Marty is witness to the
spectacle:

> Quite without preparation he had found himself star-
> ing at a horrible halucinatory [sic] double-image of
> himself and [the dead man's] shirt. He was both
> standing upright and wearing that pierced, lifesoaked
> shirt and at the same time lying pierced and life-

soaked himself on the ground after having flung it
away from him, while somewhere up behind him out
of eye range he could nevertheless see a weird, tran-
scendental image of his wife Marty's head and shoul-
ders superimposed among the foliage gloom of the
trees looking down at the two images sadly. . . . *I'm
so sorry. So sorry for you.* It was said with all of that
vitality and force-of-life lifeforce Marty had so much
of in her.[30]

The passage represents, in a moment that crystallizes the uncanny of war, a
terrifying breakthrough of consciousness: of death and the feminine, of the
end and the beginning, and of the uncertain limits of the self. Yet in the
course of time, Bell also realizes that the war reduces not the enemy other
but *us* to automata, as he whistles to himself "I am an automaton" to the
tune of "God Bless America," realizing further that his inhumanity ironically improves his ability to function in combat.[31]

In a still more revealing passage, the novel later takes up this theme again
in order to anatomize the dynamics among beauty, race, sexuality, and the
uncanny; the passage in question involves Bell's experience of a malaria
nightmare in which Marty is giving birth. Bell has been thinking of her and
her lover—because he is sure that she has one—and in his dream his fear
takes on unexpected dimensions. The dream initially spotlights his conde-
scendingly affectionate view of his wife's childlike aspect—a view that mirrors Burke's sense that beauty is linked with helplessness and generates feelings of superiority. Bell dreams that Marty cries out, "'I'm pushing! I'm
trying!' in a child's brave voice.'" As the baby emerges, however, "Bell sat
aghast in horror, embarrassed, disbelieving, and strangely acquiescent, and
watched the coal black baby come lasciviously the rest of the way out of the
beautiful, beautifully white, shaved crotch of his wife. The color contrast
was strangely gorgeous, oddly satisfying, suddenly very sensual. And more
bluntly painful than anything Bell had ever felt in his life." Still dreaming,
Bell realizes that he is sexually excited by the sight of this birth scene, then
looks again only to discover that the infant "wasn't black it was Japanese."
Ruminating on his dream, the socially progressive Bell later speculates that
when men at war think of their wives, their fantasies give rise to feelings of
racial hatred, and he considers these dynamics in terms of what he calls
"sexual esthetics."[32] Thus uncanny terror, emanating from the "beautiful"

source of "a certain lustful pleasure," and from radically destabilized identities (what Kristeva calls the "destructuration of the self"),[33] provides Bell with an etiological rubric for comprehending the drive to wage war.

Revealingly, Burke's reflections on obscurity as a property of the sublime also have racial and gender dimensions. He relates the story of a blind boy who regained his vision at age thirteen or fourteen and was made uneasy by the sight of a black object. Later, Burke reports, "upon accidentally seeing a negro woman, he was struck with great horror at the sight."[34] Although Burke usually links darkness with sublimity, and the feminine with light, life, and beauty, as Mitchell notes, this anecdote signals a psychic and rational confusion: "The double figure of slavery, of both sexual and racial servitude, appears in the natural colors of power and sublimity."[35] (Thus, much as the French Revolution created gender trouble for Burke's conceptual framework, so too does this interplay of race and gender. One might recall, here, Sula's claim, in Toni Morrison's novel, "'You say I'm a woman and colored. Ain't that the same as being a man?'").[36] To be sure, compared with Burke, Jones's novel offers a more self-aware modernist depiction of how the uncanny destabilizes other aesthetic categories and shapes the representation of war. Specifically, the generically conventional formula of paternal mastery over parturition is here reconceptualized as an issue of the politics of race and gender and what Bell calls "sexual esthetics," the uncanny beauty that motivates men to hate the enemy other and make war. Self-reflexively, Bell's ruminations provide something like a theory of why the mastery of parturition is important to the combat genre.

Malick's film considerably expands the novel's attention to the luminous tropical beauty of the setting and to the eerie dialectic of beauty and war, especially through images that frame the astonishing variety of the natural world—its shifting sunlight and sea light, land and mist, and its variegated fauna and flora.[37] But while Jones attributes many of his more revelatory moments to Bell and creates Private Witt as a minor character, Malick makes Bell (Ben Chaplin) and Witt (Jim Caviezel) physically and vocally similar doubles of each other and gives Witt the more significant role. Witt, in fact, speaks the film's first words, asking in voice-over, "What's this war in the heart of nature? Why does nature vie with itself? Is there an avenging power in nature, not one power but two?" The words accompany a prologue, not based on a specific scene from the novel, in which a crocodile slowly sinks into green waters, an image linked by a lap dissolve to a shot of the base of an enormous tree, which in turn cuts to a worm's eye view of a light-filtering canopy of leaves—a romanticist's vision of a sublime cathedral in nature.[38] Moreover, like Freud's crocodile, this one is also tied to a focus on the maternal, and it will rhyme with imagery of woman as both the idealized bearer of children and as the harbinger of death, the "ma(w) of war."

After these initial images, Witt's connection to the natural world is quickly established as being less centered on a conflictual sublime than on the Edenic, lyrical beauty of the native Melanesians' world, epitomized both by the joyful play of the Melanesian children in the clear sea and by a beautiful smiling Melanesian mother who washes the head of her child, as if in a baptismal gesture, as she stands in a shallow pool. In a mind-screen flashback, the elements of beauty, the feminine, nature, and the maternal are soon expressly counterpoised by a further element, death, as Witt recalls his own mother and reflects on her deathbed scene at home, presumably a return of a familiar repressed, a manifestation of the uncanny. Although visual details of the mind-screen are domestic and lovely, Witt remembers not only his inability to find the "beauty" in "her going back to God," but also his belief that the immortality must be in the calm with which she faced the end. (Later, Witt's double, Bell, finds beauty in a vision of his gentle, lovely wife, whom he imagines wading into water and beckoning him toward death and the sea—images that recall both the crocodile's movement and Tadzio's summoning Aschenbach at the end of *Death in Venice,* as well as the waters or amniotic fluid of birth. This mind-screen vision gently aestheticizes the uncanny association of the feminine with death and enables Bell to advance during battle.)[39]

There is much that aligns Witt with the aesthetics of beauty and tranquility in Malick's film. For one, there is actor Caviezel's gaunt, ethereal elegance (enhanced by the film's lighting)—a look that, like the elongated human forms in mannerist painting (in El Greco, for example), signifies spiritual beauty and the longing for transcendence. Similarly, Witt's preference for being AWOL with the peaceful, family-centered Melanesians to fighting the Japanese, as well as his concern and compassion for his fellow soldiers, links him to the values of beauty and tranquility. His repetition of the Melanesian woman's baptismal gesture when he comforts a wounded soldier by trickling water from a canteen on the man's head reinforces this point, as does his attentive presence at other soldiers' dying moments, when he tries to glimpse the beauty and immortality in these events.[40]

Although Witt seems to be yet another instance of what Zoe Sofia terms the "cannibalization of women" in post–Vietnam War films, his status not as Everyman but as odd man out overtly differentiates this feminized character from typical 1940s masculine ideals. Significantly, he also enacts a relation to maternity very different from that of the soldiers in *The Big Red One;* whereas they "manage" the maternal (and implicitly manage death in the process), he expressly aims to incorporate the maternal without obviating it and thereby affirm and preserve a kind of spiritual beauty and serenity in the face of the battlefield deaths that inevitably come too soon.[41] His ability to incorporate the other extends to his sympathetic ability to "hear" the voice-over of a dead Japanese soldier, who is entirely buried save for his face, which looks like a sad human mask in the earth.

At the same time, Witt's initial vision of beauty also has an uncanny double, one he sees only after he himself has been immersed in the horrors of battle, and this doubling recalls Freud's view that whereas the double is initially experienced as "an assurance of immortality, he [later] becomes the ghastly harbinger of death."[42] Immediately after Bell receives a "Dear John" letter from his wife—a letter that leaves him utterly devastated—Witt discovers the fallenness of the island's native people—the human skulls lining the walls of their unhomey huts, suggesting cannibalism (to be sure, an uncanny ingestion that makes the unfamiliar very much one's own). Before, as he had remarked, the Melanesian children appeared never to fight among themselves and seemed the inhabitants of a purely harmonious world; now he sees native children whose world is marred by distrust, conflict, disease, and death. Indeed, Witt here confronts a host of native strangers, others with whom he experiences an unnerving blend of alienation and identification. His divided consciousness is further represented by a flashback to the smiling Melanesian mother, a figure who, in his recollection, does not meet his gaze but who appears in effigy, in profile, now an uncanny death-in-life figure divided from him as if by an abyss.[43]

The juxtaposition of Witt's and Bell's visions of their fallen worlds, and Marty's positioning as an Eve figure, affirms the status of these worlds as doubles, just as Witt's memory of the Melanesian mother frames the cannibalistic native society as the frightening obverse of an edenic one. In effect, Malick's handling of these elements serves as a reformulation of Jones's treatment of the uncanny, conceived in the film in pre- and postlapsarian imagery rather than in the raw, more sexually charged imagery found in the novel's account of Bell's hallucination and nightmare. One result of this transformation is that the film has more pointedly mythic overtones, dimensions that enforce the positioning of women, especially Bell's wife, in a highly conventional, disturbing, and retrograde way. Specifically, Marty's decision to divorce Bell and marry another man—her succumbing to sexual temptation—identifies her as a daughter of Eve and her betrayal of Bell as a replay of the transgression that, according to this creation myth, introduced suffering, sin, and death into the world. The focus on mythologized female infidelity to one's vow obscures the broader historical context of the military's problematic standards of sexual conduct among its fighting men; Marty, as the "enemy within," becomes as threatening to Bell's well-being as the physical enemy without.

More successful is Malick's treatment of Witt's death at the hands of a circle of able Japanese soldiers, camouflaged in nature's lush greenery. The sequence not only fulfills a familiar convention of the combat genre (in which the most sympathetic character dies), but also integrates Malick's aesthetic domains—the uncanny (because always unprepared for) confrontation with death in the form of an enemy who is, like Witt, identified with the natural world, now both in its beauty and dreadful sublimity, and who is in a sense not Witt's opposite but is instead folded back into him.

This death scene is also related to an additional uncanny effect that deserves special attention. It involves an aspect of the film that is both faithful to the novel and yet significantly different in effect. Specifically, Malick represents Japanese troops who are not reduced to automata, but who are subject to gruesome, inhumane mistreatment by an American soldier, in images that are, if anything, toned down relative to Jones's description in the novel. Jones writes: "When Charlie Dale whipped out his pliers and Bull Durham sacks and began yanking gold teeth, Fife had to turn away . . . Dale garnered many gold teeth, and an excellent chronometer which he later sold for a hundred dollars. Coming on a Japanese sitting dejectedly on a doorstoop with his head in his hands, this beautiful watch sticking out like a big diamond on his wrist, Dale shot him through the head and took the watch."[44] This depiction of horribly compromised heroism is one that viewers have come to associate with the Vietnam War film but one that has been repressed in the filmic memory of World War II—hence it generates an uncanny impact here.

Ironically, Thomas Doherty criticizes Malick for portraying the Japanese according to "revisionist intentions or commercial calculations"—that is, from the desire to capitalize on the Japanese market for American films—as well as for being too close in spirit to the Vietnam combat film. As evidence, Doherty asserts that "Japanese soldiers appear mainly as shadows in the grass or defeated victims of American war crimes (reversing the national identities in a well-known rumor of the Pacific war, a ghoulish GI collects gold fillings from the bodies of dead Japanese)."[45] On the contrary, although Malick's *The Thin Red Line* evokes the Vietnam War genre, for example, by casting John Savage in the role of the emotionally devastated Sergeant McCron, it effectively complicates masculine images from that war by showing the uncanny doubling of images of compromised heroism from World War II to Vietnam and by deconstructing a culturally sanctioned misremembrance of difference.

Still more ironic, perhaps, is the paucity of criticism of World War II films of the 1990s for their tendency to sanitize the sexuality of the American soldier. These films portray him as an ideally loyal husband and respectful foreigner, or as romantically involved with a beautiful nurse, and although he may well indulge in sexually charged banter, his fidelity and his feminized dimensions make him the radical opposite of the soldier-rapist found in Brian De Palma's Vietnam War film, *Casualties of War* (1989). Similarly underacknowledged is the collective amnesia of these World War II films regarding the U.S. military's efforts to control women's sexuality back home, and the films' neglect of important revelations, in the midst of the World War II anniversary celebrations of 1990s, about what the Japanese military euphemistically called "comfort women" (sexual slaves for servicemen), along with the U.S. government's role in helping to bury Japan's record in human trafficking. The U.S. military's complicity in this cover-up was motivated, in part, by its own reliance on the Japanese prostitution system, which was redesigned in 1945 to accommodate the needs of occupying U.S. forces. Cynthia Enloe documents these revelations, as well as the significant *similarities* between military prostitution policies on the Axis and Allied sides, and she contextualizes both in relation to sexual policies and politics of other war efforts, including that in Vietnam. (For example, Enloe reports that by the end of America's withdrawal from Vietnam, "between 300,000 and 500,000 Vietnamese women were working as prostitutes in South Vietnam. An estimated four-fifths of them were afflicted with venereal disease".)[46] The endless lines of men awaiting the services of prostitutes in Mike Nichols's *Catch-22* (1970) make connections that are worlds apart from the visions of the commemorative war films of the 1990s, but for the sake of change, these, too, bear remembering.

Keith Gordon's Uncanny A *Midnight Clear*

If the uncanny plays a vital role in Spielberg's and Malick's films, it is virtually ubiquitous in Gordon's *Midnight Clear,* an antiwar film set in the Ardennes forest in late December 1944, during the Battle of the Bulge. An uncanny atmosphere pervades the mise-en-scène, including the abandoned chateau where the young Army intelligence squad on which the film focuses makes their unheimlich "home." Inside, the place is replete with long halls, dark corners, and eerie shadows, and inside and out it is set off by unnerving sculptures—in particular, a snow-dusted stone bishop who literally holds his detached head in his hands (a reminder of Freud's equation of decapitation with castration and hence uncanniness).[47] Similarly, in the middle of a nearby snow-packed road, the corpses of two frozen soldiers—one German, one American—stand upright, doubles locked in a macabre, dancelike embrace; the squad initially mistakes them for the enemy and starts shooting. (The arrangement turns out to be a signal from a small squad of Germans that they want to meet to negotiate their surrender.) Elsewhere, a single frozen hand sticks straight up through the forest snow, and still elsewhere, a road doubles back on itself, sending the hapless American squad in a circle and creating a sickening sense of déjà vu.

Like the mise-en-scène, the cinematography, editing, and sound also convey uncanniness, making the familiar strange. For example, when three of the squad venture from the chateau on a patrol, one of them suddenly looks up in fear, and a quick zoom out unexpectedly becomes an over-the-shoulder shot, aligning the viewer with three waiting German soldiers, poised with rifles trained on the American enemy. Like a series of double takes, a countershot is jump-cut to closer and closer views of the seemingly menacing, statue-still Germans, and the Americans begin screaming, beside themselves with fear. At the end of the scene, the camera again shows the Americans from the Germans' vantage point, but only after the Germans themselves have vacated their position without firing a shot. The cinematography and editing thus position the viewer as a spectral double of the Germans, just as they make the two trios of soldiers, German and American, into strange doppelgängers against the snow. And although sound contributes to the uncanny in this scene, it does so even more elsewhere, as in the disembodied laughter and "Schlaf gut" (sleep well) that the squad hears outside the chateau at night, or in the weird rendering of the Christmas carol that gives the film its name, played over the end credits. Even the film's distanciating voice-over commentary on the army's vocabulary for death reveals the words to be filled with a terribly falsifying sense of child's play, and hence makes the familiar disturbingly strange.

The heart of the uncanny in this movie, however, is the family formed by the decimated squad of young soldiers, a group that the army originally assembled for their high IQs and presumed fitness for intelligence work. They include Will Knott (aka "Won't"), played by a young, emphatically soft-bodied Ethan Hawke (also the film's narrator); Vance "Mother" Wilkins (Gary Sinise), emotionally unstable from shell shock and from grief over his stillborn child; Paul "Father" Mundy (Frank Whaley), who once aspired to the priesthood and who, in death, becomes a Christ-like figure of veneration; and finally Will's three "siblings." Among them is Stan Shutzer, a Jewish GI whose knowledge of Yiddish ironically makes communication with the openly anti-Semitic German squad possible. Ironically, too, it is Stan's aggressive but playful act of building an anti-Hitler snowman that breaks the ice with the Germans and opens the way for them to visit the chateau, bearing holiday presents.

Of special interest is the family's uncanny "Mother," who is both an unusual variant on a combat film formula and a frighteningly familiar personification of a larger cultural construction of maternity and madness. The film develops its critique of war by generating uncanny subversions of the separation between subject and object, us and them, and it makes "her" unstable identity the sticking place. Indeed, whereas Gordon's German soldiers prove to be not the familiar Nazi automata but playful, human, and vulnerable—a group of young boys and old men back from the rigors of the Russian front, who even bear gifts like Christmas magi for their American counterparts—"Mother" is stuck in a negative stereotype, an inverted madonna, whose stillborn child presages disaster.[48]

The instability of "Mother" and his inability to be psychically reborn into the brotherhood of soldiering find vivid expression from the film's first scene. In a snow-covered field, he jumps from a foxhole and runs through the forest, throwing away his rifle, equipment, and clothing. He next appears in a clearing, squatting naked in a frigid stream, moaning and crying, an unnerving blend of despondent mother and hapless warrior. Later, in the chateau, "Mother" is also coded as the madwoman in the attic, literally holed-up there, and it falls to the siblings to safeguard "Mother" and keep him from completely falling apart. To that end, Stan initiates a plan to create the appearance that "Mother" is a hero who deserves to be sent home, and he admonishes Will that, even though the plan is risky, "For 'Mother's' sake, we should at least try."

But the madness of "Mother," his inability to be counted on as a participant in the scheme that the American and German squads jointly contrive—a plan involving the Germans' surrender after a staged skirmish—results in the death of "Father," the Germans, and Stan as well. In a film that shows the insanity of battle, there is, presumably, an ironic justice in the fact that the army gives "Mother" a Bronze Star—the one soldier overtly identified as female, crazy, and trigger happy is the publicly recognized "hero." Although the squad originally intends to obtain a medal and ticket home for "Mother" as bonuses of the fake skirmish, "Mother," ironically, receives the award for turning the skirmish real and deadly, without ever knowing exactly what happened. (As "Father" dies, he repeatedly insists, "Don't tell 'Mother'"—that is, don't tell Vance the truth about the disaster he set off). Thus the film provides an ironic destabilizing of the gendering of the heroism that it critiques. Similarly, the horrific outcome validates the troopfamily's resistance to the conventional boys-to-men war-film narrative, just as it affirms their belief in war's absurdity and in the humanity of their opponent. Yet, paradoxically, the narrative also both codes pacifism as masculine and affirms an old combat-film notion—the idea that success depends on the ability of the soldier to manage the maternal, something "Won't" can't. And as in *Saving Private Ryan*, acting on behalf of a "mother" and for the sake of appearances that are intended to please both her and the higherups proves deadly.

A Midnight Clear includes a single biologically female character, Janice (Rachel Griffin), who is also linked with death. An attractive young woman who, as shown in a flashback, helps four members of the squad fulfill their desire to lose their virginity while on leave, Janice had been engaged to a boy named Matt and had made love to him before he left to fight in Sicily, where he was soon killed. She tells the four that she had been on the brink of suicide, then lost her nerve, then met them. It is thanks to her that the four realize their goal. "Volunteering herself to all of us," Will's voice-over explains, is a "simple, lovely idea" that he and the others initially have trouble recognizing as such; nonetheless, "just before dawn, Janice comes quietly, privately to each of us." As lap dissolves link the images of lovemaking, Will continues, "We pass through the mythical barriers between boys and men, men and death. Janice takes us with her. I think I'll always feel strange about my first sexual experience, masquerading as a dead boy named Matt."

The scene is in many regards highly conventional, with a woman serving as the portal to manhood, life, and death—for like death, she "comes quietly, privately to each of us," in an act that mythically affirms their manhood, their fitness for making love and making war. What deepens the sense of uncanniness, however, is the perception that the four soldiers, too, "masquerade as a dead boy named Matt." [49] In a sense, the four are doubles of death, and their identities are blurred and made diffident even through the very "mythic" acts that are supposed to define and affirm them. The scene's emphasis on Hawke's soft-bodied physique—so different from Hanks's or Caviezel's in the other two films—reinforces his boyishness, his less than fully differentiated sexual identity, and the pathos of his going to war.

Beyond this, the film reminds us that home, the domestic, and "domestication" are not simply synonymous with the beautiful as rational or readily narratable. Instead, congruent with Freud's view, they emerge as sites of trauma and anxiety-producing epistemological uncertainty—or, for that matter, as a mise-en-scène whose beauty defines a fantasy firmly at odds with those conventional visions of "home" and oedipal identity on which the combat film traditionally depends. [50] What the film reveals as "home" or the heimlich at its warmest and most beautiful is, in fact, a scene in which "Mother," Will, and his "siblings" bathe themselves each in turn and then together bathe "Father" Mundy's dead body and wound. They position the bathtub in front of the chateau's blazing hearth, which casts golden light at once sensuously homoerotic and luminously spiritual. Their ritual of communion "resurrects Father" and "reanimates" the living through a beautiful yet eerie, even mad-seeming doubling of those Christian rituals that are designed to deny death's power. [51] In a later instance of this ritualistic motif, the young soldiers also extract the blood of "Father" from his mouth in order to use it to paint protective red crosses on white cloth to shield them all from enemy attack. The accumulation of this imagery heightens the sense of uncanny cruelty when finally the customary act of marking the corpse's identity is shown—literally hammering the boyish Mundy's jaw and teeth on his dog tag. [52] The knowledge that Mundy is dead affords the viewer little protection from a felt empathic response of pain.

The point here is not that there are no atheists in foxholes, but that, in the absence of a humane army or a sane kind of war, unorthodox rituals of resistance are needed, commemorative counterstatements of the kind the film as a whole, in fact, instantiates. Thus, for example, *A Midnight Clear* awakens the repressed of World War II to a degree that the other films do not—by focusing primarily on young boys, not fully oedipalized, battle-hardened men, as victims of war's absurd wastefulness. Released in 1992, Gordon's antiwar film also offers a powerful counterview of "domestica-tion" to the one fostered by media representations of Gulf War soldiers, whose "homey," sentimentalized side was constructed to counterpoint the images of mechanized, impenetrable masculinity embedded in the war's high-tech weaponry, a phenomenon I shall explore further in Chapter Three. (In a related vein, the film similarly counterpoints the domestic side of Arnold Schwarzenegger's war-machine masculinity in the contemporary cult movie, *Terminator 2: Judgment Day* [1991]). Finally, *Midnight Clear's* release date also makes it slightly out of step with the monumental films that began appearing some six years later, including the crassly commercial *Pearl Harbor* (2001), which succeeded in the Japanese market despite its bad U.S. reviews and contrived "from here to maternity" story line. Insofar as *Midnight Clear* shares an independent status with *The Thin Red Line* (and hence some degree of resistance to Hollywood standards), its timing and status jointly contributed to its relative obscurity, even as they appear to have in-creased its potential to imagine and remember an alternative vision of war.

Concluding Comments

My examination of the World War II combat film offers ample evidence that any consideration of the politics of aesthetic style is incomplete if it does not venture beyond the conventional dualism of the sublime and the beautiful and beyond the normative gender notions these entail. The uncanny al-ready functioned as a shadowy third term in the time of Burke and Kant. It threatened to undo Burke's aesthetic binarism of the sublime and the beau-tiful when the destabilizing interplay of race and gender was added to the mix, but also, if Kristeva is right, it in some sense informed Kant's "reasoned longing for universal peace." [53] By the end of the twentieth century, as I have explained, the uncanny also emerged as an indispensable critical term for grasping colonialist dynamics (Bhabha), xenophobia (Kristeva), and the nexus of the feminine and national identity (Molloy), but it has yet to claim its proper place in conceptual frameworks designed to comprehend the relation of aesthetic perception to the spectacle of history, especially that realized in the recent outpouring of combat films.

Further, the three combat films analyzed here can serve to remind us of the degree to which the utopian yearning for change that White describes may itself be functionally inextricable from the unheimlich. If the sublime of twentieth-century history must be represented in its unnarratable horror in order to motivate utopian longing, then these films suggest that there also needs to be some adumbration of a path beyond the horror of twentieth-century warfare, a vision not founded in nostalgic regression to nineteenth-century narrative constructs and attendant gender norms, but not oblivious to the terrors and pleasures conjoined in that messy, contradictory, earthy, other-occupied, borderline "place" Freud identified both with the repressed and with "home."

Indeed, in Kristeva's view, as a psychological phenomenon, the deep-rooted ambivalence of the uncanny can find expression in one of two trajectories. The first is the path toward paranoia and murder; the second involves an "opening toward the new" and an "identification with the other" commensurate with a recognition of the foreignness within us, our status as "strangers to ourselves." [54] Whether the films examined here figure our own strange passivity and terror in the light of the personal sacrifices of others (Spielberg), or complicate an accustomed nostalgia for an age both of "real heroes" and of edenic harmony with nature (Malick), or stage the "home front" within the war zone in order to defamiliarize both (Gordon), they take steps toward contextualizing Kristeva's hopeful second trajectory within a world shown to have been in the horrific throes of the first. If they fail to mount sustained challenges to the cultural constructs that make "woman" and "mother" the ultimate symbolic figures of the unheimlich, even in the context of war—or for that matter to the inscription of the enemy in dehumanized uncanny terms (especially in the case of *Saving Private Ryan*)—or adequately to address issues of race, each nonetheless offers moments that productively complicate the gendering of the war genre, and hence our sense of our relation to commemorations of the nation's past.

In the next chapter, my focus shifts from the World War II combat film to a presidential film set during the cold war, and to the filmic representation of a particular historical woman, one whom insiders admired for her warmth, humor, playfulness, ease with foreigners, and political experience and expertise. Regrettably, her public image as political wife and first lady, insofar as it was crafted and then imposed on her by her power-abrogating husband, largely concealed these qualities. From the 1950s onward, it often provoked observers to describe her in dehumanized terms—for example, to claim that she moved "like an automaton," or that she was "made of steel"—even as she was believed to embody a certain 1950s, self-abnegating wifely ideal.[55] Commenting on this repression and characterizing the lives of Richard and Pat Nixon during his term as president, Kati Marton writes, "The tone of the Executive Mansion is set by the relationship between the president and the first lady. A Cold War . . . raged between the East and West Wings of the Nixon White House. Much as Nixon would show contempt for the constitutional limits on the office of the chief executive, he tried to subvert the traditional role of first lady. Power would flow from only one source: Richard Nixon."[56] The symbolic role of Pat Nixon in the context of this cold war within the unheimlich Nixon White House, the larger cold war that it doubled, and Oliver Stone's mid-1990s interpretation of the Nixon presidency are topics to which I shall now turn.

Why, love forswore me in my mother's womb:
And, for I should not deal in her soft laws,
She did corrupt frail nature with some bribe,

. . . .

To disproportion me in every part,
Like to a chaos, or an unlick'd bear-whelp
That carries no impression like the dam.

III Henry VI, 3.2.153–155, 160–162

America cannot stand pat.

Richard M. Nixon

Shakespeare's Richard, Duke of Gloucester, calls up the folkloric belief that bears are born shapeless lumps of fur, to be "licked into shape" by their mothers, and this future Richard III likens his misshapenness to that of an unlicked cub, disfigured by maternal neglect. The cinema of Oliver Stone is replete with images of bad mothering, and this one seems most suggestive for *Nixon* (1995), a film that portrays the thirty-seventh president (played by Anthony Hopkins) as first and foremost a victim, not only of maternal silence and neglect, but also of psyche-deforming maternal tongue-lashings and verbal lickings.[1] Had it not been for his early, crippling experiences, the film argues, this World War II veteran and quintessential cold warrior might have succeeded in greatly reducing the arms race and limiting the threat of global war; indeed, might have served out his second term as president and speeded the cold war to a conclusion. Even in the absence of those accomplishments, documentary footage of Nixon's funeral at the end of

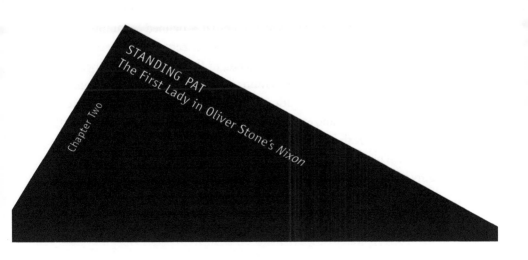

STANDING PAT
The First Lady in Oliver Stone's *Nixon*

Chapter Two

Stone's film shows Robert Dole extolling the man and asserting that the last half of the twentieth century will be "known as the age of Nixon."

Insofar as *Nixon* plays out on a world stage the dire consequences of deficient mothering, demonstrating their global ramifications, Stone's portrait of Hannah Nixon (Mary Steenburgen) reconfirms his reputation for matrophobic filmmaking with a vengeance.[2] Yet given this image of Nixon's mother, the film's sympathetic depiction of Nixon's wife (played by Joan Allen) comes as something of a surprise, and even more so in light of the striking ambivalence that Americans have expressed historically toward first ladies. Indeed, as Margaret Truman documents, from Martha Washington onward, first ladies have been "subject to political attacks far nastier in some ways than those any President has ever faced," especially when they sought to move beyond the sphere of traditional wife and mother, or when they seemed to embody their public-relations role inauthentically or robotically, as many believed Pat Nixon did.[3] Moreover, as Spielberg's *Saving Private Ryan* suggests, even the most traditionally idealized mother can become, in the discourse of national identity, an equivocal emblem. Against this backdrop, how do we interpret Stone's engaging, insightful Pat?

In part, the idealized Pat and vilified Hannah clearly function in the film as an ambivalent equation, an instance of the good mother–bad mother binarism that, according to Ann Kaplan, has served as one of North America's most potent political tools for aligning women with its shifting needs.[4] Additionally, since the very term "first lady" bespeaks a retrograde longing—for a class system the United States has supposedly transcended and for a child's idealized vision of the *first woman* it knows—it implicitly affiliates the maternal icon with a nostalgic notion of nation, conflating maternal and national ideals. The ambivalence that marks the representation of Pat and Hannah also links them to Freud's definition of the unheimlich, a concept—much like Freud's idea of the maternal—defined by ambivalence.

There can be little doubt that Stone's *Nixon* is centrally concerned with the concept of the United States as a nation, or that the uncanny powerfully shapes the film's vision, given its emphasis on doubles, alter egos, omens, specters, and compulsive repetition. Moreover, the film's focus on Nixon's repressed childhood and troubled identity boundaries dovetails with Freud's theory that the psychic origins of the uncanny are located in early repression. What is more striking, however, is the degree to which the film's uncanny imagery configures national identity through equivocal iconic images tied to Pat as first lady and as a counterimage to both Hannah and Richard, an American of whom Stone has claimed, "He is us."[5]

It is worth stressing that the cultural inscription of the historical Pat Nixon in uncanny terms considerably precedes both Stone's film and her term as presidential wife. In 1958, when Nixon was vice president, the London *Spectator's* description of her already cast the die: "She chatters, answers questions, smiles and smiles, all with a doll's terrifying poise. There is too little comprehension. Like a doll she would still be smiling while the world broke. Only her eyes, dark, darting and strained, signal that inside the black suit and pearls there is a human being, probably content not to get out. . . . One grey hair, one hint of fear, one golden tea-cup overturned on the Persian carpet and one could have loved her."[6]

The *Spectator's* portrait eerily echoes the Hoffmann story Bhabha relies on to epitomize the colonial question, but through which Molloy focuses interlocking anxieties about women and the boundaries of national identity. To recapitulate, Hoffmann's tale describes a young man in love with an automaton, a wooden doll, and in that story, the destruction of the doll and the young man's subsequent suicide have social consequences: "The history of this automaton had sunk deeply into their souls, and an absurd mistrust of human figures began to prevail. Several lovers, in order to be fully convinced that they were not paying court to a wooden puppet, required that their mistress should sing and dance a little out of time . . . but above all else . . . that she should frequently speak in such a way as to really show that her words presupposed as a condition some thinking and feeling."[7] Fittingly the *Spectator* requires Pat to perform within an equally narrowly prescribed range of activities (show a "grey hair," a "hint of fear," a "golden tea-cup overturned on the Persian carpet"). It matches the dubious humanity it ascribes to her with the unsullied foreign carpet and implies the sense of the cold-war world as a place that could "break" (in a nuclear holocaust?), and yet still paints her with a Dr. Strangelove–like smile. Thus it locates around her a troubling conjunction of the public and private, the interior and exterior, and the domestic and foreign, as well as the human and nonhuman. Paradoxically expected to serve as a *public* American symbol of the *private*, the real, and the values of home, she is judged here as unlovable and unreal in her femininity, her incomprehension, and her *terrifying* doll-like poise.

In fact, Molloy explains that in general "[t]he figure of woman stands in a metonymic but paradoxical relation to the nation," *as peripheral yet foun-*

dational,[8] so it should come as no surprise that this ambiguous representational status is magnified in the cultural standing of political wives and, in the United States, of the first lady above all. As I will argue, Stone's film conceptualizes Pat not only "ideally," as the "genuine" and the "true," but also as a double for the dreaded phallic mother to whom she is opposed, yet with whom the film at times also aligns her. An iconic figure who slips between discursive frames of reference, Pat is used to evoke multiple cold-war political contexts, and yet is delimited in ways that both protect the ideal of the president and neglect the real potential signaled by the progressive stances the historical Pat Nixon espoused.

This chapter, then, will identify and analyze the constellation of icons that Stone's film projects onto the first lady, as well as the uncannily evocative dramas that these images enact. I will examine dialectically the cultural projections that inform Stone's representations of Pat and Hannah and the ways in which these representations both define and trouble his notions of the nation and of Nixon as its key cold-war leader. Although Pat shares a certain marginality with the women characters discussed in the preceding chapter, she serves more dramatically than they as the center from which various forms of doubling emerge, and as Freud asserts, the double, above all, is indispensable to themes of uncanniness.[9]

Pat *Parrhesiastes*/Plastic Pat

Nixon codes Pat as a range of cultural icons, including Truth, a conventionally feminine emblem. Thus, in a laudatory review, Roger Ebert praises the film for casting Pat as the conscience, the voice of truth, and Christopher Sharrett recognizes that she both "[pricks] Nixon's conscience" and "alleviates somewhat the condescending or irrelevant position [Stone] assigns most female characters."[10] The film's first lady is in fact constructed as "true" or "real" on a number of levels: one is that of historical or biographical veracity—especially important to Stone given the troubled reception of *JFK;* the others involve related abstract figurations, such as conscience, family, and the "reality principle," all of which I will call iconic, since the relationship between the first lady as signifier and the contents of these signifieds is neither purely arbitrary nor merely indexical. Mediating the biographical and the iconic, *Nixon* also conceptualizes Pat as what the ancient Athenians might have called a *parrhesiastes,* someone who risks speaking the truth to a person in a position of superior power; someone whose moral virtue compels him or her to speak out in order to try to save another; someone who, in short, functions much as the Fool does in Shakespeare's *King Lear*.[11]

Indeed, the filmic Pat is identified with the "reality principle" in counterpoint to her husband. She possesses greater authenticity, moral balance, and a deeper capacity for compassion; she comprises the "real" as well as the "true," and thus confirms Molloy's perception that in discourse about national identity, the female signifies the real.[12] Further, insofar as a first lady holds the Bible for her husband's swearing-in, the film's conceptualizing of the first lady as a truth figure resonates historically; and in this regard, it evokes iconography that implies that the nation's "truth," its dominant religious code, and its first lady function in unison.[13] Within this iconography, with each new inauguration, the first lady performs symbolically in a "rebirth" of the nation.

Pat's role as truth-teller is visible in most of the scenes that include her, and although it typically relates to home-centered values, it also entails a canniness about politics. During one of these scenes, she and Nixon's advisors watch the famous televised 1960 Kennedy-Nixon debate on studio monitors. Her comments suggest that she is astute about the media and politics—perhaps more so than key players on Nixon's team, including his campaign manager, Murray Chotiner (a man whom, historically, Pat Nixon despised), and H. R. Haldeman (whom, historically, she regarded as an opportunist).[14] Instantly sensing the damage the televised debate will inflict, and remonstrating with Nixon's men for allowing her husband to proceed with it, Pat exclaims that Nixon "doesn't have to debate John Kennedy."

Pat's clear-sightedness—which recalls that of the aptly named Clara in Hoffmann's story—also emerges in a scene following Nixon's 1962 defeat by Pat Brown in the California gubernatorial race. Here, her perceptiveness and family-centered priorities contrast with Nixon's paranoid, distorted vision. He blames Castro for his loss and endorses his father's view that people are motivated by fear, not by love; she mocks these views and rejects the notion that fear motivates voters. The first in the film directly to articulate the theme of Nixon as a lost soul, she laments the destructive changes in his character and reprimands him for never seeing his daughters. She also warns him that he must be there for his family, or she will divorce him. Perceiving the threatened divorce as a painful replay of maternal rejection and lost public favor (and thus conflating mother, wife, and nation), Nixon desperately promises never to run for political office again.[15] In the following scene, he delivers the infamous "you won't have Nixon to kick around anymore" speech, a statement expressionistically filmed to contrast his mental imbalance with her grounded, family-centered vision.

Similarly, a scene set after Johnson's 1968 decision not to seek reelection humorously contrasts Nixon's self-deception with Pat's unselfishness, prescience, and normalcy. Breaking his promise to her, Nixon exuberantly resolves to throw his hat back into the political ring, and Haldeman exclaims (ironically enough), "Vietnam's gonna put you in there this time, chief." When John Mitchell reminds Nixon that he cannot afford to alienate Pat, since she sways voters, Nixon responds, "Don't worry—I'll use the old Nixon charm on her," prompting Haldeman's mocking query to the others: "The old Nixon charm? Who could resist that?" Pat's generosity and insight counterpoint Nixon's comic delusion and self-concern. Although she hates politics, resents his reneging on a promise, and wants to protect her home life, she acquiesces under the condition that he should preconcertedly choose the course that will bring him real happiness—and here, she pinpoints the critical challenge. Sometime after they win the election, she enters his White House bedroom and reaches out for intimacy, telling him, "You have everything you ever wanted. You've earned it. Why can't you just enjoy it?" but he can only unhappily circle the room away from her—the camera in close pursuit—and nervously run through a list of his enemies.

As the voice of conscience, Pat is also granted the position of articulating some of the film's most penetrating criticisms of Nixon. When the Watergate crisis deepens and he persists in hiding the truth from his family, the couple sit physically and emotionally separated at opposite ends of a long dinner table, a setting that recalls Charles Foster Kane and his wife at the end of the famous montage of meals in *Citizen Kane*—but in a degree of separation that typified the Nixons' actual White House dinners. Unlike Emily Kane, however, Pat, acting on her awareness that whatever her husband is hiding is eating him alive, tries to bridge the gap. When he rudely rebuffs her, she demands to know, "When do the rest of us stop paying off your debts?"—a question that hits home, pinpointing the cold, parsimonious economy of money and feeling, greed and insatiable need, that drive him. In the scenes that follow, she learns for the first time of the existence of his taping system—from a televised report. Later, appearing slightly drunk and aptly outraged, she advises him to burn the tapes, only to realize why he will not: "You should burn them. . . . I remember Alger Hiss. I know how ugly you can be—you're capable of anything. But you see, it doesn't really matter, at the end of the day, what's in them. Because you have absolutely no remorse. No concept of remorse. You want the tapes to get out, you want them to see you at your worst. . . . They're not *yours*. They *are* you. You should burn them." [16] Thus Stone's Pat perceptively links the tapes to Nixon's ruthlessness in the Hiss case and to his compulsion to air both his own dirty laundry and that of others. If, as Stone's Howard Hunt claims, Nixon is "the darkness reaching out for the darkness," this scene configures Pat as the bearer of fire and light from which he recoils.

This scene is important for another reason, namely, its deft dramatization of Nixon's conflation of his wife and mother. When Pat admonishes him about the tapes, a shot from his point of view reveals Hannah's uncanny image effacing Pat. Nixon, it is implied, cannot hear his wife's criticisms without hallucinating that Hannah's cold, penetrating eyes are judging him, an experience represented as fraught with the castration anxiety that Freud's analysis of the uncanny details. [17] In these moments, the film exposes his equation of Hannah with Pat as a defining pathological symptom. It suggests that since Nixon cannot acknowledge his hostility toward Hannah, he displaces and vents his anger at her by humiliating Pat, a process that enables him at other moments to perceive Hannah as a saint, but at the cost of misidentifying both women. [18] The film counters Nixon's faulty vision with Pat's capacity for clear-sightedness, a trait also opposed to Hannah's destructively pious views. Whereas Stone's Hannah claims to see into her son's soul, and thereby terrifies him, [19] Stone's Pat possesses authentic insight into his troubled psyche and offers genuine help and intimacy. During Hannah's first appearance in the film, the stern Quaker warns the boy against the worldly influence of his older brother, a warning that is excessive; during Pat's first appearance, watching the Nixon-Kennedy debate, she reacts against the misguidance her husband has received from Chotiner and Haldeman, and she is on target. Whereas Hannah is shown unable and unwilling to comfort her son about the deaths of his two brothers, Pat encourages his compassion for Bobby Kennedy when John is assassinated. And whereas Hannah fears for his soul in narrowly religious terms, Pat recognizes that he is a lost soul in human terms: he indulges in paranoia, and is unable to be comforted by the ideal of home, love, and family that she embodies. [20]

Stone's style often reinforces the idea that Pat is a truth-teller and reality check. The cinematography and editing associated with her are relatively free of the canted framing, fragmenting close shots, sudden changes in film stock, and expressionistic elements that characterize much of the film. For example, fast-motion images of clouds fleeting across the White House sky repeatedly figure events exceeding Nixon's power to control them; conversely, visual steadiness more often defines Pat, reflecting her relative normalcy and stability. More importantly, the style associated with her lacks the dimensions of prefiguration and fulfillment, time then and time now, that shape the visual web centered on her husband, a network that conjoins the sublime, the tragic, and the problematic within Nixon's quotidian and domestic life, investing it with biblical dimensions.[21] In a related vein, whereas Pat appears in televised and pseudodocumentary images within the film as Nixon's "prop," and in the film's self-reflexive moments as a series of images constructed for public consumption, the relatively unobtrusive camera work and editing that frame Pat's private moments imply that the woman behind the public persona is stable, astute, and morally grounded.

In fact, as her first appearance demonstrates, with its emphasis on her perceptive reading of the Kennedy-Nixon debate, and with the intelligence that Joan Allen accords the character, she has the wherewithal to craft her own public image. A White House photo-op honoring a disabled Vietnam vet further dramatizes her perspective on that image. The scene shows Nixon winning laughter from virtually everyone present but Pat, as he calls the war protesters "bums." Refusing complicity with his humor, Pat casts a silent glance from her daughter Julie's face to Nixon's, even as she plays the part the scene requires of her. The moment prefaces documentary footage of fallen protesters at Kent State University, editing that reinforces the rightness of her refusal to laugh, if nonetheless allowing room for questions about her quiet complicity with her husband's handling of events.[22]

The concept of Pat as ironically detached from her public "plastic" role matches the woman whom biographer Lester David praised for her pat answers—that is, for having "developed to a high art the knack of giving nonanswers to questions. She gave full replies in clichés that hurt nobody and revealed nothing."[23] Presented on television as she listens to her husband's "Checkers" speech, for example, the film's Pat seems both genuinely humiliated by this invasion of her privacy and yet able to play the obviously rehearsed scene for its pure melodrama, affectionately laughing on cue at her husband's reference to Checkers, the dog. The moment affords film audiences a reminder that like Joan Allen, Pat Nixon worked in Hollywood movies. Indeed, if the film's core idea of Pat is that she is privately a repository of the real, the film also imagines her as media-smart and, insofar as she is allowed into Nixon's world, politically astute.

Allen's award-winning performance as Pat earned the reviewers' praise, but also some criticism as a too positive portrayal. Sharrett, for one, expresses gratitude that Pat somewhat alleviates Stone's nasty gender politics, which he terms "never more troublesome" than in *Nixon*, but Sharrett also frets that, "just as Nixon seems inflated by Stone, this version of his wife looks overly ennobling for Plastic Pat."[24] The film does play down problematic facets of the historical public image. It aims instead to evoke the sort of sympathy Pat Nixon earned from the *Los Angeles Times*'s Richard Bergholz: "[Nixon] abused her perpetually but not physically. She was just a stick of furniture sitting on a stage. She was just someone who smiled and had that adoring look on her face when she'd heard the speech for the fiftieth time. We all suffered when she suffered."[25] Despite Sharrett's objections, the film's public Pat is also congruent with the woman whom Henry Kissinger once deemed "a silent patriot . . . a loyal and uninterfering female in a man's world of politics, speaking only when spoken to, and not sullying the cigar smoke with her personal opinions."[26] She also matches the person whom David describes, in uncanny terms, as a public double of her spouse: "By the necromancy of a remarkable will, she became on the surface a mirror image of Richard Nixon, with his goals her goals, his wishes her wishes."[27] This Stepford wife is an uncanny American, indeed.

Joan Allen has perfected the kind of repressed, affecting, intelligent, yet uncanny persona she plays in *Nixon*, as evidenced by her performances in *The Ice Storm* (Ang Lee, 1997) and, especially, *Pleasantville* (Gary Ross, 1998), a film in which, to borrow Molloy's phrase, "fantasies of femininity are simultaneously narratives of nation."[28] In fact, her role as Betty in *Pleasantville* concretizes the persona: Betty is a "perfect," doll-like, 1950s television-comedy wife and mother, who is transformed into a "colored," "fallen," sexual woman, an emblem for America in transition. The black, white, and grey persona that she struggles to escape is revealed, quite literally, as a death mask of conformity. Yet if Allen imbues the sadly knowing private Pat with human potential similar to that of *Pleasantville*'s Betty, in an important sense *Nixon* also limits the character, making her a nonthreatening construct of the sane and the true—an aestheticized appendage of Nixon who *embodies* the authentic. She is his "better half," not rounded with a multifaceted, complex, independent existence. The ennoblement of Pat to which Sharrett objects thus actually accentuates the uncanny Pat, even if it is an opposite to her plastic image, since it, too, dereal-izes her. In a closely related manner, Pat is defined as the ideal obverse of Hannah, and, as such, forms part of an ambivalent equation that reconfirms the matrophobia that vexes Stone's films, even as it shapes an uncanny American iconography across them.

It is worth stressing that the film's antipathy toward Hannah goes hand in glove with its underrepresentation of the hostility toward women that hallmarked Nixon's *entire* political career, culminating in his efforts to cur-tail even the traditional role of the first lady, as illustrated by his demeaning challenges to his wife's selection of White House entertainment (a first lady's prerogative), and by *his* insistence on her "Stepford wife" public per-sona.[29] In turn, Stone's underrepresentation of Nixon's bias generates un-avoidable incongruities in his film's idealized conceptualization of Pat. For example, the film finesses the question of why, if she saw through to the truth, the historical Pat Nixon did not intervene as early as Nixon's 1950 campaign against Helen Gahagan Douglas, whom he smeared as a Com-munist, "pink right down to her underwear."[30] Indeed, even though *Nixon* develops a compelling critique of the American Dream, it concurrently overlooks the historical Nixon's conflation of the threat of women and fe-male sexuality with that of Communism.[31] Yet for Nixon, evidence suggests that it was as if the House Un-American Activities Committee of the 1940s and early 1950s were the antidote to the *unheimlich* house where women rule. His perception of Communism and intelligent women as twin threats colored not only his singularly savage attacks on Helen Douglas, but also his later disparagement of Hillary Clinton, whom he privately referred to as "what we used to call a *red-hot*," a "real lefty like Eleanor Roosevelt."[32]

Moreover, the blurring of women and Communism even affected his view of Pat, as suggested by the fourth Nixon-Kennedy debate, not included in the film, in which he insisted on the need for U.S. escalation in the arms race and inadvertently voiced hostility toward more than the "reds": "America cannot stand pat," he claimed. "We can't stand pat for the reason that we're in a race, as I have indicated. We can't stand pat because it is es-sential with the conflict that we have around the world, that we not just hold our own . . ."[33] In this thrice-repeated Freudian slip, Nixon conjoined the abhorrence of Pat with that of Communism, and the loathing of an un-canny image close to home with the fear of the cold war's ultimate Other. To be sure, this imagined intolerance for Pat, this need to risk "going over" or too far, that his poker metaphor projects onto the American people, seems to have been quite undifferentiated from his own unconscious impulses. Nonetheless, by conjoining the threat of Communism with an aversion for "pat," Nixon's blunder spotlights a single irrational basis for the anti-Communist hysteria and the misogyny of the cold-war constituency for whom he spoke.[34]

Whistler's Mother/Weimar Mothers

Nixon not only counterpoints the public and private faces of Pat, one a doll-like media construct, the other an abstract, domesticated truth figure, but also codes her image in terms of an additional contrast pair: on the one hand, James Whistler's *Arrangement in Grey and Black, No. 1: Portrait of the Artist's Mother* and on the other, the archetypal mother figure of Weimar cinema, specifically that of the street film as interpreted by Siegfried Kracauer. The first of these remains the ultimate popular American icon of idealized motherhood, despite Whistler's formalist intentions, and has been acclaimed for its "powerful grasp of the Protestant character."[35] The second, because of Kracauer's influence, has become part of a defining image of German protofascist regression, an interpretation based on a pattern in which a protagonist's retreat from the world drives him back to the protective arms of his wife or mother, arms Kracauer reads as stand-ins for the fascist nation's embrace.[36]

Stone visually aligns Pat with the Weimar mother figures early in *Nixon*, when, after losing the presidential election to Kennedy, a profoundly dejected Nixon turns to her for consolation. Situated on the left side of the screen, facing right, in a composition that strikingly evokes the famous shot of a wife mothering her defeated husband in Karl Grune's *The Street*, Pat cradles her husband's head on her breast, as he surrenders to her (figures 2.1 and 2.2). In Kracauer's reading, the Weimar film image depicts a desire to pull back from the world and return to the maternal womb, a regression Kracauer saw as symptomatic of Germany's readiness to submit to authoritarian power.[37] Tellingly, as recent scholarship has shown, Kracauer's reading also dovetails with cold-war theories that pinpoint bad mothering as the source of "political deviance," whether fascist or communist.[38]

Stone uses Pat to evoke Whistler's painting in a scene set the morning after the assassination of President Kennedy. The Nixons appear largely in separate frames in this scene, as Nixon peruses *New York Times* headlines at

Fig. 2.1. Nixon (Anthony Hopkins) retreats to the cradling embrace of his wife Pat (Joan Allen) in Oliver Stone's *Nixon*.

his desk, and footage of Jackie Kennedy and her young children appears on a television set. Repeatedly viewed in left profile, à la Whistler's *Mother*, her head and hands accented, Pat sits on a sofa positioned at right angles to her husband's desk. The film aligns this iconic reference with Nixon's point of view, perhaps implying that this is in some sense Nixon's projection, although the sequence also naturalizes the association of Pat with Whistler's *Mother* by means of dialogue and of the well-known images of Jackie with her children. In the dialogue, Pat offers motherly advice as she attempts to intervene in her husband's paranoid self-concern. For his part, Nixon fixes on the Kennedys' failure to invite him to the funeral and complains that Bobby and Teddy hate him; Pat counters by urging sympathy, encouraging him to call Bobby, and reminding him that he "knows what it means" to lose a brother.

The maternal icons drawn from Weimar and Whistler seem opposites, both in their connotations and in their orientation within the frame. Yet these doubles serve related functions. The physical proximity of Nixon and Pat in the former points up Nixon's childlike dependency; the physical distance between Nixon and Pat in the latter, congruent with the inherent austerity of Whistler's image, signals the cause behind the grown man's neediness. Indeed, both the shot-countershot and the mise-en-scène in this evocation of Whistler heighten the feeling of alienation between Nixon and Pat. As a result, it foregrounds a paradox in the cultural status of Whistler's image: though popularly seen as an icon of ideal American motherhood, it is austere and abstracting rather than warmly affective (figure 2.3). By exposing unacknowledged ambivalence, the scene thus implicitly transforms the quotation of Whistler into a critique of America's idealization of the institution of motherhood. Given the images of Jackie and the fact that Pat is herself a future first lady, Stone's commentary also extends to the ideas embedded in the nation's notion of its first lady as an ideal.

Fig. 2.2. The defeated protagonist of Karl Grune's *The Street* retreats from the world to find solace in the maternal bosom of his wife.

Fig. 2.3. James Abbott McNeill Whistler (1834–1903), *Arrangement in Grey and Black, No. 1: Portrait of the Artist's Mother* (Anna Mathilda McNeill, 1804–1881), oil on canvas, 1871.

Driving home the ambivalence of the Whistlerian image and enforcing the logic of the film's maternal icons is a second, brief evocation of the same painting two scenes later. Black-and-white pseudodocumentary footage shows Hannah, shortly before her death, giving an interview, in a composition situated in the right half of the frame. Sitting in a wheelchair facing left, profiled in a high contrast long shot, her hands in her lap, she appears austere and unsmiling. Two windows in the background recall the two paintings in Whistler's portrait, and light floods through them, suggestive of annunciation iconography, but, tellingly, the light reaches Hannah only intermittently. A subsequent close shot spotlights her hands.[39] The scene stresses Hannah's austerity and lack of warmth both visually and through dialogue based on a historical interview. When an interviewer asks, "Do you think your son will ever return to politics?" Hannah answers, "I don't think he has a choice. He was always a leader." The reporter continues, "Do you think he'd make a great president, Mrs. Nixon?" "If he's on God's side, yes," is her cool reply.

In effect, Stone deconstructs the difference between Whistler's mother and the motherly Weimar street film figure as part of his critique of American social history. His portrait of Hannah implies that, despite the way their children idealized them, mothers of her generation were responsible for the failed promise and the fascist leanings of Nixon's generation of Americans. (As Stone's Nixon says, addressing a portrait of JFK, "When they look at you, they see what they want to be. When they look at me, they see what they are.") There are at least two problematic aspects of this approach, however. First, as I will discuss below, the canonical interpretation of the Weimar imagery is troubling in some of the same ways that Stone's oeuvre in general is troubling, for it carries implications of matrophobia and homophobia. Second, in the economy of the film's maternal images, Pat and Hannah come to have an exchange value that repeatedly threatens to efface Pat. In other words, it is not only Nixon's confusion of his mother and wife that is at issue in the film, and not only the tension between the plastic and true Pats, but also Stone's ambivalence about the place of women in American culture. If Stone's Nixon, in a sense, substitutes Pat for Hannah when he retreats after the 1960 defeat, Stone's chosen iconography follows suit, allowing Pat to function both as a stand-in for Hannah and as the heavily freighted symbol of a terrible legacy of loss and unmanning, allegedly both in Weimar Germany and in Nixonian America.

To appreciate the vexing nature of Stone's critique of the maternal in American culture, it is necessary to see how he fleshes out Nixon's childhood and the extent to which he identifies the etiology of Nixon's neurosis, his abuses of presidential power, and his acts of inhumanity with the specter of destructive mothering. Discussion of these elements will in some ways require a detour from my focus on Pat and thus a repetition of Stone's tendency to efface Pat with Hannah. Nonetheless, the digression aims to illuminate one of the symbolic loads that Stone makes Pat carry.

Stone narrates Nixon's childhood in Whittier, California, in black-and-white flashback segments that evoke a rigidly moral world of the past. Often the most compelling portions of the film, these flashbacks are united by their focus on Hannah's pathogenic role. The first, set in 1925 when Nixon was twelve, conveys a defining moment in his relationship with her: a confrontation about his dishonesty. Hannah reprimands him for succumbing to Harold's influence and accepting a corn-silk cigarette behind the family's store. When he denies these things, Hannah pulls back saying, "Richard, we have nothing more to talk about," words that prompt a confession and apology. Hannah then warns, "Thy father will have to know of thy lying. I expect more from thee, Richard." When he promises never to disappoint her again, Hannah confides, "Then this shall be our little secret. Remember that I see into thy soul as God sees. Thou may fool the world. Even thy father. But not me, Richard. Never me." Chillingly, the boy responds, "Mother, think of me always as your faithful dog."

The scene implies a great deal. Foremost are Hannah's rigorous moral standards and her dubious methods of control—withholding affection, threatening exposure and paternal brutality, claiming godlike powers of surveillance, and insisting on unconditional obedience. The paternal brutality is vividly defined in the very next scene as a castration threat, when Hannah's husband, Frank, first refuses to remove his bloodied butcher's apron at the supper table, then says grace in the form of a stern warning to his sons.[40] Richard's terror of his father emerges as second, however, to his dread of displeasing his mother, who has the stronger claim on him. These scenes also reveal the boy's need to rebel against her puritanical godliness, with its conditional love and harsh standards. The flashback suggests as well his deep-felt need to engage in deception if he is to gain some measure of autonomy without losing a semblance of maternal love.

The boy's abject submission to his mother's authority forecasts his authoritarian adult personality, a personality that Stone conceives along the lines of the typologies theorized in the matrophobic, heterosexist cold-war discourse on totalitarianism. Examples include Frankfurt School readings of gender destabilization and so-called sexual and political deviance in Weimar culture.[41] Stone evokes these typologies most disturbingly in his homofascist portrait of J. Edgar Hoover. Yet Stone similarly links Nixon's authoritarianism to his lukewarm heterosexuality, which Stone dramatizes through Nixon's retreats from Pat's amorous advances. In a related manner, Stone makes Nixon's fascist proclivities echo those of Charles Kane. In him as in Kane, the appetite for love exists on a grandiose scale, and most significantly, America's love becomes for him a double of the desperately needed thing that the mother's love was for the child.[42] Lost maternal love renders him a figure of poignancy, whereas the inability to provide that love marks Stone's Hannah as the harrowing specter that robs Nixon of the potential greatness that the film claims for him.[43] Stone's Kissinger laments, "Can you imagine what this man would have been if someone had loved him?"—a statement that, to be sure, either effaces Pat by conflating her with Hannah or intentionally casts aspersions on them both.

The idea of Hannah's harmful influence not only defines Stone's treatment of Nixon's totalitarian impulses, but also haunts virtually all of the major themes that Stone finds in his life, including those of fratricide, of death as an ally, and of Nixon as the possessor of a special destiny. In a key sequence, images of the assassinations of John and Robert Kennedy give rise to Nixon's remarks that "Death paved the way, didn't it? Vietnam. The Kennedys. It cleared a path through the wilderness just for me. Four bodies"—that is, the Kennedy brothers and Nixon's brothers Harold and Arthur.[44] The film immediately flashes back to 1933, when Nixon was nineteen, to his memory of the final stages of his brother Harold's losing battle against tuberculosis. Images of the charming twenty-three-year-old coughing up blood give way to a moment after the funeral in which Hannah chastens Richard, offering him an admonition that this is God's will and that his brother's death frees up family money to further his education.[45] Thus Stone's Nixon is inevitably haunted by survivor guilt, and Hannah's words deepen it and prevent healthy grieving. Yet another flashback, triggered by John Kennedy's assassination, replays the death of Nixon's brother Arthur at age seven and Hannah's harsh rebuff of twelve-year-old Richard when he threw his arms around her skirt for solace. Hannah's failure to console him again explains his emotionally deficient present. In the film, Nixon's drive for success is predicated on the blinding need to give these early deaths meaning, but no success can make good the losses, and Stone's film reveals a Nixon trapped in compulsive repetition, reenacting the uncanny traumas but never working through them.

The flashback that narrates Harold's bloody death also forms a subtext for a dinner scene on the presidential yacht in which Nixon discusses with his aides the bombing of Cambodia. Referring to himself in the third person, as if beside himself, Nixon argues that "without risk there is no heroism, there is no history. Nixon was born to do this. Give history a nudge. If Cambodia doesn't work, we'll bomb Hanoi if we have to. That's right, and if necessary, we'll drop the big one." Ominous music and reaction shots of the others' stunned faces identify Nixon's idea as deranged. Horrifically, blood flows from the steak on his plate, unnerving him, and the camera cuts from the dark flow to a shot of the dark river, an image that metaphorically extends the imagery of blood and death that originates with the "sacrificed" Harold. Some moments later, now gazing off the yacht at the Potomac,

Nixon denies that he could offer condolences to the parents of the youths killed at Kent State. "Nixon can't," he claims. This Nixon is Hannah's son, as Stone imagines her—a man crippled in his capacity to mourn, driven to win at all costs, and possessed by the conviction that death and success are inextricably linked in the confederacy of forces that shape his destiny.

Stone also implicitly lays blame for the 1971 Christmas bombing of Hanoi at Hannah's feet. Documentary footage, accompanied by the voice-over of a BBC reporter, details the assault: "In a surprise Christmas bombing of Hanoi," the reporter explains, "President Nixon today delivered more tonnage than was used at Dresden in World War II. It is, without doubt, the most brutal bombing in American history." Nixon's motivation for the savage twelve-day attack, carried out against the advice of his aides, finds articulation in the film's previous scene, the historic meeting between Mao and Nixon. Here, the cold warrior's much-acclaimed opening up of China becomes the context in which Mao, through some of the film's purely fictive dialogue, opens up a window into Nixon's soul: "You're as evil as I am," Mao tells him. "We're both from poor families. But others pay to feed the hunger in us. In my case, millions of reactionaries. In your case millions of Vietnamese." Nixon is taken aback, momentarily shocked into recognition. "The real war is in us," Mao continues. "History is a symptom of our disease."

Indeed, Stone presents Nixon's impoverishment as an emotional one, and the monumental brutality that comes of it serves above all as an ironic indictment of Hannah's generation of matronly do-gooders. Thus, beyond Whistler's mother, Stone molds Hannah to conjure numerous silent film satires of female crusaders and temperance types.[46] Unlike Brodie, Stone attempts little explanation of Hannah's circumstances or of the contributing factors behind her maternal deficiencies, thus enforcing her status as stereotype. (In contrast to Stone, Brodie points to Hannah's depression and notes that, "Although her husband worked hard, five years of marriage brought for Hannah Nixon only poverty, shabbiness, and constant comparison of her husband with the respectable, gentle Quaker father she had left.")[47] Conversely, Stone's dehumanized Hannah, though she feeds the poor and homeless, seems all judgment and duty, the succinct source of Nixon's emotional hunger and the embodiment of a long history of Protestant repression, a history that the film also evokes through the extreme restraint of the automatized public persona of "Plastic Pat."[48]

Mona Lisas and Mad Hatters

The *Nixon* screenplay identifies Pat in terms of still another cultural icon, as the "'Mona Lisa' of American politics";[49] that is, as a classic first lady and lovely enigma, indeed, as an aesthetic object whose beauty depends on the aestheticization of concealment, wherein an uncanny potential is rendered unthreatening. Although there is no doubt that Pat Nixon often played her cards close to the chest, making her difficult for the public to know, the historical record reveals a good deal more about her than Stone's icons suggest. Above all, the evidence indicates that she was in the process of finding her political footing even as the Mad Hatters around her—like the men in the Elton John song—lost theirs.[50] At a time when Nixon seemed trapped in the psychotic side of the uncanny, a place where "the boundaries between *imagination* and *reality* are erased," she seems to have moved increasingly toward Kristeva's model for a healthy trajectory of the uncanny, wherein openness toward the new and identification with the other become the foundation of sociality.[51] Disparagingly described in uncanny terms by the press, Pat Nixon nonetheless appears to have responded to others in a way that suggests she was comfortable with the uncanny within.

Specifically, biographical studies reveal a woman who developed the courage to give public endorsement to progressive ideas, and although *Nixon* downplays her liabilities, it also elides the independent political views that she eventually espoused—her identification with women's issues, with draft dodgers, and with a range of cultural others.[52] By the time of her husband's landslide reelection in 1972, she was no longer content to play the prop; she was speaking out. Even though her husband opposed women's wearing pants and believed that universal education is "a terrible idea, especially for women," Pat Nixon expressed support for women's rights, including the right to an abortion.[53] She also asserted, "I would campaign for women candidates, even if they were not Republicans."[54] Further, she pressed her husband to appoint a woman to the Supreme Court, although he took no heed. In 1972 she spoke in favor of amnesty for Vietnam draft dodgers and deserters, as long as they performed volunteer work in order to earn their way back.[55]

History demonstrates the film's curtailment of her image in another way. She came to be a first-rate goodwill ambassador precisely to the kind of nations that Nixon and Kissinger deemed peripheral to their foreign policy and felt free to treat badly—Cambodia, Pakistan, Bangladesh, India, and Chile, among others. Indeed, her trip to Lima after an earthquake in 1970 and her four-nation trip to Africa in 1972 even earned Charles Colson's praise for finally giving the Nixon presidency a *human* face: "Mrs. Nixon has broken through where we have failed. She has come across as a warm, charming, graceful, concerned, articulate person."[56] The trips demonstrated, too, that in marked contrast to her husband, Pat Nixon was at ease with people of various nationalities, races, ethnicities, and disabilities.[57] The historical Pat Nixon's nonreifying response to "strangers without" provides a telling alternative to the problematic filmic construction of the uncanny first lady in *Nixon*.

Doubtless, Pat Nixon's trips to so-called marginal nations were authorized, in part, because her worth, like theirs, was undervalued. In fact, Betty Boyd Caroli reports that "her assignments were sometimes treated as jokes. Rather than building a significant spot for her in some project that would complement her husband's work, John Ehrlichman explained that he had sent her off to 'do the Indians' (visit a reservation) in order to keep her quiet and get her out of sight"[58]—an echo of Freud's assertion that the unheimlich is that which should have remained hidden.[59] Ehrlichman's sexism and racism here are interconnected, and together they shed light on the American unheimlich. To hide the woman "at home," concealed in the nation's interior borders, among the Indian nations—nations within the belly of the nation—or to dispatch her as far from home as possible, in foreign places at the extreme borders of the nation's perceived interests: these are the imagined alternatives. Together, they mirror her paradoxical positioning in the discourse that defines the American uncanny. Significantly, the Nixon administration's blindness toward peripheral zones, its misreading of the postcolonial world, has come back to haunt the United States, since the importance of those zones—if not that of Pat Nixon's diplomacy—has become clearer in time. According to Tony Judt, a debunker of Nixon revisionism, "Ironically, [American interests suffered under Nixon and Kissinger] because Kissinger was so caught up in the 'big' picture that he and Nixon . . . made a cumulative series of crucial missteps in the 'peripheral' zones whose significance they dismissively underestimated. . . . [Their] overall objective—the advancement of the permanent interests of the United States—was probably further from attainment at the end of the Nixon-Kissinger era than at the outset."[60]

Stone, however, tacitly accepts Nixon's grandiose assessment of what was lost in the international arena as a consequence of his forced resignation. In the epilogue, Stone's voice-over asserts:

> "Nixon always maintained that if he had not been driven from office, the North Vietnamese would not have overwhelmed the South in 1975. In a sideshow [sic], Cambodian society was destroyed and mass genocide resulted. [At this point, a documentary clip from Nixon's funeral shows Robert Dole asserting that the second half of the twentieth century will be "known as the age of Nixon."] In his absence, Russia and the United States returned to a decade of high-budget military expansion and near-war. Nixon, who was pardoned by President Ford, lived to write six books and travel the world as an elder statesman."

Stone's point is that the nation was diminished in Nixon's absence. Stone's claim, along with the video clip from Nixon's funeral and the ethereal rendering of "Shenandoah" that plays over the credits, participates in the broader reclamation of Nixon that occurred during the mid-1990s, a time when contenders for the Republican presidential nomination vied for the label of the candidate whom Nixon would have endorsed had he still been alive. Stone's epilogue tacitly accepts the myth that credited Nixon with near greatness in the realm of American foreign policy—a myth that imagines Nixon as a leader whose misjudgments and bad timing undermined potential genius and heroic accomplishment in the service of his country.

Stone's perpetuation of the foreign-policy myth, despite his apparent leftist allegiances, is inextricably tied to his foundational belief in a very different sort of myth, the kind enacted in *The Oresteia* and elaborated in *The Golden Bough*. That is, Stone invests so heavily in stories of sacrificed father-kings and wicked mothers, of quest and conquest, that he fails to question the narrative shape that these impose on American history. When Nixon says, "They need to sacrifice something, y'know, appease the gods of war— Mars, Jupiter. I am that blood, General [Haig]. I am that sacrifice, in the highest place of all. All leaders must finally be sacrificed," Stone plays the statement straight.[61] An overhead shot of Nixon and Haig, moving like chess pieces across a checkered tile floor, gives the notion visual force, as does the red carpet onto which Nixon walks. Later in this scene, Pat appears in a white robe, a swanlike Valkyrie gently escorting her husband to Valhalla. Far from challenging the myths in question, she is thus subsumed within them as she is linked with death, in yet another figuration of the aestheticized uncanny.

There is no sense here of the historical Pat Nixon's political stances and diplomatic successes, accomplishments that deserve to be remembered most for the missed opportunities they point toward. Yet, of course, her admirers more often applauded the self-effacing persona that Stone, too, honors at the film's end. In Nixon's farewell address to the White House staff, he eulogizes his mother while ignoring his wife; the film counters Nixon's symptomatic oversight by cutting to a close-up of the tearful, gaunt Pat, again dressed in white. It thus pays tribute to Pat's long-suffering loyalty as well as to her iconic status as first wife, mother, and "lady." The Pat so honored, however, has been reduced to a kind of silent specter, haunting the margins of our cultural consciousness.

Surprisingly, it is Pat Nixon herself who hints at an alternative vantage point on the "first lady," one that also survives in the closing moments of *Nixon*. Specifically, she provides a small "proof" of her humanity that is quite different in character from those proofs required of the young women in E. T. A. Hoffmann's story and from those required of Mrs. Nixon by the London *Spectator*. Just before Stone's voice-over participates in the broader cultural reclamation of Nixon in the mid-1990s—one op-ed headline, playing on Mel Brook's legendary "Springtime for Hitler," termed it "Springtime for Nixon,"[62]—another image emerges, one that in some small measure provides a historical refutation of the construction (including Stone's) of the uncanny Pat. In documentary footage of the changing of the guard and the Nixons' exit to an awaiting helicopter, Pat Nixon reaches out and kisses the new first lady, Betty Ford. As a simple gesture of compassion and support, the act was typical of her and meshes with White House reporter Helen Thomas's claim that, far from being a plastic doll, "Pat Nixon was the warmest First Lady I covered and the one who loved people most."[63] As an unaffected gesture of solidarity between women, the image also evokes developments of the 1970s in ways that Stone's film does not even begin to imagine. Indeed, this fleeting image is not only utterly unprepared for by *Nixon* but is also without counterpart in *Guarding Tess*

(Hugh Wilson, 1994), *Air Force One* (Wolfgang Petersen, 1997), *Primary Colors* (Mike Nichols, 1998) and a host of other 1990s films that portray presidential wives. For just that reason, this ephemeral moment of *cinema verité*, in which the *other* Nixon defines *herself*, may ironically be the most suggestive vision inscribed in Stone's film.

In important ways, the repressions and revisions that *Nixon* enacts identify Stone's political vision as a throwback to a 1960s pre-women's-movement American liberalism, affiliating him with an ideology associated with the fallen leaders of that decade, albeit his thematic and political range also extends beyond these categories. Further, the film's elisions and re-assessments suggest his struggles as a disaffected Vietnam War veteran, coming to terms in the mid-1990s with the complex cold-war legacy of the dying fathers who fought World War II—when the nation emerged as an unequivocal moral and military victor and the masculine military hege-mony seemed quite simply beyond question. In this respect and others, Stone's film can be viewed as the completion of the trajectory of his Vietnam War films of the 1980s, the decade during which that subgenre flourished. Tellingly, Stone's work also bespeaks his uninterest in addressing the partic-ular legacy of the Vietnam War that resulted in increased gender, ethnic, and racial diversification in the military and increased reliance on working-class enlistments, developments that ironically functioned in part as out-growths of the women's and civil rights movements, important elements of which had often been strongly pacifist. This tangle of issues, as focused in a Gulf War film, is the subject that I shall consider next.

As a televisual war and media event, Operation Desert Storm, like Prospero's magic, was directed toward rectifying past losses. Packaged, censored, and promoted as *not* the Vietnam War, the conflict in the Persian Gulf was to dramatize what Susan Jeffords has memorably termed the remasculinization of America, coupled with a derealization of civilian suffering.[1] Whereas photographs of napalmed Vietnamese villagers had once haunted the national conscience, injured and dead Iraqi women and children became, in callous Pentagonese, mere "collateral damage." Whereas televised reports of the barbarism of the 1968 massacre at My Lai once rendered American soldiers alien, televised images of American troops in the gulf revealed familiar everyday heroes, fighting for family and friends.

Historically, the Gulf War stood in contrast to the Vietnam War in an-

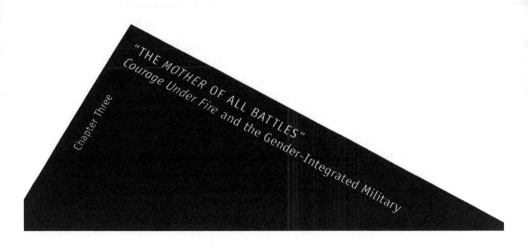

Chapter Three

"THE MOTHER OF ALL BATTLES"
Courage Under Fire and the Gender-Integrated Military

culture at large. They have also complicated U.S. relations with Arabic cultures, as Osama bin Laden's deadly reaction to the presence of gender-integrated American troops on Saudi soil made clear.

To date, *Courage Under Fire* (Edward Zwick, 1996) remains the most complex and compelling Hollywood feature film to engage this history and these anxieties. Set during the 1990–1991 Gulf War and the ensuing months, the film depicts an investigation into the heroism and death of a white female army captain, Karen Walden (Meg Ryan), a helicopter pilot and single mother who is posthumously nominated to be the first female recipient of the Medal of Honor for combat.[4] An African-American officer, Lieutenant Colonel Nathaniel Serling (Denzel Washington), is assigned to the inquiry as his "second chance" to atone for having given an order that, in the chaos of battle in Desert Storm, resulted in the death of another soldier, his friend Boylar—a fiasco that the army covers up.

Serling's quest leads to a series of flashbacks, stories that are presented both as mind-screens and as narratives that are videotaped or audiotaped as evidence. The young crew members of a Black Hawk helicopter, whom Walden reportedly saved from the Iraqis, offer Serling one story, a group narrative that a videographer captures. Members of Walden's male crew offer him conflicting reports—of how she and her crew relieved the young men pinned down by the Iraqis, of the subsequent downing of Walden's medevac helicopter, of the long night spent fighting off the enemy, and of the hotly disputed circumstances of her death. Resisting the army's pressure for a quick confirmation of her medal-worthy status—and an instant public-relations coup—Serling doggedly pursues and eventually uncovers the full truth, earning personal redemption in the process.

To its credit, the film articulates a complex vision of the Gulf War, not a simple antidote for the post-traumatic stress of Vietnam. It depicts the traumas that war begets as inevitable outcomes—regardless of smart technologies, broad public support, or racial harmony in the ranks. In fact, it points toward the increased likelihood of friendly-fire disasters accompanying increased sophistication in weapons technologies. The film also criticizes military and government manipulation of the media—the distortion and sacrifice of truth for the sake of photo-ops, public-relations capital, and patriotic feeling—and it contextualizes this manipulation in relation to Nixon and the Watergate scandal through its focus on incriminating tape recordings, including an audiotape of Serling's disastrous error. The film also goes a long way toward valorizing the ethnic, racial, and gender diversity that was an important goal of the U.S. Army in the 1990s. As this chapter argues, although the film's narrative affirms the combat-worthiness of the woman warrior, the heroic integrity of the black officer who challenges the system, and the ideal of the integrated army itself, *Courage Under Fire* is also defined by images, elisions, and subtexts that point equivocally to other historical moments and cultural vantage points that erode and destabilize its overtly forward-looking vision.

Contexts and Controversies

Because the film speaks to a knotty set of cultural issues, I shall preface my argument with a sketch of its historical contexts, including media and filmic developments before and after its release. Paramount among these is the issue of integrating women into the military, a context that encompasses (1) sexual harassment and scandal, (2) the interplay of race and gender, and (3) the interplay of gender and technology, especially the machinery of war and representation.

During the 1990s, the vicissitudes of gender integration in the armed services were charted as well-publicized incidents of sexual harassment and scandal—public-relations disasters for the U.S. military, given its express aims of integration and equality. The infamous Tailhook naval convention, at which, by the women's own accounts, eighty-three female officers were sexually abused at a Las Vegas hotel, is the best-known early episode.[5] Although it eventually led to several high-level resignations, including that of the navy secretary, Tailhook and its handling did little to counter perceptions that the violence-based military culture remained sexist at heart.

Even before Tailhook, the stress-filled, uncertain months immediately prior to the Gulf War were marked by problems of sexual assault and abuse on military bases. Indeed, according to Lynda Boose, at the time of the Iraqi invasion of Kuwait "probably more American women recruits were concurrently being raped on military bases by their fellow soldiers than Kuwaiti women had been by the Iraqi military. In fact, the instance of reported rape and sexual assault at U.S. military training installations escalated so dramatically in the months leading up to the war that finally the Pentagon and the chairman of the Senate Armed Services Committee were embarrassed into ordering investigations."[6] This escalation is all the more ironic given the propagandizing of the war by means of a trumped-up story that Iraqi soldiers ripped infants from their incubators, an action seen as integral to the enemy's larger "rape of Kuwait."[7] Adding further complexity to the dialogue was the attention the mainstream American press finally paid, in 1995, to a story that the American military had long wanted buried: its complicity with the Japanese government's system for making prostitutes available to U.S. servicemen during the occupation of Japan after that country's surrender in 1945.[8]

It was not until after the release of *Courage Under Fire*, however, that sexism in the military received its most intense military and media scrutiny. Some of the key events included: (1) revelations of sexual harassment and rapes at the army's training base at Aberdeen, Maryland (allegations of which arose in the fall of 1996, identifying a ring of male drill sergeants who reportedly extorted sex from female recruits); (2) the trial of Sergeant Major Gene McKinney, charged with sexual misconduct; (3) revelations of adultery in the careers of Air Force First Lieutenant Kelly Flinn, Air Force General Joseph W. Ralston (nominated as chairman of the Joint Chiefs of Staff), and others, including Commander in Chief Bill Clinton; and finally, (4) the horrific 1995 abduction and rape of a twelve-year-old Japanese schoolgirl by U.S. servicemen—one of a host of crimes against women and children enumerated in an early-1997 full-page *New York Times* ad run by a group of seven thousand Japanese opposed to the U.S. military presence in Okinawa.[9]

Discussion of these scandals was made both more volatile and more complex by the fact that several of them involved African-American servicemen. All of the men accused of sexual misconduct at the Aberdeen Proving Ground in Maryland were black, and Gene McKinney, similarly accused, was the first African American to hold the position of sergeant major, the highest army rank for an enlisted man. Characterizing the problem of race and sexual harassment in the military, Ian Fisher observed, "When warriors who are white are accused of sexual offenses, the questions raised seem to be about the military itself . . . But when the accused are black, the questions inevitably become more complicated, raising old suspicions about how justice is dispensed in America, particularly when race and sex intersect."[10] Indeed, D. W. Griffith's racist images of the black soldier Gus, who forces his attentions on a Southern white woman in *The Birth of a Nation* (1915), and is horribly punished for his transgressions, come all too readily to mind. Insofar as debates about sexual harassment in the military were shadowed by this melodramatic legacy, they shared ground with the controversies generated by the O. J. Simpson and Rodney King trials, touchstones that form the subject of a pioneering study by Linda Williams.[11]

Just as pernicious myths about the sexually predatory nature of black men formed a troubling backdrop to the public discourse on sexual misconduct, so too did sexist myths and double standards concerning female credibility. The McKinney case illustrates this point as well. In March 1998 a military jury found McKinney not guilty on eighteen counts of sexual harassment and guilty on only one charge, obstruction of justice. Not surprisingly, his five women accusers felt the military had betrayed them. During the trial, the defense suggested that it was the women themselves who were guilty (of racism), even though one of them was a Puerto Rican of African descent. She protested to the press: "I wanted to yell . . . 'how dare you say that to them when you look at my brown face?'"[12] It was as if a woman of color in this context had been metaphorically kept out of sight, just as the unheimlich is, even though she was physically present at the trial, because her presence destabilized the tidy identity binarisms of race and gender.

According to Kelly Flinn, the first woman to fly the nuclear-weapons carrier B-52, testifying on behalf of a woman friend who had been sexually assaulted by a pilot helped to precipitate her own downfall. The man pleaded guilty and was convicted, but retaliated by providing prosecutors with a list of men with whom, he claimed, Flinn had had sexual relations.[13] The eventual result was that in the spring of 1997 Flinn was forced to resign after being charged with adultery, lying, fraternization, and disobedience.[14] It was not the first time her opposition to sexual harassment boomeranged. During her days at the Air Force Academy, someone had written "cunt" on the message board on her door, and she insisted that the incident be investigated. As a consequence, she was ostracized and, along with her entire squadron, grounded for the upcoming holiday weekend.

The hostility and severity that Flinn experienced in the air force stood in contrast to the support and leniency afforded General Joseph Ralston, a candidate for chairman of the Joint Chiefs of Staff in the spring of 1997. Although he withdrew his candidacy once his affair became public knowledge, unlike Flinn, he was never pressed to resign.[15] Flinn's example raised many questions in the public media: How pervasive is the double standard in the armed forces? Is the lesson of her story that a virginal woman can fly a B-52, but a sexually active one—like the deflowered Brünnehilde of Germanic myth—must be divested of power? By all accounts, Flinn was an outstanding aviator and officer who had had an ideal public-relations profile. Since her case seriously damaged efforts to recruit women, some analysts speculated that there were those within the military who had desired precisely that effect.

However one chooses to interpret Flinn's story, it came to exemplify the complexities of gender integration, combat technology, and media representation in the late twentieth century, complexities whose compass the Gulf War had importantly expanded and focused. As a result of "smart bombs" and contemporaneous developments in the weaponry and culture of the U.S. military, the Gulf War was the first to call into serious question the distinction that had limited women to noncombat assignments. In the words of Richard Rayner, "The gulf war demonstrated that the distinction between combat and noncombat troops is meaningless on the modern technological battlefield." [16] Yet if combat technologies worked in part as equalizers, iconographically most weaponry remained rigidly aligned with masculinist and phallic ideas of power. The ironic result, argues Robyn Wiegman, is that female integration into the military created the very context in which "the exteriorization of the masculine body as technology most effectively functions, enabling the fetishization of masculinity that heightens, even as it displaces, the warrior symbolics once solely attached to masculine bodies." [17] Simply put, phallic technology neutralized the threat female combatants posed to the reborn masculinity of the Gulf War—and to war in general as a privileged arena of masculine display. (It follows, therefore, that the epithet used to undermine Flinn was intended to serve notice about where a woman's claim to phallic power stops.) Perhaps no example better illustrates the dynamic Wiegman details than the film *G.I. Jane* (Ridley Scott, 1997), wherein the battered but defiant heroine "muscles" her body through boot-camp endurance tests and proves her ability to "take it like a man." "Jane" validates phallic power by telling her abusive commanding officer to "suck my dick," simultaneously disavowing and emphasizing her own "lack" and inaugurating a grim new primer of "dick" and "Jane" in the process. Clearly, then, the fetishization of masculinity in weaponry did not hasten the dawn of an age when military might could be an equal opportunity resource.

If masculinist technologies continued to be allied with fetishized masculine bodies, masculine psyches kept a human face in 1990s representations, partly through their alignment with the domestic sphere—a development much discussed in film and media studies. Commenting on televisual im-

ages of the Gulf War, Wiegman explains that these representations rede-
fined masculinity, moving it simultaneously in opposing directions: first,
toward the "remasculinized" warrior ideals of the post–Vietnam War era,
with their impenetrable, "smart" technological armor; and second, toward
the "more nuanced masculine interiority" represented in the post–cold
war media ideals of masculinity.[18] Wiegman further asserts that "media coverage of the Persian Gulf War worked the tension between these masculine
performances, moving between narrative stagings of the male soldier's interiority—his love, fears, and tears for family and friends—and the technological armature that enables masculinity to both signify and exceed corpo-
reality itself. In this context, technological performance defines the public,
while the male soldier, as the body, signifies the private interior realm."[19]
The result both complicates the old alignment of the feminine with the private sphere and the masculine with the public, and displaces the feminine
so that "the domestic emerges not as the difference of an 'other's' interiority but as the psychic content of masculinity itself."[20]

Pointing to a corollary cinematic pattern, Robert Burgoyne notes that
"the search for alternative masculinities has been identified as a dominant
motif of 1990s Hollywood films," and that this search resulted in a shift "to
a more internal, psychologically nuanced model of male identity," of the
kind associated with melodrama.[21] To be sure, as Homer's portrait of Hec-
tor in *The Iliad* demonstrates, melodramatic elements informed depictions
of epic combat masculinity even well before the ancient Persians warred
against the ancient Greeks. The technological and social pressures of the
1990s, however, motivated attempts to reformulate masculinity to reflect
particular postmodern, post–cold war pressures.

Certainly the need for an alternative heroism based on masculine interiority was congruent with President Clinton's so-called dodge of the Vietnam War and resulting inability to be defined by the standard paradigm of
masculinity. In fact, the media images of both 1990s commanders in chief
illustrate the difficulty of balancing the bipartite masculinist performances
Wiegman outlines. If George H. W. Bush came to be aligned with the technology of battle, and Clinton with melodramatic spectacle, neither fully
spanned the gap. Indeed, Clinton's confession in August 1998 of sexual im-
proprieties, combined with his order of a counterterrorist strike against fa-
cilities in Afghanistan and Sudan just three days later, seemed to widen the
gap dramatically. And, despite Bush's and Clinton's association with figures
such as Colin Powell and Madeleine Albright, Bush's legacy of racist ad

campaigning (Willie Horton) and Clinton's of sexual self-indulgence mark 1990s masculine icons in symptomatically troubling ways.

The Woman Warrior of the 1990s

On the face of it, *Courage Under Fire* deals with the interrelated matters of gender, race, war, and representation in progressive, even idealistic terms. The film grants the problem of sexual harassment weight and consequence, depicting it not only as sexual misconduct but also as a means of undermining a woman on the job. At the climactic moment in the conflict between Walden and the mutinous gunner Monfriez (Lou Diamond Phillips), he tells her, "There's no way you're taking away my weapon, cunt." The problem represented in the film (as in Kelly Flinn's experience) is not that she is being pressured by a desirous superior officer. Nor is it her competence—quite the contrary, since her competence itself threatens a "taking away" or emasculation. The problem of sexual harassment, as *Courage Under Fire* compellingly depicts it, is one of masculine turf marking, of maintaining the masculine military hegemony through abuse and humiliation.

The film also seems progressive in its use of melodramatic conventions to imagine the gradual growth of a bond between black and white, male and female, based on the moral fortitude of its hero and heroine—a shared "courage under fire" that transcends even the boundary of death. Additionally, the film keeps the legacy of Vietnam in focus, without simply encoding the Gulf War as post-Vietnam Viagra. It partially deconstructs the difference between Vietnam and the gulf, visually and acoustically registering uncanny parallels between these conflicts and criticizing government manipulation of media coverage in the process. Further, strikingly like *Saving Private Ryan,* it honors heroism in the face of, or in spite of, a calculating public-relations effort by the army higher-ups to enshrine symbolic women. Yet it does so with an important difference: it vindicates the woman not as a producer of soldiers but more centrally as soldier herself. *Courage Under Fire,* then, attempts a progressive view of the complex relationships among trauma, truth, and the political-military manipulation of the media, as well as of ethics, gender, and combat.

Despite these aims, however, *Courage Under Fire* also relies on strategies through which various social problematics run interference for each other in obfuscating ways. That is, key issues—including but not limited to that

Fig. 3.1. Karen Walden (Meg Ryan) celebrates the completion of her military schooling in the gender-integrated U.S. Army.

of gender difference—function as mutually diverting decoys. In the process, cultural and historical vantage points emerge that controvert the film's progressive vision and contradict its overtly egalitarian ideals. My interest lies in delineating the limits of the film's forward-looking vision and especially of its progressive inscription of women's history.

Like *Rashomon* (Akira Kurosawa, 1950), *Courage Under Fire* presents a series of narratives that center on a brutalized woman, but unlike *Rashomon*, it ultimately both establishes an unequivocal truth about events and distinguishes clearly between reliable and unreliable narrators.[22] The summary view her copilot, Rady, offers of Walden is that "she was a soldier"— tough, resourceful, and in control—and this view is presented stylistically as objective and accurate. Conversely, Monfriez's flashback narrative, wherein Walden's tightly framed face is drawn with fear and uncertainty, emerges as a self-serving falsehood. In Monfriez's distorted account, Walden hysterically fired a handgun at him rather than let him take control and rescue her. Monfriez presents himself as rough, tough, and in charge. The facts that Serling uncovers expose his lies and validate the words in

Walden's army file—that she was a "woman of exceptional moral courage," with the strength to address unpopular issues. Crewman and medic Ilario (Matt Damon) also reveals a conclusive piece of the narrative puzzle: Monfriez led a mutiny against Walden, then shot her in the belly after erroneously concluding that she was shooting at him, not at an approaching Iraqi. To avoid being court-martialed, Monfriez told the helicopter pilot who flew the rest of Walden's crew to safety that she was already dead, thereby dooming her to certain, terrible incineration by napalm. Before her death, however, by means of her ingenuity and leadership and by keeping up M-16 fire as the others evacuated, she succeeded in saving both the injured Rady, whom her crew was about to abandon, and the crew of the downed Black Hawk helicopter.

Serling's ostensible conclusion from these facts is that when it comes to soldiering, gender (like race) is unimportant; what matters is whether you can do the job, and Walden could. Indeed, like Mulan in Disney's *Mulan* (Barry Cook and Tony Bancroft, 1998), "Jane" in *G.I. Jane,* and the female troopers in *Starship Troopers* (Paul Verhoeven, 1997), Walden is a 1990s filmic woman warrior with the "right stuff." She turns out to be exactly what the army and White House public-relations people wanted: in the words of General Hershberg (Michael Moriarty), Serling's commanding officer, "one little shining piece of something for people to believe in." Unlike M. Larry Lawrence, the former U.S. ambassador whose body was disinterred from Arlington National Cemetery once it was discovered that he had fabricated his war record,[23] Walden is no phony and no public-relations embarrassment. Unlike First Lieutenant Michael J. Blassie, the air force pilot and casualty of the Vietnam War whose remains were buried in the Tomb of the Unknown Soldier, even though his identity was known, Walden's remains are not indiscriminately used for public-relations purposes—thanks to Serling's inquiry and recovery of the facts, *his* courage under fire.

Missing in action from the film's depiction of this "truth," however, is Walden's own experience, her subjectivity. For if Walden is an object of projection and manipulation for the public-relations machine that the film critiques, she is certainly one for the film itself, despite its disavowal of such methods. As a result, she is only the ostensible center of the narrative. In contrast to the agonies of guilt suffered by her crewmen, her ordeal is never visually represented or experienced from her point of view. The narrative rules of the text—the fact of her death and the general restriction of the audience's knowledge to match what Serling knows or learns—render her vantage point impossible. Thus the film disregards her as the subject of her own story, using her life and death as the occasion for male-centered tales of war, melodramas of masculine selfhood, or personal psychograms of traumatized youth. Fitting a pattern traced by works such as Sally Potter's film *Thriller* (1979) and Elisabeth Bronfen's book *Over Her Dead Body*, the woman is "murdered" in order to give full expression to the heroism and suffering of the souls of the male characters.[24] By ventriloquizing her voice through the mind-screens of others, the film denies Walden enunciation as a subject.[25] Indeed, it is only partly overstating the case to say that Walden's death is the film's Hitchcockian MacGuffin.[26]

At the most obvious level, support for this idea comes from the film's ending, which directs attention away from the particular political conditions and implications of Walden's demise and toward Serling's acts of remembrance, understanding, and contrition. To be sure, within the world of the film, one reason Monfriez's lethal and symptomatic sexism finally fails to garner the public scrutiny that Serling's mistake attracts is, ironically, that the public's strong desire to enshrine a woman hero militates against it. And when Walden's heroism is duly celebrated at the end of the film, this heroism creates the bankable political capital that the film's sleazy White House public-relations man wanted—"There is not going to be a dry eye from Nashua to Sacramento," he predicts. But if the film criticizes this manipulative pandering to the public and the reduction of the woman to a commodity fetish, it also validates the summative view the president offers in his memorial speech in praise of her: "Only death tests and proves the power of our bond to others." That is, Walden's self-sacrificing heroism is honored, but the particulars of her experience as a woman are finally subordinated to and subsumed within a universalizing vision of model military service. The ending affirms a soldierly ideal for which, in very different ways, both Walden and Monfriez give up their lives and one to which Serling dedicates his.

The film's depiction of mourning for Walden also blurs her subjectivity. In sharp contrast to the parents of Boylar, the friend whom Serling accidentally killed, Walden's parents are never shown being informed about or in any way responding to the circumstances of their daughter's death. The film's conclusion entirely avoids the question of whether her parents know that she died from so-called friendly fire. Indeed, the act of coming to terms

Fig. 3.2. Altameyer (Seth Gilliam) and Walden (Meg Ryan) prepare to embark on a life-changing helicopter rescue mission in Edward Zwick's *Courage Under Fire*.

with the meaning of her death is displaced from her parents and daughter onto Serling. It is subsumed under his quest for personal redemption through the reclamation of a soldierly ideal.

Moreover, a sense of mourning for Walden's crewmen, Ilario and Altameyer (Seth Gilliam), overshadows that for Walden. Torn between allegiance to the rebellious Monfriez or to Walden as their commanding officer, they garner sympathy for the impossible choice they face—betray the rules of male camaraderie in battle or betray the military hierarchy of rank. The contrast between Ilario's formerly hefty physique and his emaciated state reveals the psychic price he has paid, making him a figure of considerable pathos. A boyish chain-smoker and heroin addict, he becomes a symbol of youth and innocence prematurely lost. Altameyer, the young black soldier dying of abdominal cancer in a veteran's hospital—a cancer that rhymes with Walden's stomach wound—is haunted by recurring, guilt-ridden visions of the napalm flames that engulfed her. "Oh, Jesus! The fire!" he exclaims, and the camera, slowly zooming in on his face, sympathizes with his plight.[27] His words give his suffering a biblical dimension; his hell becomes more horrible than the flames that instantly consumed Walden. As an effect of this audience positioning, the film generates considerably more concern about the potential damage to young men in the gender-integrated military than about how women such as Walden—or her young daughter—might survive and succeed in that world. Serling's wife, Meredith (Regina Taylor), reflects, "It took me a long time to figure out how to be an army wife without totally obliterating myself." [28] Evidently, the film mirrors a culture that has yet to figure out how a woman can be a soldier without herself being similarly obliterated.

The Gulf War and Vietnam

In *Courage Under Fire*, napalm signals a double flashback, both to the trauma-laden moment of Walden's demise and, uncannily, to U.S. history in Vietnam, with its legacy of loss and shattered manhood. Contemporary discourse about the Gulf War identified smart bombs, Patriot missiles, and other advanced technology as protection from the kind of "emasculation" suffered by U.S. soldiers in Vietnam. From its beginning *Courage Under Fire* situates its protagonist, Serling, within a scenario that sets up a contrary statement. The opening juxtaposes a prefatory montage that emphasizes the familiar, distanced, abstract, cool green-and-grey video-game-like imagery documenting U.S. success in the air war, to a decidedly unfamiliar view of the ground war—a scene of terrible trauma against which technology affords no "Desert Shield." Rather than merely creating a humanizing counterpoint to cold masculinist technology, as television coverage of the war commonly did, the film's opening sequence shows a nighttime tank battle marked by fatal confusion and fiery death, in which sophisticated night-vision equipment contributes new possibilities for error even as it makes nighttime battle possible. When Serling "lights up a friendly" and kills fellow soldiers, his mistake simultaneously reflects these new hazards and functions as a metaphor for the Vietnam War, a conflict in which, according to films such as *Apocalypse Now* (Francis Ford Coppola, 1979) and *Platoon* (Oliver Stone, 1986), America was essentially at war with itself.[29] When Serling is passed over for a promotion in the months after the war, he seems, like Boylar and Walden, a fatality of the conflict, for, in his words, the army "buries him" alive—another uncanny motif—by assigning him the job of investigating candidates for medals. His sense of defeat also repeats that of the earlier war and aids in the film's deconstruction of Vietnam / Gulf War.

The film is highly conscious of the failure of the earlier war and is haunted by the horrific rate of suicides among its veterans.[30] Like its central concern with post-traumatic stress and suicide, its focus on the M-16, its recurrent sounds of whirling Cobra helicopter blades, and its repeated return to helicopter shots of the napalm that incinerates Iraqis and Walden alike all point back to the revenant of Vietnam. Other reminders are even more overt. These include the character of Gartner (Scott Glenn), the *Washington Post* reporter and Vietnam veteran who uncovers Serling's story, and Hershberg's painful memories of informing the families of the casualties of that war. Serling tells Hershberg, "With all due respect, this is not Vietnam," but Serling's own drunken, desperate plea to Gartner for clarity, heroism, and rightness points strongly to a connection between the conflicts: "I just want to get something clear this time, just want somebody to be a hero, want to get something right." Indeed, the flames that kill Boylar and haunt Serling in his dreams visually echo the film's napalm imagery and thereby reinforce the sweeping symbolic dimensions of Serling's quest. The film develops such symbolism in a way that denies the Gulf War, with its technologically advanced weapons systems, the status of unambiguous antidote to masculine failure in Vietnam.

At the same time, Serling's quest to lift himself up from his plight as a tarnished hero is fully successful. This is in no small part because his mission also forms the basis for a critique of military cover-ups (especially of Gulf War friendly-fire incidents), propagandizing, and public-relations manipulations, instantiated in the army's lie and Serling's subsequent, entirely reluctant dishonesty about his fatal error in judgment. In effect, the trauma Serling experiences results not just from the manner of his friend's death, but still more from the Army's dishonesty about it and deliberate suppression of the facts, provoking even deeper recollections of Vietnam.[31] It is this larger, symbolically resonant configuration of trauma that structures the entire film. For as Barbara Johnson notes, "Lived time is anything but continuous . . . Things don't happen when they happen . . . neither intentionality nor reaction can naturalize trauma into consecutive narrative."[32] Serling's heroism consists in tunneling back to get at the truth—behind the woman warrior, within himself, and, symbolically, behind the earlier war— as well as in working through rather than merely reenacting the trauma, as Monfriez does. In other words, his heroism comes from constructing history, or at least a version of it, and from directing Gartner to the tape of the tank battle that reveals the truth about Boylar's fate.

Serling is visually aligned both with Norman Schwarzkopf (seen on a television screen being interviewed on *Larry King Live*) and with Colin Powell (shown in a photograph), and he comes to share their stature because of this mission. As quester for redemption and truth, he becomes simultaneously Walden's rescuer and the hero who bucks his superiors to force the media images into alignment with fact—"the whole, cold truth of what happened over there," he calls it. Not coincidentally, the tape played for the press near the end of the film that documents Serling's fatal error also reveals, for the first time, his heroism in battle—his order to army tanks to turn on their lights, thereby differentiating them from enemy tanks. This light illuminates truth, unlike the light given off by the napalm that silences Walden.

The Vietnam War is not the only latent meaning of the recurring images of napalm; nor is *Courage Under Fire* merely a text about that legacy. Its more thoroughly repressed meaning comes into focus when we recall that napalm is chemically thickened gasoline and that U.S. motivation for intervening on behalf of Kuwait had everything to do with access to oil and the U.S. dependence on oil, topics the film never directly engages. In other words, the most genuinely latent meaning and historically uncanny aspect of the napalm imagery is grounded in the film's contemporary contexts—crudely put, masculinity and the oil that powers many of its technological expressions.[33]

Monfriez, Serling's guilty double, is the character in whom the symptoms and significance of this suppression are most discernable. Like Serling, Monfriez is a dedicated "good soldier" who "lit up a friendly," but unlike Serling, Monfriez harbors both a deadly sexism and an inability to work through his trauma and guilt. Monfriez's horrific attack on Walden is coded as a rape. He tells her, "There's no way you're taking away my weapon, cunt," then keeps the SAW (Squad Automatic Weapon) away from her and, misconstruing her actions, rips her belly open with it. Acting out rather than working through the scene of her death, the traumatized soldier finally drives his convertible directly into the path of an oncoming locomotive. As gasoline explodes into flames, the film comes closest to exposing the links between its napalm imagery and the stakes of the Gulf War. The internal combustion that propels Monfriez's masculinity, no less than his car, feeds on gasoline—and together, gasoline and masculinity form rough synonyms for the deadly economic and emotional stakes of the war. To state this idea in other words: whereas Buster Keaton's Johnnie Gray in *The General* (1927) struggles with trains, guns, swords, and other phallic war-making tools to achieve an absurd heroism in the Civil War South, his latter day counterpart, Johnnie "Night Train" Monfriez, as he calls himself, also struggles to master masculine symbols only to be engulfed by internal-infernal flames. Tellingly, an echo of the pattern Monfriez embodies marks the shift in the *Lethal Weapon* movies (Richard Donner, 1987, 1989, 1992, 1998) from a direct focus on Vietnam vets in the first installment to an almost incoherently plotted array of gasoline-fueled, pyrotechnic, masculinist displays in *Lethal Weapon 4*.[34]

Racial History

Commenting on the interplay between race and gender in American culture, James Baldwin explains that "a black man and a white man can come together only in the absence of women: which is, simply, the American legend of masculinity brought to its highest pressure, and revealed, as it were, in black and white . . . On the North American continent . . . white power became indistinguishable from the question of sexual dominance."[35] On the face of it, the alliance between Serling and Walden in *Courage Under Fire* adumbrates a world in which Baldwin's characterization of America has finally been outgrown—black and white, male and female, *can* come together under a shared code of moral courage and physical bravery. The film's title certainly befits Walden and Serling equally, even though Serling is the central hero, and the film's overt vision embraces the idea that there is a deep bond between them.

The issue bears closer scrutiny, however, for the film supports an alternative reading: namely, that when a black man, on probation and under orders from his white superior officer, is compelled to write the history of a white woman so that he can achieve reintegration into the brotherhood of arms, the need for that woman to be absent or dead is patriarchally overdetermined. And to extend this reading, the film suggests that the black man's mission remains, by cultural necessity, one in which his masculinity is an overriding concern and his bond with the idealized white woman can exist only across the ineluctable border of her physical inaccessibility. Serling/Washington functions as Walden/Ryan's rescuer, indeed her emissary from the grave—"Karen Walden sent me," he tells Monfriez—but just as in *The Pelican Brief* (Alan J. Pakula, 1993), in which Washington protects Julia Roberts, the white woman is always at a "safe distance." In short, *Courage Under Fire*, like other films of the 1990s, offers further support for James Baldwin's claims.[36]

The problematic closure strategies of *Courage Under Fire* reflect most tellingly on these dynamics of race and gender, and they are worth describing in detail. In a sequence that crosscuts between the White House Rose Garden ceremony honoring Walden and Serling's disclosure of the terrible truth to Boylar's parents, Serling increasingly occupies a space of domestic and psychological interiority. Images and events are progressively interiorized. Absent, like Walden, from the media-worthy spectacle that honors her, he chooses this moment to acknowledge his culpability to his dead friend's father and mother. His plea for forgiveness takes place in the living room of their stately Virginia home. The film lingers on Serling's tearful face as Boylar's father encourages self-forgiveness, then cuts to the tearful face of Walden's daughter as she receives her mother's medal and the nondiegetic, eulogistic music that bridges these scenes swells on the soundtrack.

The scene in the White House Rose Garden dissolves to Arlington National Cemetery, where Serling places his own medal on Walden's gravestone as Walden's voice-over reads her farewell letter to her parents—a letter about service and family that has been recovered thanks to Serling's efforts. As Walden's voice-over continues, another dissolve takes us to Serling's home, where he and his wife, from whom he has been alienated, are reconciled in a warmly lit embrace. Finally, Serling steps out on his porch and glances up at the sky. The film cuts to his mind-screen, which contains cool gray apotheosizing images of Walden flying upward in her chopper, away from the ruins of the disastrous tank battle scene where Serling remembers standing, his gaze following her ascent; the shot then fades to white. The film now cuts back to Serling's face in the present—a face full of the unimpeachable integrity that Denzel Washington can bring to his characters—then fades to black, as the timpani continue the film's closing music. Visually and acoustically, events are comprehended within his awareness and brought to closure for the spectators.

Ostensibly, the army emerges as a great equalizer here. It unites black and white, wealthy and poorer, male and female, transcending historical divisions while focalizing events through the heroic African American's purview. Indeed, earlier, when Serling learns that the army has opted to pass him over but will not, according to his commanding officer's words, "hang [him] out to dry," Serling is juxtaposed with an image of the state flag of Georgia, a banner that features a prominent Confederate cross.[37] This image activates the connotations of lynching embedded in the "hanging" phrase, casting doubt on the army's trustworthiness. In the later scene, however, Serling acts as his *own* man, on his *own* need to be accountable, and on his desire to force the army to be accountable, too. Yet when a black man is forgiven by a wealthy white Virginia man for past misdeeds, as the two talk in the latter's white-columned plantation-style home, making all well, something else is at stake. The subsumption of the memory and trauma of the Civil War is evident. So too is that of the first great U.S. war film, *The Birth of a Nation*, with its reliance on melodrama and crosscutting, its horror of miscegenation, and its horrifyingly poisonous racism.[38]

Add the metaphorical rape of Walden by Monfriez, Serling's guilty double, abetted by her crew, as well as the film's echoes of *Rashomon*, and it becomes clear that the myth of the black rapist looms troublingly close—a myth that retains its force despite its inversion of the historical fact that it was white plantation owners who raped black women. In *Courage Under Fire*, the black man redeems himself for the act of killing a white man by "saving" a white woman who is apotheosized as a soldier, hypostatized as a mother, and denied actual presence and subjectivity. Insofar as the film attempts to displace real sexist issues through its focus on Serling, it slips into other, still more troubled waters by furiously desexualizing a black man's fascinated study of an idealized white woman, the "shining piece of something for people to believe in."

The film's treatment of sex, race, and ethnicity has additional problematic dimensions. Its insistence on picturing the U.S. Army's racial and ethnic integration in overtly idealized terms helps to obscure the anti-Arab animosities that fueled U.S. motivation to enter the war in the first place. It thereby further obfuscates the import of the rhetoric of emasculation and feminization through which that national animosity was voiced; for example, in the misogynistic, homophobic phrase "bend over, Saddam" that U.S. bombardiers inscribed on the ordnance they dropped on Iraq. Instead of acknowledging anti-Arab bias and its role in global politics and power dynamics, *Courage Under Fire* tends toward an uncritical acceptance of much of the familiar visual and verbal rhetoric of this aspect of the war, including President Bush's accenting of "Saddam" to sound like "sodomy" or "sadist" and the shared sexualized vocabulary through which Serling and other male soldiers bond. That is, they speak of fighting in Vietnam as "humping in the Delta" and of the Iraqis as "ragheads" and "fuckers." (More specifically, the disturbing references to "ragheads" are made by Monfriez, in his own flashback narrative, and by Lieutenant Chelly, a forthright young white southerner from the Black Hawk crew.) The effect is a conflation of the rhetorics of war, ethnic stereotyping, and sexual conquest with an ancient Western pedigree. (Zwick's later film *The Siege* [1998], which depicts terrorist bombings of New York City and the subsequent curtailment of civil liberties, deployment of federal military forces for civil law enforcement, and incarceration of Arab Americans, ostensibly criticizes ethnic stereotyping. The film's *visual* vilification of Arabs nonetheless provoked criticism from a number of reviewers.)

In general, then, the avoidance of broader Gulf War politics in *Courage Under Fire* and its reduction of Iraqi soldiers to distant, sexually coded figures correlate with its displacement of Karen Walden as a subject in her own story. The film fails to bring into coherent, critical focus its own symbolic discourse on both subjects. And just as the soldiers' metaphors of rape double Monfriez's expressions of disdain toward Walden, Monfriez himself targets not only the Iraqi dictator's "mother of all battles" but also Walden's womb. These intersecting global, sexual, and racial politics often coexist in the film as mutual diversions and smoke screens, generating what must be seen to some degree as unconscious, uncanny resonances.

"The *Mother* of All Battles"

No aspect of the film is more replete with intractable contradictions than its treatment of motherhood—a motif first introduced with Saddam Hussein's infamous slogan, heard in the film's prologue, indicating the primordial and exemplary enormity of the battle to be waged. Similarly, a maternal mythos has also been evoked in the discourse about the gender integration that this "mother of all battles" initiated. In Rayner's words, "Some perceive that we're witnessing the birth throes of another [revolution]," one wherein "America [is] creating its own Amazon warrior myth, the equivalent . . . [of] the woman memorialized in a Soviet realist movie, riding into town at the head of a Red Cavalry troop, then heading out again three days later, leaving behind the child to which she'd given birth." [39]

To be sure, the war genre has traditionally been male-centered, and when it has included women, it has often reduced gender to biology by equating women with mothers, as illustrated, in part, by the World War II combat films I discuss in Chapter 1. At times these maternal figures emblematize a nation (Germania or Britannia, for instance) and demand loyalty, rescue, or defense; [40] at other times, they are particular mother figures, defined according to a binary view of women: "good" ones motivate their sons and husbands to become good soldiers; "bad" ones subvert this kind of development, engendering in its stead pathology, emasculation, and death. The loyal, patient wife and "good mother" also welcomes soldiers home with a show of support, just as wives and mothers greeted soldiers returning from the Gulf War with yellow ribbons, a gesture that became a popular media image inspired by a popular song.

The historic importance of the good mother–bad mother dichotomy to the war film has been well documented,[41] as has an obverse masculinist myth tying soldiering to death. William Broyles, Jr., asserts that "for men, [war is] at some terrible level the closest thing to what childbirth is for women: the initiation into the power of life and death."[42] Similarly, military historian Martin van Creveld claims that "men have made war their special province because they cannot reproduce."[43] According to this logic, they fight to protect those of their kind who can. Conformably, before the Gulf War, white American mothers living in the Middle East were displayed in media images as being at risk.[44]

The mothers in *Courage Under Fire* are all idealized, in keeping with war-film genre protocols: Boylar's mother, Serling reports, cried her eyes out when he informed her of her son's death. Serling's wife, Meredith, has figured out how "to be an army wife without obliterating [herself]," and thus skillfully cares for their children's emotional needs in her husband's absence, routinely driving their young son Brian twelve blocks so that he will not fall off his bike in front of his friends. (She even cheers for Walden, saying "good for her," when she learns of Walden's posthumous nomination for a Medal of Honor.) Walden's mother succeeds both as mother and grandmother. Finally, Walden herself is unequivocally idealized as a single mother both in the descriptions that her parents provide and in the shots that juxtapose her with her daughter, Anne Marie. Even Walden's soldierly acts of violence are implicitly motivated by maternal protectiveness toward her crew, a domestication of female aggression that tends to render that aggression more socially acceptable.

As a biologically maternal soldier figure, however, Walden is a problematic figure, as the flashbacks attributed to Ilario reveal. A young man who is emotionally childlike, Ilario is closest to Walden of all her crew, having served with her for over two years and having known her family. His initial flashback shows her as powerful, in control, and protective, patting and covering his head when the bullets fly. Two-shots of the pair together, with frequent tight-framing and close-ups, also signal their deep emotional tie. In addition, in the two sequences in which he narrates his memories to Serling, Ilario is juxtaposed with pools of water. The first scene is of a swimming pool full of splashing, playing children—a scene that prompts Ilario's nostalgic yearning for childhood's freedom from the need to think about consequences. The second is an isolated lakeside setting, shown in autumn, that he loved as a child. Walden's name, of course, conjures up yet a third pool—the pond made famous by Henry David Thoreau. Clustered together, these images suggest Narcissus's inability to tear himself away from his watery reflection—Lacan's mirror stage—and hence Ilario's emotionally arrested state. Such imagery implies that the maternal Walden, no matter how fine a soldier she was, is the wrong sex to perform the crucial tasks that the war genre demands: initiating young males into the symbolic order of war and inaugurating them into manhood. When Ilario sides with Monfriez against Walden in the moment of crisis, Ilario's need for male leadership is made clear. Like Orestes, he then assumes the status of a matricidal son, later becoming a boyish figure of pathos, who chain-smokes and shoots up heroin to keep the Furies at bay. He remains arrested and suicidal, a lost soul who might instead have been a fine soldier.

Additionally, Walden's biological maternity has implications of monstrosity, as Ilario's final flashback reveals. After Monfriez takes his rifle away from her and, misconstruing her actions, shoots Walden in the belly, she refuses to let any of her mutinous crew near her. In the staccato phrases and vocabulary of a soldier, she growls that, after all, she "gave birth to a nine-pound baby, asshole. I think I can handle it. We stay with Rady." The phrasing and epithet align her speech with the terse vocabulary of the male soldier, whereas the content of the dialogue, including her protectiveness of Rady, identifies her as maternal; she says she can take it like a man because she has taken it as a mother. In fact, despite Monfriez's later denial that anyone fired the M-16 during the crew's evacuation, she goes on to keep up the M-16 fire that protects both helicopter crews. The sequence codes her as male, female, and neither—an Amazon and a variation on the phallic mother against whom, as audiences of the *Alien* films know, fire is the only effective weapon. Her coding also recalls the transvestite or gender-destabilizing mayhem that provoked Edmund Burke's distrust, as I discussed in Chapter 1.

In contrast, male soldiers' assuming maternal functions is not problematic at all. Men are shown to mother each other better than a woman could and without compromising their masculine credentials. Thus, Serling cannot talk to his wife about his guilt, his nightmare flashbacks to Boylar's death, or the army's cover-up, but he can talk about these things with Gartner, the male reporter and veteran. Serling and Gartner can bond because Gartner spent time "humping in the Delta." (Similarly, Serling bonds with the all-male crew of the Black Hawk helicopter when one of the soldiers refers to the Iraqis as "fuckers," corrects himself, and Serling replies, "You got it right the first time." Everyone laughs.) When Serling tells Gartner about the tape documenting his deadly error, Gartner mothers him: "Eat something [handing him a bag of take-out food]. You look awful." The shot-countershot here conveys their closeness and contrasts with the distance between Serling and Meredith, with whom he communicates only by phone.

Similarly, the most personal moment of bonding between Serling and his commanding officer, General Hershberg, is couched in unmistakable terms of maculinist-maternal care. Insisting that he always has Serling's best interests at heart, Hershberg reminds him, "[I'm] your friend who nursed you, patted your back, pushed promotions, fucking burped your kids at their baptisms—and I know about the drinking." As for Serling, it is a sign of his recovery that, in the film's final sequence, he is tending his son's bicycle, in effect taking over the parenting role from Meredith. Just as Captain Miller in *Saving Private Ryan* trusts his sergeant to be his mother ("I thought *you* were my mother," he jokes) but distrusts the alliance between military public relations and an actual grieving mother, so *Courage* validates maternal intervention only insofar as it is mastered and enacted by men.[45] (Here, too, are further echoes of *The Tempest*, in which Prospero takes over for the dead and missing mothers of both Miranda and Caliban.)

Maternal imagery, however, is more complex than these examples of male appropriation reveal. This complexity derives from technological and cultural exigencies. Specifically, maternal imagery shapes the opening battle scene, which is played out in a lunar desert landscape made surreal by the green cast it takes on when viewed through the soldiers' night-vision devices, technology that, as I noted earlier, both enables battle and expands the potential for error. Green is also reflected on the faces of the men within the tanks' red-lit interiors, and the juxtaposition of colors intensifies both, heightening the tanks' womblike aspect and the cool green of the killing apparatus. A tank forms the mise-en-scène of the successful male-mediated birth scene in *The Big Red One* (1980). Here, however, the tank from which

Boylar struggles to escape appears in Serling's nightmares as the scene of a baptism—or perhaps an abortion—by fire. In short, Serling fails to "nurse" his young charge as Hershberg claims to have "nursed" Serling. The scene of Boylar's death accords with Andreas Huyssen's theory that technology in its feminine aspect is culturally coded as dangerous or treacherous.[46] More precisely, the film initially codes the body of the tank, with its androgynous blend of phallic and womblike parts, as a realm of potential confusion and chaos—not unlike Walden's combat identity. It codes it, as well, as a conjunction of the womb and tomb, places that meet in Freud's concept of the maternal as unheimlich.

Because the tank scene is played out both in Serling's dreams and in Iraq (ancient Mesopotamia, a part of the globe that an earlier generation of scholars called the cradle of civilization), its larger symbolic import also demands a symptomatic reading. That is, the narrative requires an analysis of those collectively denied historical contradictions that underpin it, what Fredric Jameson terms the "political unconscious."[47] Just as ontogeny recapitulates phylogeny, the Boylar-Serling narrative provides clues about the film's repressed history of East-West relations, a history in which the West has persistently coded the East as feminine, inferior, fecund, and treacherous. In this tradition, the so-called Muslim Orient is a society defined by its threateningly undifferentiated sex drive; it must be brought under the dominion of Western patriarchy—"ravished and won," in Edward Said's words[48]—so that the United States can master the historical traumas it projects onto and associates with that region.[49]

Accordingly, the film's preoccupation with birth and technology also suggests the significance of the West's vaunted display of technological superiority over Iraq: the goal of that display was to align anew the disruptive Muslim Orient with the feminine while making possible Western patriarchy's appropriation of the East's mythic generative power. Indeed, since, as Jean-François Lyotard explains, the Greek *techné* is "the abstract from *tikto* which means *to engender, to generate*," technological mastery in an important sense implies, by definition, reproductive mastery—even and perhaps especially in the Hollywood combat film.[50] The United States and its military thus achieve a born-again masculinity and regenerated patriarchy, spoils of war the film initially questions but ultimately affirms when Serling's use of light and reason to differentiate tanks and avert catastrophe is finally revealed. Indeed, the eventual playing of the tape that demonstrates his error in judgment ultimately serves as powerful proof of his lifesaving initiative and leadership. It is perhaps no surprise, then, that at the time of its release, *Courage Under Fire* was criticized not for contradicting its own egalitarian ideals by relying on biologically and sexually determinist concepts of identity, but for creating a "potential feminist paragon" as its heroine in the war against Iraq.[51]

Conclusion and Additional Film Views of the Gulf War

This analysis of *Courage Under Fire,* with a focus on repressed history, on doubling in the figures Serling and Monfriez, and on eerie maternal imagery, has been concerned with key manifestations of the unheimlich, the conjunction of the homey and unhomey, the familiar reencountered as strange. In *Courage Under Fire,* the uncanny as the anxiety-producing return of the repressed is discernable in the film's layering of war references, from the American Civil War to the Vietnam and Persian Gulf Wars, and in the themes of soldierly fratricide and matricide, as well as in the concern with the "mother of all battles." It is also discernable in the allusions to the Watergate scandal and in the positional paradox of Karen Walden. On the one hand, she is half of the mother-child dyad that encapsulates the values of hearth, home, and nation that soldiers fight to protect; on the other, through her lonely stand as a soldier-protector, she defines the battle line or periphery, the "line in the sand," to use George H. W. Bush's phrase, which demarcates the reach of America's globalized interests. This paradoxical positioning is a relatively new variant on what Molloy recognizes as an often reiterated theme: the "inside/outside dichotomy that places women, hearth, and home at the center or foundation, and, at the same time, on the periphery of the civil state."[52]

In the chapter that follows, this study will explore the unheimlich in relation to woman, the nation, and globalization by examining two films that depart in significant ways from the Hollywood model. But before I turn away from questions emanating from the filmic treatment of the Gulf War, a brief consideration of David O. Russell's technically and thematically innovative post–Gulf War film, *Three Kings* (1999), and Nina Menkes's avant-garde *The Bloody Child* (1996) can productively round out the present discussion. Russell's film does not directly engage gender integration in the military or attempt to work through the legacy of Tailhook, the Gene

McKinney and Kelly Flinn scandals, and other events that form a critical historical context for *Courage Under Fire,* yet its concern with a maternal subtext uncannily echoes elements in *Courage Under Fire.* Its very title refers to the three magi who visited the most renowned mother and child in Western culture, and its narrative echoes its title in offering a triplication of the mother-child dyad as motivation for action. The film's soldier-of-fortune protagonists, upon seeing one of Saddam's supporters murder an Iraqi mother, are quickly transformed from purely mercenary soldiers to somewhat less mercenary ones, undertaking a rescue mission à la John Sturges's *Magnificent Seven* (1960). Moreover, one of the protagonists, Troy Barlow (Mark Wahlberg), draws motivation from his wife and young child back home and, once captured, finds this motivation counterpointed by the tragic personal history of his pedagogically minded Iraqi torturer. As the film advances this narrative, it develops a progressive critique both of the computerized televisual construction of history that marked contemporary packaging of the Gulf War and of globalization and commodification after the American model. Yet its multiple inscriptions of the maternal as an emblem of home-front values and boundaries not to be crossed serve to reinstate the traditional place of the feminine uncanny in America's imaginary construction of its history, keeping these symbolizations as formatively and problematically alive as ever.

A radically different treatment of the uncanny of the Gulf War emerges in *The Bloody Child.* Like *Courage Under Fire,* this film focuses on an investigation into a woman's death, a male soldier's guilt, and a military environment often hostile to women. Unlike *Courage Under Fire,* however, Menkes's film both rejects Hollywood conventions of history, narrative, and character, and concerns itself with what phrases such as "collateral damage" conceal. It focuses, as well, on the kindred spirits of Caliban's mother and Ariel's first captor, the abject witches, and the forces they symbolize. Moreover, *The Bloody Child* resuscitates its slain woman-witch character not to give us her story or to trigger our tears, but to remind us about her history-less status. If films that criticize media manipulation—including *Courage Under Fire* and *Wag the Dog*—often remind us that women and children are the shortest route to easy tears, *The Bloody Child* is a feminist film that defamiliarizes "women and children" in order to redeem them both from this kind of melodramatic manipulation and from historical oblivion.

My next chapter examines films that adhere to the Hollywood narrative paradigm more closely than Menkes's film, even as they find ways to revise that paradigm with reflexive strategies that illuminate how U.S. history is constructed and contested and how women's voices can shape and redefine it. Although the films in question emphasize domestic arrangements and have obvious novelistic qualities, they refuse to respond to the kind of retrograde desire for realistic, romance-inflected nineteenth-century historiography that, in Hayden White's view, is incompatible with a politically responsible representation of twentieth-century developments. As a result, their director, John Sayles, provides some of the most compelling reflections on American history and the unheimlich that emerged in the 1990s.

"Our history [as a theme park] is our future here,
not our past."

tourism developer in *Limbo*

As Julia Kristeva avows, any encounter with the uncanny—that stranger within and without who challenges the borders of identity—provokes a choice: "To worry or to smile, such is the choice when we are assailed by the strange; our decision depends on how familiar we are with our own ghosts." [1] For Homi Bhabha, the location of that conundrum, both spatially and temporally, is on the border, in the interstices, and the sort of art that expresses the groundwork of choosing necessarily revivifies the past. That is, this kind of art "does not merely recall the past as social cause or aesthetic precedent; it renews the past, refiguring it as a contingent 'in-between' space, that innovates and interrupts the performance of the present. The 'past-present' becomes part of the necessity, not the nostalgia, of living." [2] The process, in short, is quite distinct from one of evoking an idealized past to assimilate a problematic present, or of constructing a whitewashed present as an antidote to an intractable past. What is at stake is the deconstruction of the boundaries of the historical "in between."

In recent films by independent filmmaker John Sayles, the defining elements in his depictions of contemporary America have been precisely such encounters with the kind of "past-present" that Bhabha theorizes and precisely such moments of choosing as Kristeva invokes. With that in mind, this chapter explores the following questions: In Sayles's *Lone Star* (1996) and *Limbo* (1999), what is the nature of his films' familiarity with the historical specters that people their particular locales, the southern- and northernmost geographic borders of the continental United States? What

Chapter Four

"FORGET THE ALAMO"

Lone Star, *Limbo*, and the Limits of the Nation

qualities define the in-between spaces of his films as these films revivify the past? And finally, what is the relationship in these films among the uncanny, the feminine, and the boundaries of the American nation?

The two films in question constitute companion pieces, even doubles of each other, in a number of ways. They share cast members, including Kris Kristofferson, who plays a Western-style heavy in both: the racist Charley Wade in *Lone Star,* the shady Smilin' Jack in *Limbo.* They further share Vanessa Martinez, who plays a teenager caught in a troubled relationship with her mother in both: the young Chicana Pilar Cruz in *Lone Star* and the alienated, imaginative Noelle De Angelo in *Limbo.* The two films also flesh out the problems and pleasures of midlife heterosexual couple formation, as they simultaneously raise questions about the forces that define family, home, and community. In both, as in many Sayles films, storytelling plays an important part, and competing stories express conflicting perceptions of familial and community identities. Both, too, deploy familiar tropes of landscape and history, innocence and corruption, in order to narrativize state and nation. Perhaps most strikingly, however, both films use the symbolically charged figure of a daughter-storyteller to represent and call into question the multiple borders that shape national and state identities.

If the parallels between *Lone Star* and *Limbo* are striking, when these films are viewed in the context of contemporary international cinema, still more extensive mirroring emerges. First, the two Sayles films share patterns that Maureen Molloy spotlights in the New Zealand films *Heavenly Creatures, The Piano,* and *Once Were Warriors.* These include the following: (1) complex or problematic mother-daughter relationships, (2) the casting of daughters as storytellers, and (3) uncanny motifs such as doubling, mutilation, and the return of the repressed. A further shared characteristic is the presence of broad configurations of unhomeliness, rooted in women's paradoxical relation to national identity. To quote more extensively from a passage by Molloy I cited briefly in my introduction:

> The figure of woman stands in a metonymic but para-
> doxical relation to the nation. Many theorists [hold]
> that 'the nation' is premised on an inside/outside di-
> chotomy that places women, hearth, and home at the
> center or foundation and, at the same time, on the
> periphery of the civil state. This ambivalence recapit-
> ulates the immanence of the unhomely in the home

for women. For women, the nation (or the home) can never be simply that which is comfortable, warm and intimate. But there is more to this than meets the eye. This ambivalence of woman to nation recapitulates the ambivalence of woman to the modern human subject, both human and not fully human, both necessary and repressed, both bounded and unbounded. The uncanny, with its implications of doubling, merging, and return of the repressed, is the expression and the effect of the feminine. The lack of boundaries, surety, and the return of the archaic make it also a powerful expression of the postcolonial nation.[3]

Given the implications of these phenomena and motifs, their range is all the more noteworthy, and, impressively, it extends to the development of the young singer-storyteller Nicole Burnell in Canadian filmmaker Atom Egoyan's haunting *The Sweet Hereafter* (1997), as well as the fringe existence of the two young women, Isa and Marie, of Erick Zonca's *The Dreamlife of Angels* (*La vie rêvée des anges,* France, 1998), and of the youthful doubles Yuliet and Fabiola in Carlos Marcovich's *Who the Hell Is Juliette?* (¿*Quién diablos es Juliette?* 1997), not to mention Sayles's own rather gentler *The Secret of Roan Inish* (1994).[4]

Significantly, in Molloy's view, the New Zealand films depict a bleak vision: Although they disrupt an earlier fantasy of New Zealand national unity that was founded on the illusion of harmonious race relations, despite the colonialist past, these 1990s films replace that fantasy with an unheimlich idea of nation that is threatening, strange, and, like the uncanny itself, gendered feminine. Instead of inscribing an accommodation of or opening up toward the range of differences that includes that of gender, they perpetuate an ancient formula wherein female sacrifice becomes a prerequisite to the process of defining and redefining national identity. In Molloy's words, "The nation is configured as woman but almost unbearably, as a dead woman—Honora, the good mother [of *Heavenly Creatures*]; Grace, the good daughter [of *Once Were Warriors*]; Ada, the mutilated [of *The Piano*]. Is this Irigaray's truth made visible—that the polis is necessarily formed on the death of the feminine? If so, these films are profoundly pessimistic."[5] That is, they express a milieu that has responded in fearful, retrogressive ways to the crises of postcolonialism, with its massive reconfigurations of the social and economic landscape. Of the films' unheimlich elements, Molloy also observes, "It is not only the internal features of these films that are uncanny but the reiterations between them—the reapparition of narratives of femininity that echo the old stories of female-to-female treachery and the ways in which female sexuality both secures and undermines home and nation. Each is about secret female worlds, muteness and speaking, merged identities, betrayal of relations between mothers and daughters leading to mutilation and death."[6]

Whether the other films that I have named here generate a similar view of nation is no simple question. Even if they all confirm Bhabha's insight that liminality informs the postmodern, postcolonialist condition, they also refer to geographically and historically discrete situations. Thus, the cold, northern, urban, industrialized France that forms the setting of *The Dreamlife of Angels*, with its oppressive class stratification and problematic, homogenizing American pop-culture presence, differs from the snowy rural community, with its deceptive surfaces and vulnerability to commercializing interests, of Egoyan's Canada in *The Sweet Hereafter*, and so on. But it is worth asking whether, in sharing many of the uncanny elements that connect the New Zealand films, Sayles's *Lone Star* and *Limbo* also exhibit the retrogressive dimensions that Molloy detects in them, or whether Sayles's work offers alternative visions and challenges to conventional female encoding in the narrative of nation.

In fact, since *Lone Star* and *Limbo*, like the majority of Hollywood films, focus on male protagonists, Sayles's work might appear to be relatively less progressive. Specifically, his films center on middle-aged men who bear the familiar contours of a certain kind of 1990s American movie masculinity: Survivors both of failed marriages and of troubled relationships with their fathers, they work at jobs that mismatch their desires; they are also loners living in their hometowns, burdened by a past that returns to haunt them, a past in which death and issues of guilt and innocence figure importantly. Further, both men turn away from their loner status to form bonds with female characters whose identities are in some way enmeshed with the locale.[7]

Additionally, as Janet Walker explains, *Lone Star*'s structuring concern with oedipal conflicts identifies its lineage with male-centered traumatic Westerns, films that both call up and conceal "the violence of the father-son relationship" and "the inevitable ambivalence of inheritance" in the context of a U.S. history of bloody conquest. Whether based on oedipal struggle or, like *The Searchers*, on so-called bad blood about the captivity of a Euro-

American by Indians, "the traumatic Western embeds a narrativized version of history contextualized by familial and/or racial differences as its originary trauma."[8] Each of the New Zealand films, in sharp contrast, centers on girls and women and thereby, in Molloy's reading, "challenges the usual tropes of nationhood, displacing the young male hero, and the figure of woman as mute ground to be defended, with a fierce and active female creativity."[9]

Yet, as I will argue, in Sayles's films female characters move to the center of the narratives in both expected and unexpected ways, becoming figures whose social liminality not only serves as a synecdoche for the geopolitical identity of their respective locales, but also as the means by which alternative visions of the present and future, as well as the personal and cultural, find articulation. At the same time, the concept of female creativity serves a crucial role in Sayles's films, especially in *Limbo*, wherein—just as Molloy observes of the New Zealand films—"the plot or character is built around a specific female creativity—be it fantasy, storytelling, or music making";[10] in *Limbo* it is all three. And whereas the New Zealand films are tinged by a nostalgia for a presumably more innocent age, Sayles exposes nostalgia, especially Eisenhower-era nostalgia, to a trenchant critique.

To be sure, the colonial or imperial power that gives rise to corruption, violence, and loss in the New Zealand films has its counterpart in the racism, political corruption, and crassly exploitative commercialism indicted in Sayles's films, but as Molloy contends, in the New Zealand films female sexuality is also identified as a destructive force: "Ultimately, [these films'] displacement [of the young male hero] is recouped by a violence that reiterates the disruptiveness of female sexuality."[11] Conversely, in Sayles's work, although female sexuality may also be framed as disruptive, a trigger to violence, and a conduit to uncanny repetition, it is nonetheless affirmed—remarkably, even when the reach of its disruption extends to incest.

Lone Star

Lone Star begins with the discovery of a ghost from the past, a man's skeleton found on an old army shooting range in the desert. Called in to investigate, Sam Deeds (Chris Cooper), the sheriff of the border town of Frontera, Texas, suspects that the remains are those of Charley Wade, a notorious "bribe and bullets" sheriff from the 1950s, and he further suspects that his own father, Korean War veteran Buddy Deeds (Matthew McConaughey), killed Wade. Along with Hollis Pogue (Clifton James), Frontera's current mayor, Buddy had been one of Wade's deputies, and he later became the town's sheriff—in fact, a legendary lawman remembered and respected by the diverse ethnic groups of the town for his welcome differences from the lethally racist Wade.

In another sense, the film begins much earlier, with the complex Texas history that Pilar Cruz (Elizabeth Peña), a local high school teacher, sums up for her class in a critical moment of storytelling:

> Okay, we have the fight against the Spanish with bloody conflict for dozens of years till they're finally defeated in 1821 and Mexican independence is declared. Anglo settlers are invited to colonize the area, and by the time they begin the movement against Santa Anna, they outnumber the Mexicans here by four to one. The war between Mexico and the Anglo forces ends in 1836 with the formation of the Texas Republic. Texas joins the United States as a state where slavery is *legal* in 1845, after the so-called Mexican war, then secedes to join the Confederacy in 1861. The Confederacy is beaten, and the restoration period is marked by range wars and race wars and all these paralleled by the constant battles between both the Mexican and Anglo settlers and the various Indian nations in the area.[12]

In the film's present, the Mexican-Americans form the majority, a fact with significant ramifications for local politics, including controversies about how history should be taught by teachers such as Pilar, how figures such as Buddy Deeds should be publicly remembered, and how the town should promote itself and its history to tourists. (Tellingly, while discussing tourism with town leaders, Sam derisively terms Frontera "the gateway to inexpensive pussy" across the border. The reference symptomatically links male soldiers, prostitution, and male tourists, just as it identifies women, once more, with social margins.)[13]

At another level of history, the film gestures toward its own beginnings and cinematic language through the self-reflexive elements of mise-en-scène that accompany Pilar's lecture on the formation of the state and nation.[14] Seated in the classroom, half-listening to Pilar, an African-American student draws a flip-book depiction of a muscular man, a shot-putter in motion, in a fully diegetic "shot" within the film frame that mimics the antecedents of animated films and thus evokes the early history of the movies. This is one of several metacinematic moments in the film that effectively frame and contextualize the languages and dialects of cinema as scripts of history. By playing cinematic language off Pilar's lecture in this way, the scene creates a kind of dialectic that engages the various forms of history, both as story and as marker of the borders of identity. In this case, even though it is obviously not the student's intention, his muscle-man drawing can suggest the *caudillos* or strongman patriarchs who held power throughout the 1800s in the region of which Frontera is part, and one of whose metaphorical descendants in the 1950s, on the Anglo side, was Charley Wade. Thus there is a covert connection between the teacher's and student's "dialects."[15]

Sam, Pilar, and the student animator, Chet Payne (Eddie Robinson), are also products of the three genealogies around which the main plot and subplots center. Chet is the son of U.S. Army Colonel Del Payne (Joe Morton), who has recently been posted near Frontera, his hometown, where Otis Payne (Ron Canada), the father from whom he has long been estranged, still lives. Chet is curious about Otis, the owner of the sole local bar frequented by African Americans, and Chet eventually learns from him that the family descends from a complex, racially mixed heritage, the black Seminoles, expert trackers who worked as mercenaries for the whites—a past echoed in Del's present army career and one Sayles describes in Shakespearean terms in an interview: "You can move up [in the contemporary army] as long as you're willing to be the Ariel of the piece, as long as you're willing to be the mercenary, the hired gun."[16]

Whereas the film works toward a sense of the imminent, healthy reconciliation of Del and Otis (aka Big O), effected in part by Chet's desire for familial connection, the stories of Sam and Pilar evolve more equivocally. In the film's climax, Sam finds out that it was Hollis, not Buddy, who killed Wade when Wade was about to shoot young Otis (Gabriel Casseus) in the back, and that the three kept it a secret. Sam chooses to preserve the secret, an act that spares Hollis and the tall tales he has lovingly told about Buddy, yet also leaves a cloud of suspicion over Buddy, whose legendary lawman status and past interference in Sam's love life put an enduring strain on their relationship. Sam also reunites with Pilar for the first time since their parents—his father and her mother, Mercedes, a prosperous Chicana café owner—separated the young sweethearts in high school, apparently because of their ethnic difference. (A local bartender, in fact, speaks nostalgically of Buddy as someone who discouraged mixed relationships.)

In the scene that marks Sam and Pilar's initial reunion, they dance to Freddie Fender's "Desde Te Conozco" on the jukebox ("Since I Met You, Baby," a tune that fuses Hispanic, black, and white rock-and-roll history), in a nighttime world for two set off cinematically with special lighting and lap dissolves, culminating in their lovemaking.[17] Yet what Sam discovers while investigating Wade's death is not only that Buddy was unfaithful to his mother, but also that he and Mercedes were lovers, and that Buddy fathered Pilar after Wade killed Mercedes's husband Eladio Cruz—hence, the watchful, disapproving gaze that Mercedes directs at Sam and Pilar as they move closer to each other again in the present. The revelation of their blood tie is withheld until the final scene of the film, set in the long abandoned drive-in where Buddy had separated them as teenagers, and where they now come to the decision to remain a couple, a choice made somewhat easier by the fact that she, for medical reasons, can no longer bear children.

Lone Star's stunning plot revelation led some critics to compare it with *The Crying Game* (Neil Jordan, 1992), in which the racially and sexually ambiguous Dil (Jaye Davidson) reveals his penis. But whereas in *The Crying Game,* as Sharon Willis astutely observes, "the big surprise credited with reframing the picture becomes the *whole* picture,"[18] reducing a variety of differences to the single one between a man and a woman, *Lone Star*'s revelation has the opposite effect. Sam and Pilar's hidden kinship and, even more, Pilar's mixed parentage, are critical in reframing and complicating the film as a whole, since they signify a kind of ultimate challenge to and deconstruction of the socially inscribed hierarchy of differences that shape ethnic, generational, state, and national identities, along with the diverse historical perspectives in which they are rooted. Similarly, like Payne family history, the Cruz-Deeds history registers the complex social reality that Americans have always been multiethnic, and that this is not only a "postmodern" phenomenon.

What merits special emphasis, however, is the fact that it is the woman's part to function as the ultimate figure of difference and its undoing. In a sense that is fundamental to the film, Pilar's identity is uncanny, the thing long familiar—as shown by the couple's feelings that they had a special connection from the beginning—yet hidden and repressed.[19] Correspondingly, she signifies the Mexican historical identity that preceded and underlies the Texan one insofar as it has been repressed, a symbolic role buttressed by her bilingualism and her work as a history teacher who challenges the hegemonic, Anglocentric paradigm of the past. Different from the tragic mulatta of such films as Douglas Sirk's *Imitation of Life* (1959), Pilar has a conflict with her mother about her identity, but is ultimately affirmed in her rebellion against Mercedes's American social conservatism, with its anti-Mexican bias, and affirmed as well in her choice to distance herself from the traditional historic divisions in order to heal and find pleasure in a counternarrative of the couple.

Various dimensions of the film come into focus through the inscription of Pilar in these terms—that is, through her challenge to established national boundaries, a challenge she vocalizes, while seated before a blank movie screen, in the film's resonant, border-shattering last words, her imperative to forget history as the story of limits and divides: "We'll start from scratch. Forget all that other stuff. You know, that history—to hell with it, right? Forget the Alamo." First, there is the hybrid, multidialect nature of the film's style, its aesthetic, generic, musical, and linguistic mix, a blend that conjoins not only elements of the classic Hollywood Western and detective genre (Sam's world, in effect), but also, more overarchingly, those associated with Latin American magic realism, the Mexican *telenovela*, and the local Spanish language (Pilar's). As Sayles explains, in different moments *Lone Star* encompasses cinematic styles that range from the editing of the classic Western showdown (especially in the first flashback narrated by Hollis, about Wade and Buddy's face-off in 1957), to a more expressionist mode (especially in the last flashback, in which Hollis and Big O share the narrative point of view and Hollis's shooting of Wade is filmed with the dialogue muted and jukebox blues music dominant).[20]

Formally, what is most innovative and striking, and what unites these and other flashbacks, is the fluid movement into and out of the past that Sayles, as editor of the film, effects—transitions that take place without cuts, fades, or dissolves but *within* the shot. These transitions to the past align the film not only with the structure of trauma, as Walker demonstrates, but also, in their seamlessness, with magic realism, a style identified with Latin American visual and narrative aesthetics.[21] Ultimately, these magic realist mixed temporalities reveal the inescapable contemporaneity of the past, how, in Bhabha's words, "The 'past-present' becomes part of the necessity, not the nostalgia, of living." And it is this style that increasingly qualifies and complicates the film's Anglo- and androcentric elements, counterpointing Pilar's history lesson, even as it conforms with Fredric Jameson's insight that Latin American magic realism relies on the uncanny or a return of the repressed as a significant reference point for challenging the nostalgic, Eisenhower-era-oriented historiography of the glossy, post-modern Hollywood history film.[22] Simply put, *Lone Star* relies on magic realist aesthetics not for pastiche but to expose the past-present, a framework ultimately summed up in the symbolism of Pilar.

By the same token, the revelation that Pilar and Sam are half brother and sister finally belongs not principally to the generic world in which the lonely cowboy and schoolmarm form a couple, as in *The Gunfighter* (Henry King, 1950), nor even to the world in which the detective solves the mystery that turns out to be that of the woman's identity, as in *Chinatown* (Roman Polanski, 1974) or *Devil in a Blue Dress* (Carl Franklin, 1995), but instead to the world of Mexican television soap opera, the telenovela, wherein, by convention, blood ties that prohibit romance and sexual intimacy are made known at the last possible moment—just in time to prevent a violation of the taboo.[23] Sayles's radical step is to have the couple in effect meet the ghosts and still follow their desire, deliberately choosing to cross the line of moral and public opinion. Accordingly, in *Lone Star* the violation of the incest taboo functions less like a standard oedipal narrative, centered on the forbidden desire of the son for the mother or mother substitute, and more as a way of heightening the *frisson* created by the transgressive, destabilizing dissolution of difference—that is, of exposing those illicit and covert connections between the law and the *mojado* ("wetback"), the Anglo North and La Raza of the South, male and female, center and margin, not to mention Hollywood and Latin American linguistic, musical, cinematic, and televisual styles—in order to de-define and radically deconstruct the borders of nations.

Indeed, if Sayles's films (unlike Spielberg's) generally eschew melodramatic excess, here he appropriates a tradition of Mexican melodrama, long shaped by its willingness to exceed the dominant Hollywood paradigm, and ratchets it up even further. Ana M. López's account of Mexican melodrama, with its "excess [that] explicitly defies the Hollywood dominant," affords a revealing simile for understanding the context of that excess and hence Sayles's affiliative gesture. She explains, "Like Caliban in Shakespeare's *Tempest*, the colonized must use the colonizer's 'words'—the imported cinematic apparatus—and learn the colonizer's language before he or she can even think of articulating his or her own speech: 'You taught me language and my profit on't is I know how to curse.'"[24] In short, Sayles's ending shows that he, too, has learned the Latino art of cinematic cursing.

The scene in which we first see Pilar and Sam take steps toward an unwitting violation of this taboo also speaks metacinematically. Set in the local drive-in, where the 1972 B-grade Filipino film *Black Mama, White Mama* with Pam Grier is playing, the scene reveals Sam and Pilar as teenagers forced from their car by Sheriff Buddy, who orders Hollis to take Pilar to her mother and tell Mercedes "where they found her," while Buddy takes it upon himself to deal with Sam. The movie being screened is, as Sayles explains in an interview, a kind of female version of *The Defiant Ones* (Stanley Kramer, 1958)—a prison-escape film wherein black and white are literally bound together, whether they wish to be or not—but clearly a version of that movie with a much more marginal and female-centered status.[25] It is as if Sayles recognized that the prohibited, necessarily hidden desires on which he focuses are matched by this category of movie, screened in the borderline public-private context of the drive-in, for teenagers, those in that difficult space between childhood and adulthood. Sayles observes:

> That's where people came together. In *The Last Picture Show* it was an indoor theater, the place where all the kids met and our society was created. To a certain extent, [my thought was,] Okay, this is where we were torn apart, the last place we were together. It's a funny thing, you're alone but you're together. You're in a social experience, but you're in your own little car, and it's in the dark, so there's a certain amount of anonymity to it. But also the sense at the [end of the film] that they are looking at the screen as if something may come up, but the screen is wasted.[26]

The location is, then, a kind of limbo set, a dilapidated, in-between place in the process of dissolving into something else, and a counterpoint to the present-day relationship of Sam and Pilar, whose choice to remain together returns them to the borders of respectability and community and whose future is a kind of blank screen, which they will have to fill and transform. As such, the location engenders an image of American social identity that fundamentally challenges, for example, the iconic images of the heartland as home in *Saving Private Ryan*.

Thus, there is a sense of openness in the film's ending that, with its focus on incest, was controversial, though not nearly so controversial as the radically unresolved ending of *Limbo*. The relative acceptance of *Lone Star's* conclusion seems to have been due to its plot, which gradually builds toward the dramatic revelation of Pilar's pivotally symbolic identity—in effect, a summative deconstruction of the historical borders that, by convention, define the identities of citizen, state, and nation. But there is also another facet of the relation of woman and nation that emerges through *Lone Star's* ending. Namely, if Colonel Del Payne has been "willing to be the Ariel of the piece," as Sayles says, in the end Pilar proves unwilling to be the Miranda, the docile daughter whose obedient heart and socially sanctioned marriage melt away the boundaries between political factions. Indeed, as the example of Shakespeare's Miranda reveals, women have historically had their private identity and emotional life subsumed by and made a token of the public sphere as part and parcel of guaranteeing the legitimacy of state-sanctioned identity, and this kind of subordination, whether applied to royalty, first ladies, or socially sanctioned womanhood more generally, is what Pilar expressly refuses. Her willingness to "forget the Alamo" means negating hegemonic history and social convention for the sake of an existential choice; and in her choice of couple formation, in sharp contrast to Miranda, she elects not to serve or ensure a future that affirms the patriarchal community's self-perpetuating needs. Hence the hilarious irony of the classic country-and-western song that plays over the closing credits, "I Want to Be a Cowboy's Sweetheart." She does want this, it is true, but no cowboy's sweetheart from the 1940s or 1950s would have sung out that choice and been his sibling, too.[27]

Limbo

Like *Lone Star*, *Limbo* is peopled by ghosts. Set in contemporary Juneau (Port Henry in the film), it tells the story of an Alaskan locale with a rich natural and multiethnic history, a legacy that tourism developers threaten to reduce to one giant Disney-style theme park. *Limbo* is also the story of Joe Gastineau (David Strathairn), a man whose past is troubled by thwarted potential and shipwrecked possibilities. A Port Henry native, Joe might have been either a professional basketball player, but for a career-ending knee injury in high school, or, later, a successful fisherman, but for a freak accident that cost the lives of the two other men on his boat. He now works as a handyman for a pair of middle-aged, entrepreneurial lesbians who have recently moved to the area. At a wedding reception, he meets Donna De Angelo (Mary Elizabeth Mastrantonio), an itinerant folk-rock singer who has worked all around the United States—as she says, in "thirty-six states and the territory of Puerto Rico"—with the result that her only child, Noelle, feels rootless, neglected, and resentful. Nonetheless, performing songs forms an indispensable source of creativity for Donna, her means of telling the story of her life, whether she is breaking up with a man (as she is at the wedding reception, where she sings "Better Off without You"—not the best song for the occasion) or expressing interest in a new one, as she does when she sings about Joe at the Gold Nugget lounge. Here, as in the hangouts of Frontera, storytelling is a major pastime, a way of sorting out history, community, and identity, with the important difference that at the Gold Nugget, it is also a form of entertainment for tourists, who visit the place while listening to tales about its colorful history related by a young woman guide. Although Donna's relationships with men have been a series of disappointments—something her daughter resents—singing offers reliable satisfactions, especially when she "hooks into a song" and puts it across to her audience, providing live entertainment of a different order from the kind sold in packaged tours.

Joe's particular ghosts reemerge when he, Noelle, and Donna accompany Joe's half brother, Bobby, on a boat outing, only to discover that Bobby has been involved in some shady business with drug dealers, men who end up boarding the boat and killing him one night when the others are below deck. Fearing for their lives, the three swim to shore on a completely isolated island in the Alaskan wilderness. They find an abandoned, ramshackle cabin that is in the process of being reclaimed by the forest and take shelter there. Joe experiences déjà vu because he has placed Donna and Noelle's lives in danger; specifically, he has a nightmare that replays the death of the two men aboard his fishing boat, one of them the younger brother of Smilin' Jack, a local bush pilot who "does whatever pays best or what he can get away with," in Joe's words. Nonetheless, Joe, Donna, and Noelle begin to form something like a family, especially when Noelle discovers a diary and reads it aloud to the others each evening by the fire. The film ends with the three waiting on the shoreline together as a plane approaches, Donna having chosen to move out into the open, the other two following. Has Jack come alone to rescue them, or has he returned as a mercenary, along with the drug dealers who want Joe, Donna, and Noelle killed to cover the other murder? Notoriously, the film's last image leaves its audience in limbo, not knowing what will become of the provisionary family as they wait on the shore.

As this summary suggests, *Limbo*, like *Lone Star*, emphasizes the pressures that the past and conflicting stories about the past bring to bear on the present. But whereas *Lone Star* recounts border history in part through its innovative cinematic flashback techniques, *Limbo* moves from initial visions of Alaska's past as a washed-out promotional video or tourist developer's theme park to an encounter with forces that are considerably less tame. And whereas *Lone Star* builds slowly toward its dramatic revelation of Pilar's pivotally symbolic identity—that is, toward a deconstruction of the historical borders of Texas, the United States, and Mexico—*Limbo* uses female characters overtly throughout as symbols of problematized geopolitical identities, synecdoches in a narrative network that holds the two halves of the film together. *Limbo* simultaneously generates a mood infused, far more than that of *Lone Star*, with an ambient uncanniness. Indeed, this feeling is even evoked by the film's title, which a trailer for the film defines in the following ways: (1) the dwelling place of forgotten souls, (2) a state of oblivion or neglect, (3) a place or state of arrested possibilities, (4) a condition of uneasiness and apprehension, and (5) a condition of unknowable outcome. To be in limbo is to be caught in an in-between space, a place where the borders of identity are unsettled or arrested, a locale haunted by the ghosts of the repressed—an arena that, as Molloy has shown, is culturally gendered female, a facet that sheds light on the hostile reception that greeted the limbo ending of the film.

Limbo uses a prefatory promotional video to set up a good deal of the film, and it is a satirical creation by Sayles, manipulated to suggest age and authenticity. Like the 1950s promotional film that opens *Heavenly Creatures* and the opening shot of *Once Were Warriors*—a *trompe l'oeil* billboard advertisement sporting not the native Maori's dislocated world but a tourist's dream image of New Zealand—Sayles's video focuses on a place made both familiar and strange. Narrated in customary male voice-over style, it touts Alaska's "panoply of flora and fauna, the like of which is seen nowhere else on the planet," while showing stuffed animals—both children's toys and taxidermists' products—sporting conspicuous price tags. In parallel fashion, the narrator catalogs the diverse peoples who have inhabited the area through time, while visuals reveal Mexican workers putting heads and costumes on the bodies of plastic Eskimo dolls, the kind of dehumanized image that Bhabha identifies with the cultural uncanny of postcolonialism. Gendering the place female, the voice-over also recalls the people who responded to Alaska's "siren call" to pursue "the promise of untold fortune," words ironically matched with images of present-day white-haired tourists. Even before this video, *Limbo*'s title sequence includes underwater shots that show large salmon teeming in a man-made hatchery, imagery that conjoins defining features of Alaska's past and present with a disquieting, uncanny eeriness. According to Sayles's DVD commentary, this fish imagery also suggests "souls in the waiting room, finding out whether they go to heaven or hell or limbo." Yet since the word "limbo" is slowly spelled out over the crowded fish, this place itself is already clearly limbo.

In the film's diegesis, the first symbolic human counterpart to the state of Alaska is a young bride dressed in white. Her outdoor wedding reception, with majestic white-peaked mountains as a backdrop, provides the context against which *Limbo* introduces and satirizes debates about Alaska's future, debates in which loggers and tourist interests (and, less conspicuously, environmentalists) contend. During the reception, the bride's father, a wealthy tourist-industry developer, argues with a lumberman against simply clear-cutting the Alaskan forest and suggests, cynically, that loggers should "quit with the chainsaws when [they] get to where people [in the tourist boats] can see"—a "solution" that will maintain the illusion of "virgin" forests as it forwards the commercial vision of Alaska as theme park—in effect, an uncanny place, only outwardly alive. And in a cynical variation on Shakespeare's Antonio's "what's past is prologue," the father then insists that where consumerist value is concerned, "Our history [as theme park] is our future here, not our past"—and nearly in the same breath he exclaims, gesturing toward his daughter, "Would you look at her? She looks like a million dollars!"

Thus, his words succinctly connect the bride with money, the fecund daughter with the state's and nation's future. In her white wedding gown, the bride is an embodiment of the soon-to-be-ravished (clear-cut, drilled, and commercially exploited) "virgin" territory and of Alaska's status as "America's last frontier" (so named in the opening promotional video), the ultimate boundary and prize. Expanding the scope of the symbolic economy that equates bride, wealth, and state, much as Prospero does in *The*

Tempest, the father makes a speech at the wedding banquet, standing flanked by his daughter and his wife, and boasts, "This has been for us a land of opportunity." Here, the bride's symbolic function in Sayles's social satire overtly extends beyond Alaska to include all of the United States, a larger brave new world.

Functioning as additional and less conventional symbolic female presences are the lesbian couple Lou (Rita Taggart) and Frankie (Kathryn Grody), who also first appear at the reception. Relative newcomers to the area, they suggest, in part, an alternative Alaskan future to the one embodied in the developers' schemes, since for these women the traditional push west to find freedom involves carving out and defending a place at the edge of a stubbornly heterosexist society. Living in a house suggestively poised near the border between land and sea and relying on their skills as contract and criminal lawyers, the couple are affirmed even as they are gently satirized. Although they quibble like an old married couple, they gamely refuse to be intimidated by a testy local fisherman, Harmon King, who wants to reclaim a valued fishing boat and license that they have legitimately taken over.[28] They also succeed in bringing Joe back to boats and fishing, the one kind of work that, to him, makes everything else seem merely a simulacrum—in his words, "secondhand."

As Sayles's comments about the film's opening imagery of the salmon hatchery reveal, *Limbo* also generates an analogy between the area's human inhabitants and its salmon, an analogy focused through another symbolic female character, one who exists in the film both as a familiar kind of troubled adolescent and as the embodiment of a pervasive Alaskan anomie—namely, Noelle. She, too, is introduced at the reception, but her symbolic role becomes clear only with a story titled "The Water Baby" that she creates and reads aloud for her high-school English class. It describes a father with a video camera, recording events in slow motion, and a mother who gives birth to an infant, "wet and cold" with a "bluish pallor," gasping for air, its gills "lined with crimson." Hers is an unmistakably self-referential story, its central image of the water baby an objective correlative for her sense of being a fish out of water, of having a marginal and submerged identity in a cold, fluid world, of having landed in Alaska but not being connected to her mother's warmth, the place, or a vibrant future.[29]

The film expands this symbolism further in the scene that follows. After reading her story in front of the class, Noelle appears in a mind-screen shot walking through the corridors of her school as an insular outsider, hallucinating distorted sounds and perceiving that she is being dwarfed, crowded, and stared at. The moment eerily replays the film's opening underwater footage. Similarly, her story's reference to the crimson-lined gills recalls a haunting image from earlier in the film in which bright red blood drips onto writing paper from a slit Noelle has made with a razor on the underside of her upper arm. The reference also resonates with a shot of Noelle regarding herself in the mirror, then holding an opened pair of scissors to her face, a pointed end close to her eye, in a mirrored image that is initially match cut with a mirror reflection of Donna performing at the Gold Nugget. In a related moment, as Joe and Donna, on a first date, watch teeming fish thrash and die, Joe explains that salmon "stop eating when they head in," and Donna recalls that Noelle, too, stopped eating for a while and had to be nourished intravenously. Donna's words thus signal another analogy between Noelle and the fish, eerie doubles of each other and symbols of the locale. Finally, Noelle's terrible woundedness also resonates with images from the "slime line" of a salmon canning factory that appear early in the film.

The relation between Noelle as storyteller and Alaskan identity in limbo, on the border, is developed still more extensively in the survival story that comprises the last part of the film. This portion of *Limbo* both enforces and unsettles the sense of congruency between the identity of state and nation and female identity established by the film to this point. In effect the segment begins with an image of "men with guns"—a phrase that names the 1998 film Sayles made between *Lone Star* and *Limbo*. At the same time, *Limbo* matches the raw, primitive power of masculine brutality with an elemental and even evolutionary sense of family formation, both in the diary Noelle reads and in her interaction with Donna and Joe. Revealingly, it is Noelle who discovers the murdered Bobby's cold, white hand as she walks along the pebbly shore during the day, a hand that resembles a form of sea life, sticking up uncannily out of the rocks, a symbol of his victimization by primitive violence; it is Noelle, as well, who brings the old familial conflicts to the surface, especially in her story-reading and story-crafting capacities, but also in her oedipal conflicts with her mother and her feelings of attraction toward and competition over Joe.

The diary offers an uncanny doubling between its author and Noelle. The diarist, Anne Marie Hoag, was an only child like Noelle and was apparently about Noelle's age when she lived in the cabin with her parents. Her father, the object of Anne Marie's sympathy, had been disabled on a logging job and, needing another source of income, decided to raise blue foxes for their pelts in this remote place where, reenacting a familiar American story, he could easily have the land. In contrast to her father, her mother had been reluctant, going "on about how she will miss female company and how I will have to be her special friend." After the first few entries, the diary stops, but Noelle's "reading" does not. That is, Noelle pretends to read aloud—with Donna and Joe initially none the wiser—effectively ghostwriting a fiction that obliquely expresses her profound estrangement from Donna, her fear of abandonment, and her disquiet in the unheimlich cabin in the woods with its troubled family history.

Noelle projects her own ghostly ideas of herself into the narrative of Anne Marie, again suggesting her fantasy relationship to the place. For example, in Anne Marie's voice she explains that "some days I will go for hours without speaking," and she imagines that she might be invisible; she also fantasizes that she is possessed by the soul of some long-dead Indian girl, or a she wolf, or the soul of a soaring bird who should have flown south for the winter, or, in an overt romance fantasy, that she is the beloved of a male fox who wants to carry her off to his island. As Noelle's evening "readings" continue, she describes Mrs. Hoag's fear that if she eats any more fish—the steady diet of both the family and the foxes—she will grow fins, an echo of the liminal imagery from the "The Water Baby." In the course of her stay in the remote locale, Noelle becomes increasingly feverish from her exposure to the cold, and as she sickens, her ghostwritten portrait of Mrs. Hoag darkens into a bleak hallucination. The mother, says Noelle, refuses to deal with the little foxes and also harmonizes poorly with her daughter in song (a clear reference to Donna's singing and Noelle's dissonant feelings toward Donna and Donna's work). Noelle also narrates that Mrs. Hoag steals the warmth from the dwelling—that is, she hides the axe for chopping firewood and is emotionally distant; when she sleeps with Anne Marie, she pulls heat from her rather than giving her warmth. Further, Noelle's imagery identifies the mother with death: Mrs. Hoag is a "black spot" who, despite her fundamentalist religiosity, refuses to celebrate Christmas (another self-reference by Noelle), yet who kills all the foxes, even the kits, because she thinks that they are "Satan's handmaidens." She burns her husband's face with hot bacon grease and, in Noelle's last reading, finishes by hanging herself. "We won't bury her on the island. She made me promise," Noelle "reads." Like one of the vixens who appears to have eaten her litter in Noelle's account, the mother of Noelle's fantasy is the devouring, vengeful mother, an embodiment of the paranoid and lethal aspect of the unheim-lich that Kristeva defines, whereas the father and daughter Noelle imagines are partners and helpmates, the mother's innocent victims.

If Noelle's narrative imagines a cold, unhomey female destructiveness, it also depicts such destructiveness as a facet of Alaska itself. The diary narrative that Noelle invents is the one place that expressly names the word and the place of the film's title, a word that the film makes resonate with Alaska's past, present, and uncertain future. In the fictional portion of the diary, the uncanny aspect of this limbo becomes clear. The father in Noelle's narrative identifies the time and place they are living in as limbo: "Papa calls it limbo because it sure isn't heaven, and it's too cold to be hell." Indeed, the diary's story is set in the dead of winter, a time when, as Joe explains, people in Alaska kill each other just for something to do. Moreover, like the cold, eerie opening images of the film over which the film's title is gradually spelled out, Noelle's ghostwritten story depicts a cold, raw state of nature and the cycles of reproduction and death. Describing the foxes, she reads that "the terrible birthing has begun," an echo of the salmon teeming in an underwater shot, their cycle of spawning and dying converging in fulfillment of what Joe will later call "a pretty hardwired" pattern that leaves no room for other options. Supposedly, he says, humans are smarter than that, but for the Alaskan settlers that the ghostwritten diary recalls, sexuality and death, reproduction and destruction, also go hand in glove.

Here, more starkly than in *Lone Star,* are uncanny echoes of the elements that Molloy discusses in the New Zealand films: the "old stories of female-to-female treachery," the focus on "the ways in which female sexuality both secures and undermines home and nation," the concern with "secret female worlds, muteness and speaking, merged identities, betrayal of relations between mothers and daughters leading to mutilation and death,"[30] and the vision of a place identified with and defined by a dead woman. Here, too, is that familiar sense of the inhospitable nature of home and nation for women, who are situated as both center and periphery, necessary and repressed, human and not fully human, narrowly defined and indeterminate.

In *Limbo,* however, there are counternarratives as well. First, the Hoag family story that Noelle tells is not the only fiction she spins. It has a counterpart in the story she presents to Joe as the truth about her own absent father, a tale in which, to use Kristeva's phrase, "psychic contents take the place of material reality."[31] Noelle recounts that her father is a celebrity composer whose photo has appeared in *People* magazine and who is also the father of her two half sisters and a half brother. Noelle further claims that she is cut off from them all because of Donna's wishes. Later, however, when Noelle blames Donna for their current life-threatening predicament, for having taken the trip to try to impress Joe, Donna tells Noelle the truth about her father and exposes the fiction about him that, it turns out, Donna helped create. When Noelle was small, her mother attempted to compensate for her father's absence and neglect by sending Noelle presents in his name. The result was Noelle's idealization of him, evidenced in her refusal to get rid of a dollhouse, even though she did not like it, because she thought it was a gift from him (an unheimlich gift, to be sure). Donna now reveals that she crafted this fictive caring and giving father in the tradition of the Easter bunny and Santa Claus, a revelation that deepens Noelle's feelings of loss and alienation but that also makes her confront a truer, less patriphilic picture of the past.

No less significantly, before the last diary "reading" Donna discovers that most of the diary's pages are blank and that Noelle's "reading" is her own nightmarish invention. Donna's response is one that signals growth in her character and parenting. Whereas, before, she offered Noelle emotional bribes—"Do this for me and I'll love you forever," for example—now she realizes the depth of Noelle's sense of betrayal and despair, and she weeps as she listens to her daughter's final "reading." Seeking to reassure her in this inhospitable "home," Donna tells her that the mother in the story did something that she would never do—abandon her daughter: "I would never leave my daughter, no matter what."

At this point, the film itself shows a resolve to challenge and change the historical fictions on which family, state, and nation have conventionally been founded, as it offers a promising counternotion of family in the one being formed. A contrast with the family ultimately established in *The Piano* is revealing here: In that film, the family is constructed at the price of Ada's extraordinarily forceful creativity, her "voice," since her piano playing is possible only through the clicking of a man-made metal finger, the replacement for the one her husband Stewart chopped off; in Sayles's film, the family imagined fully accommodates female connection and creativity. Not only does Donna cradle her sick and sleeping child, but she and Joe also agree to arrange their lives so that Donna can still travel and sing, and Joe, whom Noelle likes, will care for Noelle during Donna's absences. The music and lighting lend warmth and a sense of optimism to the scene in the cabin when the two strike this agreement. At the same time, a lap dissolve from Donna's warmly lit face to the cold grey of a mountain face both links and tellingly contrasts the woman and the place, just as it pointedly sets Donna apart from the fatal Mrs. Hoag of Noelle's dark fantasy.

The final scene is neither pessimistic nor optimistic but a redefinition of the question of the future. No longer focused on the issue of mother-daughter betrayal, the film now turns to the problem of to whom the future belongs: "men with guns" and the overwhelmingly commercial interests, or people seeking to start over as members of communities and families on alternative terms. Indeed, quite probably, one of the reasons viewers felt betrayed by Limbo's unresolved ending is that the personal story functions to represent a larger, open-ended, collective narrative of a state and nation with all futures left in doubt. The film's unanswered questions thus encompass not only heterosexual couple and family formation, but also the question of whether much of Alaska will be reduced to a simulacrum of itself, a theme park replete with dioramas of Filipino workers in salmon-factory facsimiles, as Harmon King suggests, in which history itself is reduced to what sells. More broadly, at issue is whether or not the United States will give way to an even more extreme form of the "age of access," as Jeremy Rifkin terms it, built around commodified, fabricated experiences, hyper-capitalism, and the homogenization of our history, natural resources, and cultural diversity in the name of commercial gain for the few (who will live, perhaps, in Stepford-style residential theme parks, peopled with virtual wives). Or will something of the better values posited by the film preserve more of the past and our natural heritage, while simultaneously defining the nation so that woman and home, foreigner and family, find a more successful synthesis? Rifkin argues that to avoid the former, it is necessary to assure

continued access to healthy and diverse local cultures. The forces of commerce, if not tempered, could devour the cultural sphere by redirecting it into commodified fragments of commercial entertainments, lived experiences, paid amusements, and purchased relationships. Losing access to the rich cultural diversity of thousands of years of lived experience would be as devastating to our future ability to survive and flourish as losing our remaining biological diversity. Bringing culture and commerce

back into a balanced ecology is a pressing concern in
the coming era.[32]

Going beyond Rifkin, Sayles has created a film that is keenly aware of the gendered symbolization that mediates the culture's understanding of these dynamics and of their particular ramifications for the personal lives of women and men. Indeed, since, as Rifkin conceptualizes it, the age of access is centrally defined by its increasingly murky borders and boundaries (the consequence of the emerging dominance of access over ownership, style over history, and hypertexts over books, for example),[33] and defined as well by its commodification of simulated experience that makes encounters with the Other safe—its canning of the uncanny, if you will—Sayles's concern with the gender of the uncanny in the narrative of nation could scarcely be more timely.

Prologue to What?

What are the prospects for the kind of better future Rifkin imagines, if we look at the evidence in the two Sayles films discussed here? And a related question: What moments do the films offer that provide evidence for or models of the better choice identified by Kristeva, the smile as a response to an encounter with the uncanny? *Limbo*'s very title and tag line ("a condition of unknown outcome"), together with its truncated ending, signal a provocative refusal to answer the question—a prologue to what?—and an attempt to disturb audiences into reflection.[34] *Lone Star,* however, offers evidence that I have not yet explored that gains importance in the context of the broader array of questions I am now posing.

Some evidence from *Lone Star* seems unequivocal in its hopeful thrust. An example is the U.S.-identified Mercedes's complete turnaround late in the film, reflected in her decision to aid rather than report the illegal Mexican immigrants who come to her for help, in particular the sweetheart of one of her male employees, a very young woman who, as a flashback from Mercedes's point of view reveals, reminds her of herself when she initially crossed the river to the U.S., aided by Eladio. For the first time, the stranger without reanimates and humanizes the stranger within her; instead of speaking as a person who routinely disparages Mexicans—for example, calling the men "*chulos* with grease under their nails"—she identifies in an accepting way with her own south-of-the-border past. The film's shift from canted to balanced framing of Mercedes and from high-angle to eye-level shots reinforces the impression of her rectification and reconciliation with her past.

The film also affirms the choice to commit one's self to an interracial or interethnic relationship, although Sayles is forthrightly dubious about whether such choices hold much potential to alter society, even as his film, through its focus on black Seminoles, acknowledges their long-standing role in shaping American history. Speaking primarily of Pilar and Sam's decision to be together, but also of that of the film's black and white couple, Priscilla and Cliff (both in the army), Sayles explains:

> It is only an individual accommodation, and that was a lot of my point with the ending, it's not going to change society. They're going to have to leave the society they're in, they can't stay in that town. You may be very very nonracial, you may be married to a black person, but if you're in the middle of the Watts riots, that's not going to help you. That individual accommodation you made has not changed the social situation, or hasn't changed it enough so that what society is still doing is going to honor your change. Interracial couples that I know are careful about where they go. If it's a black and white couple, for example, there are places with white people where they don't go, and there are places with black people where they don't go. Only on the edges of those societies is there a place for them and their kids. In the hearts of those societies, sometimes, they're just not welcome.[35]

Indeed, Sayles humorously develops this theme further in the film when Cliff's friend Mikey asks Cliff if Priscilla's family is "gonna be cool about you being a white guy?" Cliff responds, "Priscilla says they think any woman over thirty who isn't married must be a lesbian. She figures they'll be so relieved I'm a man . . ." To which Mikey wryly replies, "Always heartwarming to see a prejudice defeated by a deeper prejudice." And he continues, "But marriage, man. I did two tours in Southeast Asia and I was married for five years. I couldn't tell you which experience was worse . . . I knew she was Japanese, but she didn't tell me the ninja assassin part. Her parents acted like I was going to blow my nose on their curtains."

Thus, unlike the recent teen pics *Save the Last Dance* (Thomas Carter, 2000) and *Crazy/Beautiful* (John Stockwell, 2001), which find formulaic happy endings that affirm interracial and interethnic teen couple formation as something consonant with the American dream and professional success, *Lone Star* depicts mixed couples in terms less governed by fairy-tale, wish-fulfillment paradigms. More specifically, whereas the teen pics just mentioned use the formula of the traumatic loss of the mother to open up the space and the desire for an artistically talented blonde girl's bonding with a masculine but "mothering" black or Chicano male, *Lone Star* takes the middle-aged interethnic couple back to the site of their teenage dissociation, a place that finds them once more on the borders of respectability, needing to renounce their current jobs and agreeing to be outsiders in order to make their union work.

At the same time, the interracial romance of Priscilla and Cliff adds still another level of complexity to Sayles's depiction of these dynamics, one related to social shifts made visible during the Gulf War. Discussing the inspiration behind his film, Sayles reports noticing in the television coverage of that war that he "started seeing a lot of interracial couples, who were married and in the army. And I realized, here is what used to be, only a few years ago, one of the most racist and retrogressive parts of society, now being the place where even though it's about going and killing other people, there seems to be a certain degree of equal opportunity." [36] Thus the barrier that *Courage Under Fire* erects between the black man and white woman, as well as the context of racial and sexual friction in military harassment cases that it evokes, gives way in *Lone Star* to the depiction of military coworkers Priscilla and Cliff, who may have professional disagreements—for example, about how to discipline a young black female private—but whose commitment to each other is both strong and tolerated within the military enclave, even if not by all of Frontera's citizens, the redneck bartender played by Leo Burmester being a case in point.

If *Lone Star* acknowledges the extent to which American society is still ruled by its perception of ethnic and racial "tribal boundaries," and still curtails the freedoms of those who choose to live outside those limits, it also criticizes the false sense of belonging that emerges both from the commercially constructed group identities that consumerist culture validates and from the sanctioned, circumscribed forms of racial and ethnic integration that it promotes and exploits. An example of Sayles's critique of the superficially integrated community emerges during a heated teacher-parent meeting in which the selection of high-school history texts is the topic under debate. An Anglo mother asserts that she is not troubled by Chicano culture insofar as it is circumscribed and circulated as a commodity: "If you mean like music and food and all, I have no problem with that, but when you start changing who did what to who . . . that's what's got to stop." In this scene, the film succinctly exposes both the commonplace transformation of ethnic culture into an assortment of free-floating market products and the normalization of that process in everyday discourse.[37]

A more developed instance of such critique emerges from *Lone Star*'s depiction of American sports culture. The kind of pseudosocial participation it invites is exemplified by Sam's "high strung," psychotropically medicated ex-wife Bunny (Frances McDormand), whose name oddly echoes Buddy's and whose only sense of belonging is to a world she associates with her own father—the macho world of professional football, with its limited if highly visible racial integration, the counterpoint and complement to accepted forms of diversity in the commercialized spheres of ethnic food and music. Spouting statistics and schedules and recalling her own "altercation" at a game, Bunny, the "daddy's girl," is an extreme form of the escapist fan and sports junky, cut off from human history and belonging, inhabiting a living room where her only companionship seems to come from sports simulacra, including a life-size blow up of African-American Dallas Cowboy sports legend Tony Dorsett and the recorded games and sports coverage that steadily play on her television set.

If Sayles's Frontera, Texas, is a mosaic of diverse, fabricated enclaves, barely bonding together—its Hispanic public officials as likely to be involved in boondoggles as its Anglo ones—it is nonetheless represented as preferable to the blend of pop culture and commerce that defines Bunny's vicarious, addictive, sports-industry-based world. To borrow phrasing that Jeffrey Sconce uses in another context, she depends upon "an uncanny and perhaps even sinister component in 'living' electronic media," the television set as a "haunted apparatus" that brings the narcotizing, spectral world of sports into her unhomey home.[38] (And, like the murderous drug dealers in *Limbo*, the beneficiaries of Bunny's addiction are ultimately profit driven.)

Sayles's resistance to facsimiles of and substitutes for community also extends to his implicit critique of the practice, both in Hollywood moviemaking and in the culture at large, of treating Eisenhower-era America as the idealized, utopian reference point for the family and nation. Accordingly, *Lone Star* exposes the hidden history—the ghosts in the closets—of the Deeds and Cruz families from that period through its revelation of Pilar's origins. Sam repeatedly hears that Muriel, his mother, was "a saint," a phrase that turns out to mean she was willing to suffer Buddy's long-term extramarital affair with Mercedes, a revelation that creates dissonance between the ideal, socially sanctioned 1950s family and the material reality, which in this case turns out to be double families, the official Anglo one (Muriel's) and the socially marginal, covert Anglo-Chicano one (Mercedes's). Similarly, Sayles generates contrapuntal flashbacks, especially between the nostalgic, publicly accredited narratives that lionize Buddy Deeds in the 1950s and the more complex, hidden renderings of the past, narrated from perspectives that rarely inform the Western or detective genre or the Hollywood history films oriented toward America's so-called golden age. The latter perspectives include Chucho Montoya's eyewitness account of Charley Wade's cold-blooded murder of Eladio Cruz, rendered in seamless flashback style, and also the memory of Wade's first encounter with Otis, as recalled by Minnie Bledsoe.

If the 1950s created uncanny doubles, symbolized in the women's names Muriel and Mercedes, and if contemporary mixed couples' dilemmas are focused through a Chicana and a black woman the film names Pilar and Priscilla, and, further, if Buddy and Bunny are echoing names paired to connect the patriarchal and patriarchally dependent ghosts from Sam's past, then it would seem that the feminine as the uncanny plays an even more significant role in Sayles's *Lone Star* than my initial reading suggests, especially when issues of communities under the pressures of globalization and the age of access are factored in. Like issues of national identity, and part and parcel of them, issues of capitalist globalization find inscription in uncanny feminine terms, and Sayles's films both problematize these terms and remind us that they will continue to shape our culturally mediated encounters with the past and our ability to envision and alter our future.

The attacks of September 11, 2001, are, in an important sense, the definitive uncanny events of recent American history, given their eerie echoes of numerous disaster movies, their culprits' identities that mirror the archetypal villains of recent Hollywood cinema, and their replay, again and again, for television viewers the world over. On March 10, 2002, according to a report on France 2 television, 39 million Americans also watched the initial airing on CBS of *9/11*, a documentary directed by two French brothers, Jules and Gédéon Naudet, and American James Hanlon, a veteran New York City fireman, about the attack six months earlier that destroyed the World Trade Center and, along with it, the lives of thousands of people from around the world and hundreds of public-safety officials. The Naudets' original intent had been to document the experiences of a rookie fireman, or, as Gédéon explains in the video, "to show how a kid becomes a man in nine months," the probationary period served by rookie fire fighters—"probies," as they are called. It was a project that, not entirely unlike the study that I set forth in this present text, was overtaken by events that its makers could not have anticipated.

My far more modest project has been to chart a series of cinematic representations of U.S. history created in the closing decade of the twentieth century—films whose subjects move from World War II, to the cold war, to the techno-warfare and globalization of the 1990s. Simultaneously, I have sought to uncover the films' *unheimlich* dimensions, especially as these serve both to reveal and to veil women's lives and experiences. Although my study ends with films released in 1999, the production of history-based Hollywood films did not, of course, stop in that year, and neither did the themes and patterns examined in the preceding chapters. For example, combat-film releases in 2001–2002 include the history-based *Behind Enemy*

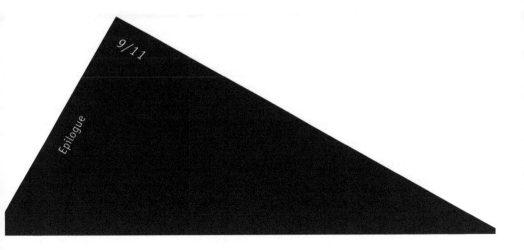

Lines (John Moore, 2001), *Black Hawk Down* (Ridley Scott; originally scheduled for release in 2002 but released in 2001, in the wake of September 11), *We Were Soldiers* (Randall Wallace, 2002), *Hart's War* (Gregory Hoblit, 2002), and *Windtalkers* (John Woo, 2002).

As a group, these films, together with those discussed in the preceding chapters, form an important context for understanding the documentary *9/11*. For indeed, what is remarkable about this documentary is not just the fact that it was transformed from a project of restricted scope into a historical document of international significance, but also, on another level, that it shapes and edits the material of the rookie's story to resemble the contemporary combat film—for example, by the way it deploys the birth metaphor (the nine months one spends as a proby) and contours the sense of history it conveys through that generic lens. To be sure, it lacks the techno-wizardry of recent combat films. Moreover, some similarities between military fighting and firefighting are already givens. These include structures, discourse, and protocols, the division of men into battalions, the use of certain hierarchical titles such as "lieutenant," the wearing of uniforms for formal occasions, the draping of the flag on the coffins of the honored dead, the opportunities that those who serve have to test their courage and to save the lives of others, and the ethnic diversity of those who serve. Other elements, however, are not givens, coming in part from the distinction between training to save lives and training to take them.

Antonios Benetatos, or Tony as he is called, is the idealistic rookie whom the French brothers selected as the center of their story, and he is a clear counterpart to the idealistic green recruit of war movies. Tony explains early on in the documentary that he "always wanted to be a hero" and that becoming a firefighter is the "only way" for him to do that. He also admits to being scared: "I'm wondering how I will actually react when there is fire flying over my head." Although the Naudets are "old friends" of Hanlon's, they, like Barry Pepper's photojournalist, Joseph Galloway, in *We Were Soldiers,* are nonetheless outsiders. Like Tony, they also seek to prove their mettle in order to be, in the men's words, "part of a family at the firehouse."

Tony must wait many weeks before being even marginally tested—he is called on to put out a car fire—and this prolonged waiting period counterpoints the formulaic building of suspense before the first engagement in many a combat film. In a moment of foreshadowing, Tony also receives instruction from the seasoned Hanlon, the two of them framed, face-to-face, by the Twin Towers in the glow of evening light. The night of September 10, before Tony's true test arrives, Jules (who has joked that the documentary is turning into a cooking show) volunteers to make dinner for everyone and serves up one leg of lamb—not the five it would take to feed the firefighters of Engine 7, Ladder 1. The mood is light, and Jules takes a ribbing for his miscalculation, but religious motifs (of being blessed, making sacrifices, and sharing a last supper) have begun taking form and recall a related use of similar motifs in A Midnight Clear.

When the long-awaited conflagration finally arrives, it is more chaotic, unintelligible, and horrific than anyone could ever have imagined. Jules enters Tower 1 with Chief Joseph Pfeifer, Battalion 1, and identifies Father Judge, the firemen's chaplain, as one of the worried onlookers; Father Judge later becomes the first official casualty of the attack and is immediately and reverently carried off by his fellows. Meanwhile back in the firehouse, Tony exclaims, "This is war. Fucking war." A retired veteran, Chief Burns, arrives on the scene, and both he and Tony, feeling compelled to help, set out for the World Trade Center. Images of white dust, smoke, and apocalyptic devastation redefine the Manhattan cityscape, recalling ghostly scenes from German expressionist cinema. The site itself, in the words of Jules, seems "the gateway to hell."

Jules and Gédéon, having been separated throughout the day, separately wonder if the other is still alive; they are shown finally reunited, embracing, speaking French. A fireman echoes fraternal sentiments that recall lines from Saving Private Ryan, as he tells Jules, "Yesterday you had one brother. Today, you have fifty." In fact, miraculously, all of the men of this firehouse have survived—even Tony the rookie, who belatedly walks back to the firehouse after having searched with the retired chief for nine hours for his fellow firefighters, not knowing that everyone from this house is safe.

Jules explains that Tony has proven himself to all his fellows and become a man; not in nine months but "in about nine hours," Hanlon adds. Yet his coming of age is also clearly something different from a typical transformation of boy to fireman, and Tony's conversion connects him with the much less heroic Upham of Saving Private Ryan as well as with Josh Hartnett's courageous, shaken idealist, Ranger Staff Sergeant Matt Eversmann, in Black Hawk Down—two Hollywood film characters who shift from idealistic, internationalist views of military operations to considerably more insular perspectives. "A lot of guys don't know if they're going to do the job any more," Tony says. "I know it's either this or the army now. I like saving lives; I don't like taking them. But after what I saw, if my country decides to send me to go kill, I'll do it now," he continues sadly. What he has described himself seeing most recently, as presented in the film, is the dead body of a pregnant woman, an ultimate motivating emblem in time of war.

9/11 is a powerful testimony to the courage and sacrifice of the men whose actions it depicts, and it is a documentary for posterity, affording an intimate view of an event that will haunt the nation for a very long time. It is also a reflection of what Cynthia Enloe calls the militarization of American culture, a process that predates the events of September 11, but was clearly, under the leadership of George W. Bush, accelerated by them and by his administration's return to a covert, cold-war style of governance.[1] Yet it is also important to remember that in the months before the broadcast of *9/11*, another, very different vision of that historical turning point could be found—if one looked for it. Written by authors such as Rosalind Petchesky, Distinguished Professor of Political Science at Hunter College, and appearing in publications such as the *Women's Review of Books,* this alternative vision insisted on contextualizing and historicizing that event even as it challenged the dominant readings of its imagery.

Enloe, for example, questioned what she terms the militarization of women's rights and bodies in the wake of September 11. She explained, "Here's the test of whether Afghan women are being militarized. If their well-being justifies the U.S.'s bombing of Afghanistan, then we are militarizing Afghan women—as well as our own compassion."[2] In her view, the irony of the U.S. decision to act on behalf of these women—women whose unhomey Afghani homes and nation were, unquestionably, sites of terrible oppression—was that militarization effectively reduced their defense from a worthy cause in and of itself to a mere by-product of another, quite different, political and military agenda.[3] (In contrast, Enloe praised African-American Representative Barbara Lee [D.-Calif.] for casting the single vote against giving George W. Bush "carte blanche to wage war.") Enloe focused on contemporary militarization of American women as well, as she criticized the decision made by the organizers of the Miss America Pageant to rely on judges with military credentials. Her critique recalls the pioneering feminist position paper on the 1968 Miss America Pageant—a paper discussed in my introduction—which indicted the militarized use of the pageant as a propaganda tool for the war in Vietnam.

For her part, Petchesky refocused the symbolism of the World Trade Center as the expression of an uncanny symmetry between doubles. She identified fundamentalist terrorism and global capitalism "as phantom Twin Towers arising in the smoke clouds of the old towers—fraternal twins, not identical, locked in battle over wealth, imperial aggrandizement, and the meanings of masculinity." Thus Petchesky saw the honor, property, and wealth that the pseudo-Islamic terrorist leader Osama bin Laden spoke of defending as a network "whose nepotism and ties to oil interests eerily resemble those of the Bush family," and she further noted the uninterest of both Bush and bin Laden in the social movements of the impoverished.[4] In her view, both leaders also appropriated religious symbolism—perhaps not insincerely but not authentically either—to justify warfare and violence, as in Bush's claim to being a promoter of "infinite justice" and in bin Laden's so-called jihad or holy war, with its mission of claiming for the Islamic "brotherhood" roughly a third of the globe. Yet Petchesky also insisted that global capitalism's most powerful weapon is not "'infinite justice' or even nukes, but infinite Nikes and CDs" (those Nikes, as I noted earlier, being to an unconscionable degree the fruits of women's sweatshop labor). And although metaphors of brotherhood form another doubled element between the two sides, "the U.S. sends single mothers who signed up for the National Guard when welfare ended to fight and die in its holy war; the U.S. media remain silent about the activism and self-determination of Afghan women in groups like the Revolutionary Association of Women of Afghanistan and Refugee Women."[5]

To be sure, the U.S. media did give attention to the story of Lieutenant Colonel Martha McSally, the highest-ranking female fighter pilot in the U.S. Air Force at the time of the U.S. war on the Taliban. Although she was head of the search-and-rescue mission over Iraq, because she was based in Saudi Arabia, McSally, self-identified as Christian, was required to travel through a stunning time and culture warp, as striking, in fact, as the shift in Kubrick's 2001 from ape women to mod-clad flight attendants. That is, McSally was compelled to wear an abaya—a long black Islamic robe covering her from head to foot—whenever she left the base. In contrast, her male counterparts were forbidden to wear Islamic garments; in further contrast, neither State Department women in that country nor U.S. servicewomen in other Muslim countries were required to wear abayas. U.S. military dress code also required McSally, as a servicewoman, to ride in the back seat of cars and to be accompanied by a male escort if going off the base. When her attempts to combat the policy discretely proved futile, she sued, claiming religious and gender discrimination and insisting on her right to be treated according to the values of the nation she serves, not be sacrificed to the proprietary and vestiary gender values of the host nation.

Significantly, her exceptional story garnered more attention than did evidence of American women's *resistance* to war as a strategy for dealing with terror, resistance that tended to be labeled traitorous when it was acknowledged at all, yet that steadily gathered momentum in the face of escalating militarism—the purportedly antiterrorist American and British invasion of Iraq in 2003. The most memorable example of denying women's resistance came in the form of Robert Kagan's appropriation of John Gray's best-selling notion from 1992 that "men are from Mars, women are from Venus," a phrase Kagan transformed into a metaphor to explain differences between American and European attitudes toward the possession and use of military might. Writing for the Hoover Institute's *Policy Review* in 2002, Kagan claimed that, "Americans are from Mars and Europeans are from Venus"—in a long essay that never once registers awareness of possible differences in attitude toward military action that might be held by Americans themselves.[6] Yet to insist that normally "Venusian" American women become "Martian" on actual martial matters begs an obvious question. By paying no attention to the gender differences the phrase he borrows was coined to describe, his work serves as a classic case of evoking and erasing gender differences in the name of promoting a unified national agenda and propagating a homogenized concept of American identity.

In sharp contrast to Kagan, Jennifer Pozner reported on a September 29, 2001, article in the *Washington Post* that includes—buried at the end—the information that, when polled, "women 'were significantly less likely to support a long and costly war' [in Afghanistan than] were men" and that "'48 percent [of women] said they wanted a limited strike or *no military action at all*'" (Pozner's emphasis).[7] Similar results emerged in a Gallup poll. Yet, as Pozner observed, "What's alarming is that politicians, pundits and the press first roundly ignored the *Post* and Gallup data about women's more conditional approach to the 'war on terrorism,' then claimed the traditional gender gap familiar from the Persian Gulf and Kosovo crises had disintegrated with the Twin Towers."[8] The greater concern about death and suffering that women expressed in these polls, and the fact that such concern was missing or misrepresented by the media, prompted Pozner to ask a critical question, reminiscent of Miranda's implicit, quickly silenced questions from *The Tempest*: Where are the women on the Sunday-morning television talk shows and in the bylines of op-eds published by the major American newspapers? Recalling that, "In the 1930s, Eleanor Roosevelt would only speak to female reporters at her press conferences, forcing newspapers to employ women journalists," Pozner urges that a comparable pressure be brought to bear on the media in the present.[9]

Questions related to Pozner's should be demanded as well of Hollywood cinema, with its post–cold war escalation in anti-Arab stereotyping, its often nostalgic, nationalistic approach to the conflicts of world history, its product placements (in the largest sense) that enforce global capitalist dynamics, and its militarizing influence on the way the public perceives past and current events, including, spectacularly, those of 9/11. For, as Petchesky avows, "all the horror of the 20th century surely should teach us that war feeds on itself and that armed violence reflects, not an extension of politics by other means, but the failure of politics; not the defense of civilization, but the breakdown of civilization."[10]

To be sure, the immediate consequences of the invasion of Afghanistan were reported benefits for some women. In particular, the number of women who felt obliged to wear burkas in the streets of Kabul was reduced to about half and the schools there were opened to girls. Yet, a year and a half after the Taliban was routed from the capital, and a year after President George W. Bush promised a sort of latter-day Marshall Plan for Afghanistan, Barry Bearak termed the country *Warlordistan,* a place where feudal chiefs hold sway, despite the people's yearning "for peace [and] good government of the type that provides safety and schools and doctors."[11] At the same time, Carlotta Gall reported on Afghani village women still trapped by deadly traditions that make them suffer one of the highest rates of maternal mortality in the world, in part because they continue to be prohibited from showing their faces to male doctors.[12]

Meanwhile, Hollywood films of the 1990s shaped the packaging and reception of the American-British invasion of Iraq in 2003, its central public-relations story being the March 23 capture and April 1 rescue (recorded on often-replayed, grainy night-vision video) of Private First Class Jessica B. Lynch, a nineteen-year-old supply clerk from Palestine, West Virginia, who was part of a maintenance unit ambushed in southern Iraq. Offering an antidote both to a recent mistake that had led U.S. troops to kill a van full of Iraqi women and children, and, more abstractly, to the symbolically charged abandonment of a woman soldier in *Courage Under Fire,* the images of Private Lynch being whisked into a waiting Black Hawk helicopter were truly made to order. From the start, news reports emphasized the filmic quality of the story, calling it *Saving Private Lynch,* although the approving nod to Spielberg glossed over his film's questions about the military's use of women for public-relations purposes. As evidence contradicting government versions of the original story mounted, however, these references gave way to cries of *Wag the Dog* and to op-ed rhetoric echoing critiques of the first President Bush's war against Iraq. Alan Hamilton summed up a widely held view of Lynch's story: "The American military obviously saw immediately what a great PR stunt [the rescue] was. They played it for all it was worth." [13]

Indeed, the analogy to Karen Walden in *Courage Under Fire* bears extension here, insofar as Lynch, through no fault of her own, became, by June 2003, a female symbol of troubling public-relations manipulation, and her story had as many versions as Walden's. Specifically, Lynch morphed from valiant woman warrior keeping up M-16 fire despite multiple bullet and knife wounds, to a slight blonde waif mistreated by her Iraqi captors and in dire need of rescue, to the victim, along with Native American Private First Class Lori Ann Piestewa and three others, of a serious Humvee accident, itself precipitated by poor military communications, a wrong turn, and an ambush. Piestewa, the first American female soldier killed in this war, was one of ten in the maintenance unit who did not survive. For her part, Lynch suffered multiple fractures, a compression injury to her spine, and memory loss, thereby becoming not the source but, like Walden, the springboard for others' versions of her capture and rescue. According to a *Washington Post* account of June 17—a correction of its earlier version of events—"Neither the Pentagon nor the White House publicly dispelled the more romanticized initial version of her capture, helping to foster the myth surrounding Lynch and fuel accusations that the Bush administration stage-managed parts of Lynch's story." [14]

Coming amidst charges that government manipulation of intelligence reports on weapons of mass destruction had created a "phantom menace"—a distortion that some found more criminally culpable than Watergate—the story of the woman from Palestine became still more symbolically freighted, its meanings encompassing not only ambivalence about women in the armed forces (now fierce fighters, now damsels in distress), but also public doubts about the Iraqi incursion itself. In this context, the photogenic Lynch also betokened the dubious means by which Bush *fils* had sought to create the illusion of Oedipal triumph over Bush *père.* In sum, as

American history folded in on itself again, the story extended patterns traced in this book that weave war and women together into narratives shadowed by uncanniness.

According to Mark Bowden, military favorite and author of the book *Black Hawk Down,* the American media, when confronted with an incomplete story, for better or for worse, tend to mold "what little [they] know into a familiar shape—often one resembling the narrative arc of a film." [15] Yet Bowden's position evades the probability, forecast by the media scramble to offer Lynch a package deal, that an equally formulaic shaping of events will emerge when more of the facts are known, and that much will be suppressed—including, perhaps, the full story of KBR/Halliburton, the oil-services giant that "rounded the bases" with Iraq. "It got rich doing business with Iraq, it got rich preparing to destroy Iraq and it's now getting rich rebuilding Iraq," as Dan Baum has documented. [16] Although at this writing, the story of the war, its stunning doubles, the media, and Private Lynch, are still evolving, all offer powerful evidence of the profound need for alternative visions of history.

Stone's *JFK* (1991), the most debated history film of its decade, famously begins with President Dwight D. Eisenhower's January 1961 farewell address, with its warning to the nation about the need for vigilance in the face of an unprecedented kind of militarization, including a permanent U.S. arms industry and "military-industrial complex"; Stone's film's epilogue, like the work you are reading, echoes Shakespeare's *Tempest* with the phrase "What Is Past Is Prologue." The words with which Stone brackets *JFK* continue to reverberate and provoke reflection in new and changing contexts. To make the past the prelude to a genuinely alternative future, however, the full range of women's voices, as forces that can recount and influence history, must become audible in a way not present in Stone's work, in the mainstream history films of the 1990s, or in the contemporary media generally. Rather than serving as militarized entities or aestheticized uncanny projections—symbols that can conceal as much of the actual woman as the shroud-like abaya does—women can innovate genuinely productive change, but only if they achieve the status of full partners, in both an active, multilateral dialogue of nations and in the history films that reimagine and narrate it.

Introduction

1. Carol Gilligan, "Teaching Shakespeare's Sister: Notes from the Underground of Female Adolescence," preface to *Making Connections: The Relational Worlds of Adolescent Girls at Emma Willard School,* ed. Carol Gilligan, Nona P. Lyons, and Trudy J. Hanmer (Cambridge, Mass.: Harvard Univ. Press, 1990), 7. Although Gilligan's work is often misinterpreted and dismissed as passé, as Susan Bordo explains, its center is a still very relevant "critique of the sexual division of labor that assigns 'female' values to a separate domestic sphere while keeping the public, male space (and 'masculinity') a bastion of autonomous selves" (*Unbearable Weight: Feminism, Western Culture, and the Body* [Berkeley, Calif.: Univ. of California Press, 1993], 48).

2. Robert A. Rosenstone, *Visions of the Past: The Challenge of Film to Our Idea of History* (Cambridge, Mass.: Harvard Univ. Press, 1995); Vivian Sobchack, ed., *The Persistence of History: Cinema, Television, and the Modern Event* (New York: Routledge, 1996); Robert Burgoyne, *Film Nation: Hollywood Looks at U.S. History* (Minneapolis: Univ. of Minnesota Press, 1997); Marcia Landy, ed., *The Historical Film: History and Memory in Modern Media* (New Brunswick, N.J.: Rutgers Univ. Press, 2000). See also Susan Jeffords, *The Remasculinization of America: Gender and the Vietnam War* (Bloomington, Ind.: Indiana Univ. Press, 1989); and Lucy Fischer's discussion of momism and World War II in *Cinematernity: Film, Motherhood, Genre* (Princeton, N.J.: Princeton Univ. Press, 1996), 92–110.

3. Fredric Jameson, "On Magic Realism in Film," *Critical Inquiry* 12 (Winter 1986): 303.

4. To cite one example, like Caliban, nonwhite male characters in Western literature and film have often played background roles, and like Caliban, some have also been conceived and punished as the would-be rapists of white women.

5. As for *Singin' in the Rain,* it is Lena's displacement that makes the very history of Hollywood in that film possible. Steven Cohan's analysis of *Singin' in the Rain* identifies some of the terms of this dynamic ("Case Study: Interpreting *Singin' in the Rain,*" in *Reinventing Film Studies,* ed. Christine Gledhill and Linda Williams [New York: Oxford Univ. Press/Arnold, 2000], 53–75).

NOTES

6. Henderson argues compellingly that the film infuses frictions between European and Native Americans with social anxieties about race relations in the 1950s, and he points to public debates sparked by the May 17, 1954, Supreme Court decision in *Brown vs. the Board of Education of Topeka,* which mandated desegregation of the public schools (Henderson, *"The Searchers:* An American Dilemma," in *Movies and Methods: An Anthology,* vol. II, ed. Bill Nichols [Berkeley, Calif.: Univ. of California Press, 1985], 429–449). The film's anti-Semitic portrait of Mr. Futterman, reinforced even by the meaning of the name—*futter* means "fodder, grub"—speaks to other prejudices of the cold war period as well.

7. Ibid., 435.

8. Janet Walker, "Captive Images in the Traumatic Western," in *Westerns: Films through History,* ed. Janet Walker (New York: Routledge, 2001), 227.

9. See Sarah Bayliss, "The Three Faces, All of Them Female, of Liberty," a review of "The Changing Face of Liberty: Female Allegories of America" (an exhibit at the New York Historical Society), *New York Times,* July 2, 2000, sec. 2, 31.

10. Helen Gardner, *Art through the Ages,* 7th ed., vol. 2 (New York: Harcourt Brace Jovanovich, 1980), 828–829. See also Walker's discussion of time in *The Searchers* ("Captive Images," 222–227). For an extended consideration of de Chirico and Hitchcock, see Matthew Wigdahl, "The Metaphysical Filmscapes of Hitchcock's *Vertigo*" (master's thesis, Univ. of Colorado at Denver, 1997).

11. Robert Burgoyne makes a related point in his extraordinary reading of the film: "In evoking memory . . . as the register of national belonging, the film simultaneously erases many of the historical events that continue to trouble the national narrative." Thus, for example, *Forrest Gump*'s eponymous protagonist narrates his socially unaware memories of the Vietnam War as the film itself engages in "parasitizing" Vietnam War genre films "in a way that empties them of their original content" and converts dissent and critique to altogether different ends (*Film Nation,* 109–110). For further discussion of the film's elision of women's history, see Thomas Byers, "History Re-Membered: *Forrest Gump,* Postfeminist Masculinity, and the Burial of the Counterculture," *Modern Fiction Studies* 42, no. 2 (Summer 1996): 419–444.

12. There are further differences between film and painting. For example, Zemeckis centers the house, positioning it literally a stone's throw from Jenny, whereas Wyeth's farmhouse is more distant and off to the right. Forrest, crippled then later healed in childhood, enters the frame to join Jenny, whereas Christina, crippled her whole life, is very much alone.

13. Gardner observes, "Wyeth's painting [in general] is a meticulous Realism [*sic*] treating of the American scene in a muted poetic way that has something of the dreaming detachment of Surrealism without Surrealism's fantasy" (*Art through the Ages,* 860).

14. As documented by the Feminist Majority Press in October 1997: "Nike women's empowerment ads aimed at the US market are in sharp contrast to the treatment of women workers in these sweatshops. Eighty to ninety percent of the workers in these sweatshops of Vietnam, Indonesia, and China are women" ("Women's Groups Urge Nike to Put Its Money Where Its Mouth Is").

15. Cynthia Enloe, *Maneuvers: The International Politics of Militarizing Women's Lives* (Berkeley, Calif.: Univ. of California Press, 2000), 291.

16. For further discussion, see Bordo, *Unbearable Weight*, 19.

17. For the complete document, see Robin Morgan, ed., *Sisterhood Is Powerful: An Anthology of Writings from the Women's Liberation Movement* (New York: Vintage, 1970), 521–523.

18. Of Jenny, Byers observes, "The assignment of all [her various] roles to one woman is much more symbolic than realistic. For instance, the coeds who posed for *Playboy* were not generally the ones who identified with Joan Baez . . . and the HIV-positive single mothers of the late 1980s were not, by and large, coeds in exclusive southern women's colleges in the mid-sixties" ("History Re-Membered," 432).

19. Jacquie Jones, "The Accusatory Space," in *Black Popular Culture*, ed. Gina Dent, Discussions in Contemporary Culture, no. 8 (Seattle: Bay Press, 1993), 96.

20. The words of Nina's response are as follows: "Some people think it's because they all got killed, but I think it has more to do with the decimation of the manufacturing base in the urban centers. Senator, an optimistic, energized population throws up optimistic, energized leaders. Now when you shift manufacturing to the sun belt and the third world, you destroy the blue collar core of the black activist population. Some people would say the problem is purely cultural. The power of the media that's continually controlled by fewer and fewer people, add to the monopoly of the media a consumer culture that's based on self-gratification, and you're not likely to have a population that wants leadership that calls for self-sacrifice. But the fact is I'm just a materialist at heart. As I look at the economic base, high domestic employment means jobs for African-Americans. World War II meant lots of jobs for black folks. That is what energized the community for the civil rights movement of the '50s and '60s. An energized, hopeful community will not only produce leaders but more importantly, it will produce leaders they respond to. Now what do you think, Senator? . . . My mother was a Panther. Huey Newton fed the kids on my block."

21. Roger Ebert's otherwise positive review rightly complains about these developments: "I didn't buy the romance between Bulworth and Nina; it's a recycling of the tired movie convention that a man in a fight for his life can always find time, in three days, to fall in love with a woman half his age. And I didn't much like the movie's ending—not the false ending, and not the real one that follows, either" (Review of *Bulworth*, <www.suntimes.com/ebert/ebert_reviews/1998/05/052202.html>). Stanley Kauffmann's review identifies problems with Bulworth's wife: "Mrs. Bulworth's behavior in public and private is hard to believe. Candidates' wives don't often upbraid their husbands in front of others for being late. And the likelihood seems dim that such a wife, in the middle of a campaign, would have an affair, in these days when investigative reporters are drooling with rapacity" ("Color Lines," review of *Bulworth*, *The New Republic* Online, <www.tnr.com/archive/060898/kauffmann060898.html>).

22. In *Primary Colors*, this tendency is far more pronounced—the teen-age black girl whom the presidential candidate may or may not have impregnated is a background figure defined simply as a glyph, motivating plot and complicating theme.

23. Safiya Bukhari-Alston, "On the Question of Sexism within the Back Panther Party" (<http://www.hartford-hwp.com/archives/45a/014.html>, March 9, 1995).

24. Sigmund Freud, "The 'Uncanny,'" trans. Alix Strachey, in *On Creativity and the Unconscious: Papers on the Psychology of Art, Literature, Love, Religion*, ed. Benjamin Nelson (New York: Harper and Row, 1958), 123–124; 122.

25. Ibid., 131.

26. *Shorter Oxford English Dictionary*, 277.

27. Freud, "The 'Uncanny,'" 152–153.

28. Lucy Fischer, *Shot/Countershot: Film Tradition and Women's Cinema* (Princeton, N.J.: Princeton Univ. Press, 1986), 193.

29. Ibid., 205–215.

30. Hélène Cixous, "Fiction and Its Phantoms: A Reading of Freud's *Das Unheimliche* (The 'Uncanny')," trans. Robert Dennomé, *New Literary History* 7, no. 3 (Spring 1976): 525–548, esp. 533–535.

31. Tania Modleski, *The Women Who Knew Too Much: Hitchcock and Feminist Theory* (New York: Methuen, 1988), 92.

32. See Tania Modleski, *Loving with a Vengeance: Mass-Produced Fantasies for Women* (New York: Methuen, 1982), 59–84; Mary Ann Doane, *The Desire to Desire: The Woman's Film of the 1940s* (Bloomington, Ind.: Indiana Univ. Press, 1987), 123–175; and Diane Waldman, "Architectural Metaphor in the Gothic Romance Film," *Iris: Cinema and Architecture*, no. 12 (1991): 55–69. See also Peter Brooks's influential work, *The Melodramatic Imagination: Balzac, Henry James, Melodrama, and the Mode of Excess* (New Haven, Conn.: Yale Univ. Press, 1976), esp. 16–20.

33. Modleski, *Loving with a Vengeance*, 31, 71.

34. Doane, *The Desire to Desire*, 144–154.

35. Waldman, "Architectural Metaphor," esp. 69.

36. Kristeva, *Strangers to Ourselves*, trans. Leon S. Roudiez (New York: Columbia Univ. Press, 1991), 191.

37. Jameson, "On Magic Realism," 316.

38. Homi K. Bhabha, *The Location of Culture* (New York: Routledge, 1994), 9.

39. Ibid., 10–11.

40. Ibid., 137.

41. Maureen Molloy, "Death and the Maiden: The Feminine and the Nation in Recent New Zealand Films," *Signs* 25, no. 1 (1999): 158–159.

42. Ibid., 160. Although Molloy's theoretical approach serves as a powerful model for my project, I consider her readings of the New Zealand films to be provocations to further reflection rather than as definitive.

43. Ibid., 159.

44. Cf. Seven-of-Nine and the queen bee leader of the Borg in the *Star Trek: Voyager* series.

45. The term derives from Alison Landsberg, "Prosthetic Memory: *Total Recall* and *Blade Runner*," in *The Cybercultures Reader*, ed. David Bell and Barbara M. Kennedy (New York: Routledge, 2000), 190–201.

46. For illuminating reflections on and complications of these traditional align-

ments, see Modleski, *Old Wives' Tales and Other Women's Stories* (New York: New York Univ. Press, 1998), 173–174; see also Modleski on Kant's theory of the sublime as it relates to contemporary horror films and to Lyotard's designation of postmodernist aesthetics as sublime ("The Terror of Pleasure: The Contemporary Horror Film and Postmodern Theory," in *Film Theory and Criticism*, 5th ed., ed. Leo Braudy and Marshall Cohen [New York: Oxford Univ. Press, 1999], 698–699). For further discussion of the uncanny and sublime in relation to theories of horror fiction and fantasy, see, for example, Ken Gelder's insightful *Reading the Vampire* (New York: Routledge, 1994), 43–48. Gelder also considers the connection of the uncanny and the sublime to national identity, yet he misses the significance of women in this context.

47. Immanuel Kant, *Critique of Judgment*, trans. J. H. Bernard (New York: Hafner Publishing Co., 1951), 102.

48. For a relevant discussion of Kant's concept of universal peace, see Kristeva, *Strangers to Ourselves*, 170–173.

49. W. J. T. Mitchell, *Iconology: Image, Text, Ideology* (Chicago: Univ. of Chicago Press, 1986), 129.

50. Ibid., 142–144.

51. Regina Janes, "Beheadings," in *Death and Representation*, ed. Sarah Webster Goodwin and Elisabeth Bronfen (Baltimore: Johns Hopkins Univ. Press, 1993), 242–262, esp. 255–256.

52. Hayden White, *The Content of the Form: Narrative Discourse and Historical Representation* (Baltimore: Johns Hopkins Univ. Press, 1987), 68.

53. Ibid., 75.

54. Hayden White, "The Modernist Event," in *The Persistence of History: Cinema, Television, and the Modern Event*, ed. Vivian Sobchack (New York: Routledge, 1996), 17–19.

55. Freud, "The 'Uncanny,'" 148–149. Freud's focus on the feeling of being haunted by the dead adumbrates the experience that the war films discussed here can provoke in spectators: that spectators, too, are haunted by the war dead, who have in effect "come back from the dead" to appear on screen.

56. Paul Rabinow, ed., *The Foucault Reader* (New York: Pantheon, 1984), 186. See also Georges Bataille, *Visions of Excess: Selected Writings, 1927–1939*, trans. and ed. Allan Stoekl (Minneapolis: Univ. of Minnesota Press, 1985), 149–150.

57. Freud, "The 'Uncanny,'" 151.

58. Ibid., 153.

59. *Shorter Oxford English Dictionary*, 1415.

60. Freud, "The 'Uncanny,'" 152. Freud also refers obliquely to the war as the reason he has not examined the foreign literature on the uncanny (123).

61. Ibid., 123.

62. This destabilization is memorably illustrated in Toni Morrison's *Sula*, with its depiction of World War I trauma and the weirdness of home. See Barbara Johnson's excellent discussion of the uncanny in *Sula* in *The Feminist Difference: Literature, Psychoanalysis, Race, and Gender* (Cambridge, Mass: Harvard Univ. Press, 1998), 74–87.

63. Derrida, "Semiology and Grammatology: Interview with Julia Kristeva," in *The Communication Theory Reader,* ed. Paul Cobley (New York: Routledge, 1996), 209–224.

64. Further complicating the uncanny's status as an aesthetic category is Freud's assertion that the uncanny is that which ought not to have been seen; that is, while Freud argues that the uncanny is an aesthetic category in its appeal to the senses and the pleasurable sense of fright it can provide, he also identifies it as a psychological and social category of things that ought to have remained hidden and out of sight. The statement has implications for visual versus purely verbal media, and can illuminate Malick's adaptation of uncanny elements from James Jones's novel *The Thin Red Line* that are discussed below.

65. Robin Blaetz, " 'You're going to live if I have to blow your brains out': War, Childbirth, and *The Big Red One*" (paper presented at the Society for Cinema Studies Conference, Pittsburgh, 1992).

Chapter 1

1. A veteran of the Korean War attending one of my film classes in the spring of 2000 was especially adamant in rejecting Malick's film. Speaking expressly on behalf of the older vets, this man objected, "Malick dishonors the American soldier of World War II." I will return to this issue and to that of the film's controversial beauty later in this chapter.

2. For a discussion of the film's reception and the range of critical responses it provoked, see, for example, Marouf Hasian, Jr., "Nostalgic Longings, Memories of the 'Good War,' and Cinematic Representations in *Saving Private Ryan,*" *Critical Studies in Media Communication* 18, no. 3 (September 2001): 338–358.

3. By the time of *You've Got Mail* (1998), Hanks's more hardened romantic lead uses a line from *The Godfather* to similar effect; namely, "go to the mattresses," meaning "go to war."

4. Richard Schickel, "Courage Underdone," review of *Courage Under Fire, Time,* July 22, 1996, 94.

5. White, *The Content of the Form,* 10.

6. Tim O'Brien, *The Things They Carried* (Boston: Houghton Mifflin, 1990), 87. In the same passage, O'Brien also asserts the beauty of war, but in terms that conflate beauty with sublimity, as it is conventionally defined.

7. White, *The Content of the Form,* 71.

8. Quoted ibid., 69.

9. Ibid. Cf. *The Thin Red Line,* in which Captain Bosche identifies Sergeant Welsh as the mother, and *A Midnight Clear,* in which Private Wilkins is known as "Mother."

10. See Stuart Byron, "*The Searchers:* Cult Movie of the New Hollywood," *New York,* March 5, 1979, 45–48.

11. Richard T. Jameson, "History's Eyes," review of *Saving Private Ryan, Film Comment* 34, no. 5 (September/October 1998): 23. Frank P. Tomasulo, in a reading much more attuned to the film's politically and historically problematic dimensions, empha-

sizes not the scene's shattering effect but its "Norman Rockwell-like" setting ("Empire of the Gun: Steven Spielberg's *Saving Private Ryan* and American Values" [paper presented at a conference for the Society for Cinema Studies, Washington, D.C., 2001]). I shall return to Tomasulo's critique.

12. A. Susan Owen, "Memory, War and American Identity: *Saving Private Ryan* as Cinematic Jeremiad," *Critical Studies in Media Communication* 19, no. 3 (September 2002): 290.

13. Ibid., 270.

14. Jeffords, *Remasculinization of America,* 105.

15. Owen, "Memory, War and American Identity," 272.

16. On the other hand, insofar as actual World War II soldiers demonstrated Miller-like "feminine" qualities, they also have been effaced by traditional representations.

17. For a valuable discussion of Spielberg's aesthetic innovations, see Thomas Doherty, *Projections of War: Hollywood, American Culture, and World War II,* rev. ed. (New York: Columbia Univ. Press, 1999), 304–310.

18. Cf. Brecht's poem "Deutschland, Bleiche Mutter" in which a German murders his Jewish brother. See also Peter Ehrenhaus, "Why We Fought: Holocaust Memory in Spielberg's *Saving Private Ryan,*" *Critical Studies in Media Communication* 18, no. 3 (September 2001): 321–337. Although I am not persuaded by Ehrenhaus's reading of Upham and of the troop's overtly Christian sharpshooter, Private Jackson, Ehrenhaus offers an important contextualization of the film.

19. Revealingly, one reviewer cracked, "[Upham] would not be such a bad guy hanging around on the Left Bank 20 years earlier, but he's not cut out for a foxhole" (Karen Jaehne, review of *Saving Private Ryan, Film Quarterly* 53, no. 1 [Fall 1999], 41). Upham is, indeed, identified as being more international than strictly American, and despite objections voiced in some popular venues to the casting of Hanks in the film, it is Davies's role that most destabilizes identity. As for the feminine positioning of Mellish in this scene, it inevitably recalls German stereotypes of Jewish males as effeminate, a position the SS fighter literally forces on Mellish.

20. Richard Schickel, "Reel War," *Time,* July 27, 1998, 19. Similarly, Roger Ebert asserts, "[The film's actors] are all strong presences, but for me the key performance in the movie is by Jeremy Davies, as the frightened little interpreter. He is our entry into the reality because he sees it clearly as a vast system designed to humiliate and destroy him. And so it is. His survival depends on his doing the very best he can, yes, but even more on chance. Eventually he arrives at his personal turning point, and his action writes the closing words of Spielberg's unspoken philosophical argument" (review of *Saving Private Ryan,* <http://www.suntimes.com/ebert/ebert_reviews/1998/07/072404.html>.

21. Tomasulo, "Empire of the Gun." See also Jacob Weisberg, "Bombs and Blockbusters: World War II Nostalgia at the Movies Is Blurring the Picture of Kosovo," *New York Times Magazine,* April 11, 1999, 17–18, and David Denby, "Good Guys," *New Yorker,* March 11, 2002, 92–93. The unilateralism of the 2003 invasion of Iraq also extends Tomasulo's point.

22. The African-American combat soldiers who volunteered to go into France to

fight the Battle of the Bulge did so even though they all, including the sergeants, had to consent to being reduced to buck privates.

23. Here he enacts a pattern reminiscent of the one Bhabha describes as being inflicted on colonized subjects, the obligation to prove one's human credentials through slightly flawed performative gestures (see *Location of Culture*, 135–138).

24. Burgoyne, *Film Nation*, 96.

25. Owen, "Memory, War and American Identity," 274.

26. Hasian, "Nostalgic Longings," 349–350.

27. To be sure, Spielberg also interweaves the world of nature with the world at war in a memorable sequence that crescendos from the singular sound of a heavy rain drop thudding against a broad green leaf to a spattering of drops that sound like bullets, to gunfire itself, first distant and then all too close. Malick's emphasis on tropical splendor is much more sustained than Spielberg's focus on nature, however.

28. Jones, *The Thin Red Line* (New York: Bantam, 1962), 237.

29. Ibid., 158.

30. Ibid., 68.

31. Ibid., 275–286.

32. Ibid., 409–411.

33. Kristeva, *Strangers to Ourselves*, 188.

34. Edmund Burke, *A Philosophical Enquiry into the Origins of Our Ideas of the Sublime and Beautiful*, ed. James T. Boulton (South Bend, Ind.: Notre Dame Univ. Press, 1968), 144.

35. Mitchell, *Iconology*, 131.

36. Morrison, *Sula*, 142.

37. In fact, Doherty criticizes the film overall for being "too pretty" and for what I am calling its uncanny dimensions: "Owls watch alertly, vampire bats hang ominously, and carrion birds circle eerily. Weirdly festive in blue and red, parrots stand out against the browns and green of the jungle and the khaki of the GI fatigues" (*Projections of War*, 314–315). The beautiful and the weird are nonetheless present in Jones's novel (published *before* the American phase of the Vietnam War), as is the pointed cynicism of Welsh, despite Doherty's claim that it is "heretical in World War II territory."

38. Contrast this with the dark sublimity of Jones's cathedral image: "A curious sense of unreality had come over all of them with the discovery of the shirt. The dripping, gloomy, airless jungle with its vaulted cathedral-like ceiling far above did not serve to lessen it" (*The Thin Red Line*, 70).

39. Freud's "The Theme of the Three Caskets," which is complemented by his later study of the uncanny, theorizes a related symbolization of death as its "wish-opposite," "not a thing of horror, but the fairest and most desirable thing in life," that has nonetheless "kept certain characteristics that border on the uncanny" (Freud, "The Theme of the Three Caskets," trans. Alix Strachey, in *On Creativity and the Unconscious: Papers on the Psychology of Art, Literature, Love, Religion*, ed. Benjamin Nelson [New York: Harper and Row, 1958], 73). These ideas illuminate the imagery of Bell's wife throughout.

40. Compare this with the words of Malick's humane Captain Staros about his men

after Colonel Tall forces him to leave his battalion: "You are my sons. I carry you inside me." The film affirms his maternalism without coding it in conventional terms of paternal mastery.

41. Malick's focus can also be contrasted with the erotic, ritualized beauty that French filmmaker Claire Denis discovers in the legionnaires of *Beau Travail* (2000), even though that beauty, too, is tied to the landscape.

42. Freud, "The 'Uncanny,'" 141.

43. The effigy or profile images seen on coins have come, by convention, to be associated with the dead—hence, for example, the recurring profile shots of Madeleine in Hitchcock's *Vertigo* to suggest that she is among the dead. Witt's death itself is shot in profile.

44. Jones, *The Thin Red Line*, 453, 464. See also 446–447. The first American combat troops arrived in Vietnam in 1965.

45. Doherty, *Projections of War*, 312. James Morrison also sees these scenes as "the clearest gauge of the film's post-Vietnam dispositions" (review of *The Thin Red Line*, *Film Quarterly* 53, no. 1 [Fall 1999], 36). Doherty's criticisms of this film's supposed commercial calculations seem much more relevant to *Pearl Harbor* (2001).

46. Enloe, *Maneuvers*, 67.

47. *Enemy at the Gates* (2001) creates a related effect by staging the initial encounter between Vassili, the Russian hero, and Konig, the German sharpshooter, in a bombed-out department store that is littered with deceptively human-looking mannequins.

48. For a further, highly illuminating discussion of this topic in the context of Hollywood cinema and World War II, see Fischer, *Cinematernity*, 102–108.

49. Elisabeth Bronfen's words help elucidate the choice made by the suicidal Janice: "The double, simultaneously denying and affirming mortality, is the metaphor of the uncanniness of the death drive, of '*Unheimlichkeit par excellence*,' grounding all other versions of the uncanny because it points to what is most resistantly and universally repressed, namely the presence of death in life and at the origin of life" (*Over Her Dead Body: Death, Femininity, and the Aesthetic* [New York: Routledge, 1992], 114).

50. I am relying, here, on Judith Mayne's definition of fantasy as "the *staging* of desire . . . a form of mise-en-scène" (*Cinema and Spectatorship* [New York: Routledge, 1993], 88).

51. Following Otto Rank, Freud explains that "probably the 'immortal' soul was the first 'double' of the body" ("The 'Uncanny,'" 141). Freud also points out that "the resuscitation of the dead in miracles, as in the New Testament, elicits feelings quite unrelated to the uncanny" ("The 'Uncanny,'" 154). It is the film's peculiar treatment of these motifs that creates the sense of the uncanny.

52. The image also eerily echoes the idea of the ma(w) of death.

53. Kristeva, *Strangers to Ourselves*, 169–173.

54. Ibid., 188–192.

55. Betty Beale and Rex Scouten as quoted in Kati Marton, *Hidden Power: Presidential Marriages That Shaped Our Recent History* (New York: Pantheon, 2001), 181–182.

56. Marton, *Hidden Power*, 185–186.

Chapter 2

1. In a 1968 campaign film, which contains his only public criticism of his mother, Nixon himself sounded this theme: "My mother used to say later on that she never gave us a spanking. I'm not so sure. She might have. But I do know that we dreaded far more than my father's hand her tongue. It was never sharp, but she would just sit you down and she would talk very quietly and then when you got through you had been through an emotional experience" (quoted in Fawn Brodie, *Richard Nixon: The Shaping of His Character* [New York: Norton, 1981], 60). Anthony Hopkins's posture, gestures, and facial expressions give a physical dimension to the character's psychic misshapenness, and in a review, David Denby aptly characterizes Hopkins's Nixon as "clumsy and trapped, a bear carrying his own zoo bars around with him . . . even into the bedroom" ("Poor Richard," review of *Nixon, New York,* January 8, 1996, 44).

2. Cf. the indictment of the soldiers' mothers in *Born on the Fourth of July* (1989) and *Heaven and Earth* (1993)—not to mention the auto-da-fé of Mallory's sitcom mom in *Natural Born Killers* (1994).

3. Truman, *First Ladies* (New York: Random House, 1995), 5, 12.

4. Kaplan, *Motherhood and Representation: The Mother in Popular Culture and Melodrama* (New York: Routledge, 1992), 45–46.

5. Stone quoted in Norman Kagan, *The Cinema of Oliver Stone,* expanded ed. (New York: Continuum, 2000), 269.

6. London *Spectator* quoted in Lester David, *The Lonely Lady of San Clemente* (New York: Crowell, 1978), 88.

7. E. T. A. Hoffmann, "The Sand-Man," trans. J. T. Bealby, in *The Best Tales of Hoffmann,* ed. E. F. Bleiler (New York: Dover, 1967), 212.

8. Molloy, "Death and the Maiden," 160.

9. Freud, "The 'Uncanny,'" 140.

10. Ebert, review of *Nixon,* <http://www.suntimes.com/ebert_reviews/1995/12/1012232.html>. Sharrett, "The Belly of the Beast: Oliver Stone's *Nixon* and the American Nightmare," *Cinéaste* 22, no. 1 (1996), 4–8.

11. Michel Foucault, "On the Parrhesiastes" (talk given as part of the Humanities Lecture Series, Univ. of Colorado at Boulder, Boulder, Colorado, October 10, 1983).

12. Molloy, "Death and the Maiden," 155.

13. The young woman protester at the Lincoln Memorial who identifies the nature of the government "Beast" for Nixon is similarly a female *parrhesiastes* figure, but one whose insight Nixon recognizes and thoroughly endorses.

14. Greg Mitchell, *Tricky Dick and the Pink Lady: Richard Nixon vs. Helen Gahagan Douglas: Sexual Politics and the Red Scare, 1950* (New York: Random House, 1998), 47; David, *Lonely Lady,* 164–165. The mutual dislike between Haldeman and Pat Nixon eventually escalated into what David calls the "White House Battle of the Sexes" and the "War between the East and West Wings." Stone gives little sense of these frictions. As for Chotiner, he is vividly characterized by Brodie, who asserts that he seriously equated Democrats and Communists (*Richard Nixon,* 175–179).

15. Truman recounts this history as follows: "After his failed 1960 bid for the presidency, she made him put in writing a promise to quit politics. A year later, when he told her that he had decided to run for governor of California, she burst into tears. When he announced, without consulting her, that he was going to run for President in 1968, she plunged into a depression" (*First Ladies,* 191).

16. Mitchell describes and contextualizes Nixon's role in the Hiss case as follows: "What would set [Nixon] apart from [most of his Republican colleagues in 1947], and would bring him to national attention, was his decision to focus his energies on rooting out domestic communism. First, he landed a spot on HUAC, which, under the new GOP leadership, immediately went after Communist infiltration of the government and Hollywood. With Karl Mundt, he drafted a bill requiring Communists and Communist front groups to register with the Justice Department, and it passed the House before sinking in the Senate. His big break arrived, however, when *Time* magazine editor Whittaker Chambers came forward to identify former State Department official Alger Hiss as a onetime Communist. Nixon was not responsible for producing the witness, but his dogged faith in the rather unsavory Chambers enabled him to take credit for breaking the Hiss case. (Chambers later revealed that Nixon's 'somewhat martial Quakerism' amused and heartened him.) Most spectacularly, [Nixon] displayed for newsreel cameras the so-called Pumpkin Papers, several rolls of microfilm of classified documents that Hiss had allegedly passed to Chambers, who hid them in a pumpkin on his farm" (*Tricky Dick,* 44). Several years later, after Nixon launched his Senate campaign against Helen Gahagan Douglas in 1949, "a key moment in the campaign came very early. Nixon's considerable support might not have meant much if the second Hiss trial (with a new judge presiding) had ended with an acquittal. If that had happened, Nixon 'would be vulnerable to charges of witch-hunting,' Stephen Ambrose later commented. But on January 21, 1950, Nixon got the guilty verdict he desperately needed" (ibid., 50). In contrast to the "somewhat martial" Quaker, Hiss had been president of the Carnegie Endowment for International Peace from 1946 to 1949. As a result of his conviction on charges of perjury, he spent over three years in prison.

17. Freud, "The 'Uncanny,'" 137–138.

18. Similarly, in his resignation-speech scene, Nixon praises his "saintly" mother and fails even to mention his wife, an oversight accompanied by camera work that keeps Pat in the picture and reminds viewers both of his omission (based on the historical record) and of his equation of his mother with his wife.

19. The soul partakes of the uncanny because, according to Freud, the "'immortal' soul was the first 'double' of the body" ("The 'Uncanny,'" 141).

20. Stone also bifurcates paternal figures in his films, showing heroes who are torn between a good father and a bad one, or between the good and bad figurations of a single patriarch, such as Lincoln. Stone's mothers, however, are much more narrowly imagined.

21. See Erich Auerbach's discussion of the biblical sublime in *Mimesis: The Representation of Reality in Western Literature,* trans. Willard R. Trask (Princeton, N.J.: Princeton Univ. Press, 1953), 22–23.

22. According to Carl Sferrazza Anthony, the historical Pat Nixon was privately very troubled by the mounting casualties of the Vietnam War (*First Ladies,* vol. II [New York: Morrow, 1991], 180–181).

23. David, *Lonely Lady,* 87. David's image recalls the tactics of Kevin Costner's aging baseball catcher in *Bull Durham,* a man who conceives of the professional athlete's reservoir of sports clichés as a deliberate ploy, a means of (not) dealing with the media.

24. Sharrett, "The Belly of the Beast," 5.

. 25. Bergholz quoted in Brodie, *Richard Nixon,* 467.

26. Kissinger quoted in David, *Lonely Lady,* 84.

27. Ibid., 83.

28. Molloy, "Death and the Maiden," 154. For a discussion of Allen's role as a vice presidential candidate in *The Contender* (Rod Lurie, 2000), see Kent Casper, "All the President's Women" (unpublished conference paper for The American President on Film: A National Conference, Westlake Village, California, 2000).

29. Nixon's fear and hatred of women, especially intelligent ones, is well documented (Brodie, *Richard Nixon,* 232–245; David, *Lonely Lady,* 164–165, 192), and discussions of Stone's problematic historiography are legion. See, for example, Sharon Willis's brief but insightful comments (*High Contrast: Race and Gender in Contemporary Hollywood Film* [Durham, N.C.: Duke Univ. Press, 1997], 257 n. 45). For a discussion of Nixon's subversion of the role of the first lady and his attempts "to impose an image of frozen perfection on his wife," see Marton, *Hidden Power,* 185–187.

30. Mitchell states that "Pat Nixon's feelings about the savagery of her husband's attacks on [Helen Douglas] were unclear" (*Tricky Dick,* 159).

31. A similar conflation characterized Nazism, which tied Communism to Jewish male sexuality.

32. Nixon quoted in Mitchell, *Tricky Dick,* 260.

33. Nixon quoted in Brodie, *Richard Nixon,* 428.

34. This is not to say that the Communist threat was sheer illusion; it was not (Allen Weinstein and Alexander Vassilev, *Soviet Espionage in America: The Stalin Era* [New York: Random House, 1999]). Yet it bears remembering that Nixon's linkage of femininity with Communist sympathizing not only worked with his public but also helped set back the cause of women in politics for years (Mitchell, *Tricky Dick,* 260–261).

35. Richard Dorment and Margaret F. MacDonald, *James McNeill Whistler* (New York: Harry N. Abrams, 1994), 142.

36. Siegfried Kracauer, *From Caligari to Hitler: A Psychological History of the German Film* (Princeton, N.J.: Princeton Univ. Press, 1947). Street films such as Karl Grüne's *The Street* (*Die Strasse,* 1923) and Bruno Rahn's *Tragedy of the Street* (*Dirnentragödie,* 1927) serve as Kracauer's models.

37. Kracauer, *From Caligari to Hitler,* 122–123. For a discussion of some of the problems in Kracauer's approach, see Patrice Petro, *Joyless Streets: Women and Melodramatic Representation in Weimar Germany* (Princeton, N.J.: Princeton Univ. Press, 1989), xvii-xxiv.

38. See Corber, *In the Name of National Security: Hitchcock, Homophobia, and the Political Construction of Gender in Postwar America* (Durham, N.C.: Duke Univ. Press,

1993), 196–198. In *Nixon,* dialogue pointedly links Nixon's brutality with German fascism, bolstering the political import of Stone's quotation of Weimar film.

39. Further parallelism between these portraits stems from the fact that before Whistler painted the portrait of his mother, her husband and two of her children had died (Dorment and MacDonald, *Whistler,* 142).

40. Use of psychoanalysis in the *Nixon* screenplay is quite conscious. See, for example, dialogue (omitted from the film) that has Nixon rejecting psychoanalysis in a way that cannot but validate it (Stephen J. Rivele, Christopher Wilkinson, and Oliver Stone, "*Nixon:* The Original Annotated Screenplay," in Nixon: *An Oliver Stone Film,* ed. Eric Hamburg [New York: Hyperion, 1995], 93).

41. For a critique of Frankfurt School theory along these lines, see Andrew Hewitt, *Political Inversions: Homosexuality, Fascism, and the Modernist Imaginary* (Stanford, Calif.: Stanford Univ. Press, 1996), 38–78.

42. Also like Kane, Nixon collects things to cover the gap of missed maternal love; in Nixon's case, tapes and achievements. And like Kane, he becomes different things to different people; the film presents him as an isolated, narcissistic man who offers a false face to others in the hope that the false self, unlike the real one, can be loved.

43. Some of Stone's other references to Welles include the opening upward pan from outside the White House fence, the cloudy night accompanied by gothic music, the biblical allusion to Cain, the "March of Time"–style newsreel—in *Nixon,* taking the form of a premature political obituary—and the alienated dinner scene already discussed.

44. Stone expands the theme of fratricide and doubling in the film to include Haldeman and Ehrlichman, when, after being forced to resign, Haldeman says that it was "Six ... six bodies"—that is, those of Haldeman and Ehrlichman as well as those of the Nixon and Kennedy brothers.

45. "This law school is a gift from thy brother. Thou art stronger than Harold, stronger than Arthur. Strength in this life, happiness in the next," she says. Harold's charm furthers the sense that he and John Kennedy are doubles. As Brodie explains, both were "handicapped by illness, but still ... exuberant, fun-loving charmer[s]" (*Richard Nixon,* 415).

46. Joe Klein later affixed the same stereotype to First Lady Hillary Clinton: "in another time, she might have been a founding member of the Women's Christian Temperance Union" ("An American Marriage," *New Yorker,* February 9, 1998, 36). Ironically, although Stone stresses Hannah's religiousness, it was Frank's that played the more obvious role in Harold's death. Against his wife's wishes, Frank sent his oldest son to a boys' "Bible school" in Massachusetts—a school straight out of *Jane Eyre,* with daily 5:30 A.M. cold showers and boys coming to breakfast with icicles in their hair. He contracted a virulent case of tuberculosis, the disease that later killed him (Brodie, *Richard Nixon,* 92–93).

47. Brodie, *Richard Nixon,* 67.

48. Arthur M. Schlesinger, Jr. mistakenly reads Stone's Nixon as the sympathetic victim of both his parents equally ("On *JFK* and *Nixon,*" in *Oliver Stone's USA: Film, History, and Controversy,* ed. Robert Brent Toplin [Lawrence, Kan.: Univ. of Kansas Press, 2000], 214), but there can be little doubt that Stone's Nixon is essentially his mother's

victim. Nor is Stone's focus on the mother unique in this context; it is matched by that of Vamik D. Volkan, Norman Itskowitz, and Andrew W. Dod. These scholars quote Wilbur Cohen, an FDR appointee, on what makes a good president. Cohen asserted, "To be President, you need to have a good mother. The father doesn't matter. You need a good mother" (Volkan, Itskowitz, and Dod, *Richard Nixon: A Psychobiography* [New York: Columbia Univ. Press, 1997], 144). The authors concur, but they qualify Cohen's statement—not to say that the father matters, but to say a "good enough mother" is needed. In an age when some insist that single-parent families are not "good enough," and others, with Hillary Clinton, that "it takes a village," the singular focus of these men is striking. They contend that Hannah Nixon was not "good enough," in part because her husband's behavior depressed her, and depression prevented her from offering adequate mothering. However, they do not follow through with this argument to draw obvious conclusions about paternal-husbandly contributions, including powerful indirect ones, to presidential personality types. Mother-blame and the American uncanny go hand in glove.

49. Rivele, Wilkinson, and Stone, "*Nixon:* Original Screenplay," 117. See also Brodie, *Richard Nixon,* 141.

50. "Mona Lisas and Mad Hatters" is the title of 1972 song by Elton John and Bernie Taupin criticizing the social inequities of New York, a city where the "rich man can ride and the hobo he can drown." Pat Nixon's allegiance to the "little guys" emerged in one of her first remarks after Nixon's successful 1968 election bid. Speaking about her vision of life in the White House, she enthused, "The guests won't be limited to big shots!" For his part, her husband quickly countered that all of their friends were "big shots" (quoted in Truman, *First Ladies,* 10–11). As Watergate revealed, many of Nixon's closest associates were also like those criticized in the 1972 song—incapable of distinguishing right from wrong or night from day, incapable of knowing "if it's dark outside or light."

51. Kristeva, *Strangers to Ourselves,* 188, 189.

52. See David, *Lonely Lady,* 153–164.

53. Richard Nixon as quoted in Mitchell, *Tricky Dick,* 261; David, *Lonely Lady,* 153.

54. Pat Nixon as quoted in David, *Lonely Lady,* 153–154.

55. Ibid., 154.

56. Charles Colson as quoted in Truman, *First Ladies,* 195. More than her husband, Pat Nixon also earned Eisenhower's praise for her work during the vice presidential goodwill tours she and Nixon made to the Far East, Africa, England, and Russia (Paul F. Boller, Jr., *Presidential Wives* [New York: Oxford Univ. Press, 1988], 405). As for Pat's own priorities on these trips, Boller explains, "Above all, she insisted on meeting women's groups in every country she visited, for she was anxious to dramatize the achievements of women in the world, and bring their problems before the public, especially in countries where their status was low. 'Everywhere I went,' she said after one of her trips, 'it helped women.'"

57. See Anthony, *First Ladies,* 195–210.

58. Caroli, *First Ladies* (New York: Oxford Univ. Press, 1987), 250.

59. Freud, "The 'Uncanny,'" 140.

60. Judt, "Counsels on Foreign Relations," review of *A Tangled Web: The Making of*

Foreign Policy in the Nixon Presidency by William Bundy, *New York Review of Books* 45, no. 13 (August 1998): 60. The brutality that troubles many erstwhile tangential zones after the collapse of Communism is further evidence of the gravity of Nixon and Kissinger's error.

61. The analogy drawn by Stone's Nixon overlooks the historical Nixon's willingness to sacrifice his daughter, Julie. He allowed her to make 150 speeches on his behalf during Watergate, exploiting her trust and never apprising her of his guilt (Brodie, *Richard Nixon*, 514).

62. Mitchell, *Tricky Dick*, 261.

63. Thomas as quoted in Truman, *First Ladies*, 190. Thomas covered first ladies from Bess Truman to Hillary Clinton. Also see Diane Sawyer's account of her first encounter with Pat Nixon (quoted in Marton, *Hidden Power*, 187–188). Sawyer recalls how Pat Nixon "did this beautiful thing that melted me when I first met her. I had written something for her and took it over and as I was going to leave, Mrs. Nixon said, 'Do you remember when you were a little girl, and just made a new friend, and didn't want them to leave and you said, I'll walk you 'halvers,' halfway home.' She took my hand and walked me halfway back. And then hugged me—just like a little girl. She was full of affection and gaiety. . . . She loved having fun. She loved it when [press aide] Frank Gannon played the piano and we would all sing and carry on. That was the Irish in her. You could even tell her a dirty joke. Well, not terribly dirty. But she was no prude. She was a real person. She got a kick out of people."

Chapter 3

1. See Jeffords, *Remasculinization of America*. An additional objective of the Gulf War was to toughen the public image of President George H. W. Bush. As Stephen Holden notes in his review of the political satire *Wag the Dog* (Barry Levinson, 1997), "The Persian Gulf War may have failed to drive President Saddam Hussein of Iraq out of office in 1991, but it certainly didn't hurt the popularity of its most vocal proponent, President George Bush. The war proved an instant political windfall, spiking up his approval ratings and banishing forever any lurking suspicion that he may have been, God forbid, a wimp. The rosy political scenario wasn't lost on Hollywood" (*New York Times*, January 4, 1998, sec. 2, 11).

2. Women made up 2 percent of the armed services in 1972 and by 1997 made up 14 percent of the army, 17 percent of the air force, 5 percent of the Marine Corps, and 13 percent of the navy (Richard Rayner, "The Warrior Besieged," *New York Times Magazine* June 22, 1997, 27). Twenty-one percent of those who joined the army in 1996 were women (Julia Reed, "Annie Gets Her Gun," *Vogue*, July 1997, 42).

3. Victoria Sherrow, *Women and the Military: An Encyclopedia* (Santa Barbara, Calif.: ABC-CLIO, 1996), 214. Women's successful performance in the Gulf War motivated the Pentagon to increase the range of positions open to women. A report from 2003 stated that "the 210,177 women . . . in uniform represent almost 15 percent of all active-duty military personnel and may occupy more than 90 percent of military career

fields" ("Warrior Women," photographs by Dan Winters, *New York Times Magazine*, February 16, 2003, 34).

4. Walden is roughly based on the actual female combatants Major Marie T. Rossi, Sergeant Theresa Lynn Treloar, and Sergeant Cheryl La Beau-O'Brien. Rossi, who died when her Chinook helicopter crashed in bad weather, was the only one of the thirteen women casualties from the war to be buried with honors at Arlington National Cemetery. Treloar, the mother of a seven-year-old, was, like Walden, known for her courage in tense situations and for her proficiency with weapons. Nicknamed "Ice Lady" because of her bravery, Treloar was the only servicewoman to participate in a top-secret assignment, a mission that brought her nearer to the Iraqi battlefront than any other American woman. La Beau-O'Brien served on the crew of a Black Hawk helicopter and died when the helicopter was shot down. It is worth noting that the first woman to receive the Congressional Medal of Honor was Mary Edward Walker, a proponent of women's rights and a physician who served in the American Civil War. Her award was granted in 1865, revoked in 1917, then restored in 1977. See Sherrow, *Women and the Military*, 58–59, 214–215, 245–246, 274–275, 314. Additionally, in his DVD director's commentary, Zwick alludes to various friendly-fire incidents during the Gulf War that were concealed by the military and that inspired the film's story.

5. As Vicki Schultz observes, "Most harassment isn't about satisfying sexual desires. It's about protecting work—especially the most favored lines of work—as preserves of male competence and authority" ("Sex Is the Least of It: Let's Focus Harassment Law on Work, Not Sex," *The Nation*, May 25, 1998, 11).

6. Lynda Boose, "Techno-Muscularity and the 'Boy Eternal': From the Quagmire to the Gulf," in *Gendering War Talk*, ed. Miriam Cooke and Angela Woollacott (Princeton, N.J.: Princeton Univ. Press, 1993), 78.

7. For further discussion of the incident, see ibid., 103, 22.

8. Enloe, *Maneuvers*, 84–85.

9. For further discussion of this last event, see ibid., 111–123.

10. Fisher, "Blacks in the Military Wrestle with Issues of Race and Justice," *New York Times*, June 17, 1997, A1, A12.

11. Linda Williams, *Playing the Race Card: Melodramas of Black and White from Uncle Tom to O. J. Simpson* (Princeton, N.J.: Princeton Univ. Press, 2001).

12. Dana Priest, "McKinney Accusers Tell of Hardships," *Washington Post*, March 16, 1998, A1, A6.

13. In particular, she was accused of committing adultery with the civilian husband of an enlisted woman. Flinn believed that she and the civilian, Marc Zigo, had "an affair of the heart," and they made a pact to lie to investigators about their relationship. Flinn lied and disobeyed orders not to see him again; Zigo broke his pact with her and described their sex life to investigators in voyeuristic detail, providing information about the kind of birth control she used and the sexual positions she favored. Sleeping with the enemy indeed. See Flinn, *Proud to Be* (New York: Random House, 1997).

14. Flinn was granted a general discharge rather than the honorable discharge she sought or the court martial that had been threatened. Her story garnered still more me-

dia attention because another female pioneer, the first woman secretary of the air force, Dr. Sheila E. Widnall, granted her the discharge. The *New York Times* characterized the event as "an extraordinarily delicate moment in the sexual integration of the American Military and its handing of sexual morality: the first female Secretary of the Air Force and the first female B-52 pilot staring each other down in a battle of wills" (*New York Times* [Sunday, May 25, 1997], 1). The lawyer who represented Flinn is named Spinner, no less. For a discussion of the Flinn family's handling of the media, see Tony Capaccio, "The Kelly Flinn Spin Patrol," *American Journalism Review* 19, no. 7 (September 1997): 12–13.

15. Ralston had the steady support of Defense Secretary William Cohen throughout his candidacy. Critics of the air force's handling of Flinn's and Ralston's cases pointed to other evidence of a double standard in the U.S. military: its historical reliance on brothels during war and its tolerance of U.S. servicemen's neglect of their out-of-wedlock children. See, for example, Katha Pollitt, "No Sex, Please—We're Killers," *The Nation*, June 23, 1997, 9. For a discussion of the U.S. Defense Department's policy on brothels, see Cynthia Enloe, "The Gendered Gulf," in *Seeing Through the Media: The Persian Gulf War*, ed. Susan Jeffords and Lauren Rabinovitz (New Brunswick, N.J.: Rutgers Univ. Press, 1994), 227. For a report on the reemergence of air force attention to the problem of rape at the academy during the 2003 war on Iraq, see, for example, Bradley Graham, "Academy Lost Focus on Assaults," *Washington Post*, June 20, 2003, A1.

16. Rayner adds, "Of the 356 combat deaths in the gulf war, 211 were among support personnel. A total of 13 women died" ("The Warrior Besieged," 40).

17. Robyn Wiegman, "Missiles and Melodrama (Masculinity and the Televisual War)," in *Seeing Through the Media: The Persian Gulf War*, ed. Susan Jeffords and Lauren Rabinovitz (New Brunswick, N.J.: Rutgers Univ. Press, 1994), 176.

18. Ibid., 174.

19. Ibid., 176.

20. Ibid., 178.

21. Burgoyne, *Film Nation*, 68.

22. As Rosenstone points out, Hollywood history avoids open or ambiguous endings: "The story is closed, completed, and ultimately simple. Alternative versions of the past are not shown; the *Rashomon* approach is never used in such works," (*Visions of the Past*, 123).

23. See *Time*, December 22, 1997, 31.

24. Bronfen, *Over Her Dead Body*. *The General's Daughter* (Simon West, 1999), an especially problematic filmic treatment of gender integration in the military, also conforms with the pattern traced in these works, as does *Three Kings* (David O. Russell, 1999).

25. Walden's posthumously read letter to her parents might be seen as an exception to this pattern, but since the film's audience hears the letter through Serling's mindscreen, its contents are mediated.

26. In a stricter sense, the fate of the M-16 is the film's MacGuffin. It provides the clue that sends Serling on his search for truth.

27. Compare his cries with Nathaniel's cries of "rings of fire—rings of fire!" in E. T. A. Hoffmann's "The Sand-Man," as Nathaniel recollects his father's death. The words are spotlighted by Freud ("The 'Uncanny,'" 135–136).

28. For a revealing discussion of the impossible pressures placed on the post–cold war "model military wife," see Enloe, *Maneuvers*, 162–166.

29. Tomasulo put this idea most directly in suggesting that *Apocalypse Now* "is compromised by chauvinism, because it focuses on *America's* suffering and self-doubt rather than on the destruction wrought on Vietnam and its people. It is as if we were fighting and killing not the Vietnamese, but ourselves" ("The Politics of Ambivalence: *Apocalypse Now* as Prowar and Antiwar Film," in *From Hanoi to Hollywood: The Vietnam War in American Film*, ed. Linda Dittmar and Gene Michaud [New Brunswick, N.J.: Rutgers Univ. Press, 1990], 151).

30. Offering an important contextualization of these deaths, Boose asserts, "the fact that some 120,000 of those who returned have by now committed suicide—twice over the number that even the war managed to kill—strongly suggests that some far more powerful source of rejection was at work in American society than any braless hippie shouting 'baby killers' could account for. It suggests that the sons of patriarchy unconsciously hear and obey a silent but omnipresent dictum written out in ancient Sparta as the edict to return from a war with one's shield or on it" ("Techno-Muscularity," 90).

31. To cite a notorious example of this dishonesty, the army tried to cover up the 1968 massacre at My Lai, in which U.S. soldiers killed at least 170 civilians—women, children, and old men—in a cold-blooded manner reminiscent of the Nazi executions of Jews. See two accounts by Seymour Hersch: *My Lai 4: A Report on the Massacre and Its Aftermath* (New York: Random House, 1970) and *Cover-Up: The Army's Secret Investigation of the Massacre at My Lai 4* (New York: Random House, 1972).

32. Johnson, *The Feminist Difference*, 81.

33. *Three Kings*, in contrast, vividly brings the issue of oil into focus.

34. Regrettably real, related images of an incomparably more horrific and unforgettable magnitude came three years later, when men on suicide missions enacted a terrorist retaliation against the United States for its actions in the Middle East. I shall return to these images from September 11 in the epilogue.

35. Baldwin, "The Devil Finds Work," in *James Baldwin: Collected Essays*, sel. Toni Morrison (New York: Library of America, 1998), 529–530.

36. See also Willis, *High Contrast*. Lou Diamond Phillips's ethnic coding further complicates the film's dynamic of race and gender by creating a conflict between minority males over a white woman. Born Louis Upchurch, Phillips is of Spanish, Scotch-Irish, Chinese, Filipino, Hawaiian, and Cherokee ancestry. See Leonard Maltin, ed., *Leonard Maltin's Movie Encyclopedia* (New York: Plume-Penguin, 1995), 700.

37. The state flag of Georgia included a prominent Confederate cross from 1956 to 2001. On January 30, 2001, as a result of a movement led by African-American lawmakers, the state adopted a new flag encompassing smaller replications of its older flags. On April 22, 2003, the Georgia Senate voted to change the flag yet again, a move successfully resisted (as of this writing) by African-American lawmakers.

38. My reading here is indebted to Mikhail Bakhtin's perception that genres have

the past embedded in them, that they both "remember" history and mold present experience in an additional way. Bakhtin further maintains that adaptation of an older genre to a new context produces "double voicing," a generic function that recasts the past as prologue precisely through the reverberative, echoing shapes that generic formulas impose on discrete events. See Gary Saul Morson and Caryl Emerson, *Mikhail Bakhtin: The Creation of a Prosaics* (Stanford, Calif.: Stanford Univ. Press, 1990), 290–292; and Burgoyne, *Film Nation*, 61. The scene I am discussing here can also be read as a revealing exception to Williams's general claim that "in post–civil rights America . . . the plantation home could no longer serve as the locus of virtue" (*Playing the Race Card*, 8).

39. Rayner, "The Warrior Besieged," 40, 56.

40. See, for example, Andrew Parker et al., eds., introduction to *Nationalisms and Sexualities* (New York: Routledge, 1992), 66–67.

41. See, for example, Burgoyne, *Film Nation*, 66–87; and Fischer, *Cinematernity*, 103–106.

42. Broyles, "Why Men Love War," *Esquire*, November 1984, 61. See also Blaetz, "'You're going to live,'" a first-rate analysis of the discourse on childbirth and war in the combat film.

43. Quoted in Rayner, "The Warrior Besieged," 26.

44. Writing in September 1990, Enloe asserted, "If there is an image that defines television's Gulf Crisis, it's a disheveled white woman coming off a 747, an exhausted baby on her shoulder. States exist, this media story implies, to protect womenandchildren [*sic*]. U.S. intervention in the Gulf would be harder to justify if there were no feminized [and maternalized] victim" ("The Gendered Gulf," 214). This media ploy is outrageously evoked and parodied in *Wag the Dog* when, through the manipulation of computerized imaging, a young woman holding a "kitten" (clearly a baby surrogate) is made to appear on television to be fleeing for her life in "war-torn Albania."

45. The need for masculine control of reproduction is also definitive for Vietnam War narratives. See Jeffords, *Remasculinization of America*, 91–94.

46. Andreas Huyssen, *After the Great Divide: Modernism, Mass Culture, Postmodernism* (Bloomington, Ind.: Indiana Univ. Press, 1986), 65–81.

47. See Fredric Jameson, *The Political Unconscious: Narrative as a Socially Symbolic Act* (Ithaca, N.Y.: Cornell Univ. Press, 1981).

48. Said, *Orientalism* (New York: Vintage Books, 1979), 311. Although Said's binary critical framework has sparked criticism, his core insight remains germane and compelling.

49. One U.S. soldier in the gulf, responding to Hussein's "mother of all battles" within the constructs of Western patriarchy, put it more simply: "Dad's coming to kick Mom's butt" (quoted in Blaetz, "'You're going to live,'" 1).

50. Jean-François Lyotard, "Can Thought Go on without a Body?" in *The Inhuman: Reflections on Time*, trans. Geoffrey Bennington and Rachel Bowlby (Stanford, Calif.: Stanford Univ. Press, 1991), 52.

51. See Schickel, "Courage Underdone," 94.

52. Molloy, "Death and the Maiden," 160.

Chapter 4

1. Kristeva, *Strangers to Ourselves,* 191.

2. Bhabha, *Location of Culture,* 7.

3. Molloy, "Death and the Maiden," 160.

4. Egoyan's film focuses more on fathers who betray their daughters than on mothers, yet it is hard not to read the apparent oblivion of Nicole's mother to her husband's incestuous relationship with Nicole as an indictment of maternal neglect. The characteristics Molloy identifies are also present to some degree in Mohsen Makhmalbaf's *Gabbeh* (1996), a film whose title names simultaneously a rug, a woven story, and a storyteller-daughter.

5. Molloy, "Death and the Maiden," 168.

6. Ibid., 167.

7. Consider, for example, the protagonists of Paul Schrader's *Affliction* (1998) and Sam Raimi's *Simple Plan* (1998).

8. Walker, "Captive Images," 247–248.

9. Molloy, "Death and the Maiden," 154.

10. Ibid.

11. Ibid.

12. In contrast to the history lesson Nina (Halle Berry) gives Bulworth in *Bulworth,* Pilar's account of the past is congruent with her character. At the same time, the fictional Pilar's ethnically mixed background counterpoints Halle Berry's actual mixed background, providing a reminder of issues *Bulworth* avoids.

13. Enloe discusses the general pattern, in many parts of the world, in which "the presence of brothels for male soldiers has laid the groundwork for the development of brothels for male tourists," a history that Sayles evokes through Sam's mocking reference; see *Maneuvers,* 68.

14. Sayles has talked at length about his filmic references and influences in *Lone Star,* mentioning, among other films, *Touch of Evil* and *The Ballad of Gregorio Cortez.* See John Sayles, "Borders and Boundaries: An Interview with John Sayles," interview by Dennis West and Joan M. West, *Cinéaste* 22, no. 3 (1996): 14–15.

15. Sayles has emphasized the importance of the strongman figure to the border region in an interview, observing that "Both Texas Anglo society and traditional Spanish society were patriarchal societies, especially on the border" (Sayles, "Borders and Boundaries," 16).

16. John Sayles, interview by Gavin Smith, *Film Comment* 32, no. 3 (May–June 1996), 61. See also Staples, "The Seminole Tribe, Running from History," *New York Times,* April 21, 2002, sec. 4, 12. This editorial discusses the lawsuit *Sylvia Davis et al. vs. United States of America et al.* in which Davis, an Oklahoma black Seminole, is challenging the tribe's decision in 2000 to deny her full tribal status and federal money—because she purportedly does not have enough "Seminole blood."

17. Sayles explains, "The jukebox holds some of their past. The song they play, 'Since I Met You, Baby,' or 'Desde Te Conozco,' is also playing on the jukebox when Del walks into Otis's place, a different version of it. That's very subtle, but some of that's how dif-

ferent cultures use the same song. It was a song that was a hit on black stations, and then it was the first hit for Freddie Fender, the first Hispanic rock-and-roll guy. He took rock and roll, black music that was becoming used by white people, and brought it to Latin America" (Sayles, interview by Smith, 64).

18. Willis, *High Contrast*, 10.

19. Molloy makes an illuminating point about incest in this context. As she explains, in Kristeva's view, "Sex, incest and murder, and contested sexual rights between mothers and daughters, not fathers and sons, lie at the origin of the foreign/uncanny. Kristeva, however, never connects this gendered origin to contemporary issues of foreignness and the nation" ("Death and the Maiden," 159).

20. See Sayles, interview by Smith, 63.

21. Sayles himself endorses the idea that these transitions are a form of magic realism (Sayles, interview by Smith, 63). To be sure, the magic realism is not as extensive as it is in *Eve's Bayou* (Kasi Lemmons, 1997), but it works to similar effects.

22. "Not the 'lost object of desire' of the American 1950s," Jameson explains, "but the articulated superposition of whole layers of the past within the present (Indian or pre-Columbian realities, the colonial era, the wars of independence, caudillismo, the period of American domination . . .) is the formal precondition for the emergence of [the magic realist] narrative style." Jameson counterposes magic realism to the postmodern history film that generates nostalgic, commodified, fetishized visions of the past, typically taking the Eisenhower era as its "privileged raw material." For Jameson, Freud's notion of the uncanny serves as a reference point for comprehending history in magic realism so conceived; that is, it illuminates the return of a repressed that complicates, contradicts, and recontextualizes Eisenhower-era nostalgia; see "On Magic Realism," 302–303, 311, 310, 315.

23. By comparison, in Hollywood cinema the threat of brother-sister incest is normally incapacitating to the hero, especially the young one, as revealed for example in the *Star Wars* trilogy. See Sarah Harwood, *Family Fictions: Representations of the Family in 1980s Hollywood Cinema* (New York: St. Martin's Press, 1997), 98.

24. Ana M. López, "Tears and Desire: Women and Melodrama in the 'Old' Mexican Cinema," in *Multiple Voices in Feminist Film Criticism*, ed. Diane Carson, Linda Dittmar, and Janice R. Welsch (Minneapolis: Univ. of Minnesota Press, 1994), 257.

25. Sayles, interview by Smith, 63.

26. Ibid. The relation of the uncanny to high school experiences is also the subject of some of the resonant personal and professional memories recounted by feminist scholar Tania Modleski in *Old Wives' Tales*, 180–181.

27. For additional perspectives on Pilar's choice, see also Emma Pérez, *The Decolonial Imaginary: Writing Chicanas into History* (Bloomington, Ind.: Indiana Univ. Press, 1999), 126; and Tomàs F. Sandoval, Jr., "The Burden of History and John Sayles's *Lone Star*," in *Westerns: Films through History*, ed. Janet Walker (New York: Routledge, 2001), 84–85.

28. Harmon King, the fisherman played by Leo Burmester, is a counterpart to a redneck bartender in *Lone Star*, also played by Burmester.

29. It is worth noting that like the female characters in the films that Molloy dis-

cusses, Noelle is both a storyteller and the inhabitant of a world that is tied in some significant way to the sea or to fish. Pauline in *Heavenly Creatures* is the daughter of a fishmonger, as is Grace in *Once Were Warriors,* and Ada in *The Piano* dives into the sea to be free.

30. Molloy, "Death and the Maiden," 167.

31. Kristeva, *Strangers to Ourselves,* 186.

32. Jeremy Rifkin, *The Age of Access: The New Culture of Hypercapitalism Where All of Life Is a Paid-For Experience* (New York: Penguin Putnam, 2000), 265.

33. Ibid., 138, 187, 206.

34. Rifkin notes that the travel and tourism industry is the top employer in the United States, just as it is in Australia, Canada, France, Germany, Italy, the UK, and Brazil (ibid., 146). Consequently, Sayles's unanswered question truly is a matter not only of Alaskan but also of national and cultural identity.

35. Sayles, "Borders and Boundaries," 16.

36. Sayles, interview by Smith, 61.

37. As suggested by the 2001 exhibit "Aztlan Today: The Chicano Postnation" at the Bronx Museum of the Arts, newer Chicano art differs considerably from that of the 1990s, insofar as it engages in "mocking Chicano as a marketing device, pushing its original political impulses onto a broader social stage and addressing the whole notion of identity through ambiguity and indirection" (Holland Cotter, "Beyond Multiculturalism, Freedom?" *New York Times,* July 29, 2001, sec. 2, 1, 28).

38. Jerry Sconce, *Haunted Media: Electronic Presence from Telegraphy to Television* (Durham, N.C.: Duke Univ. Press, 2000), 4.

Epilogue

1. Cynthia Enloe, "Sneak Attack: The Militarization of U.S. Culture," *Ms.* 12.1 (December 2001/January 2002): 15. The cold-war fear of weapons of mass destruction as a threat to the nation's survival and the cold-war response of increasing government secrecy and ends-justify-the-means policies both find counterparts in the Bush administration's post–September 11 mentality.

2. Ibid., 15.

3. Furthering her general argument is evidence from 1990 that considerable U.S. money and weaponry went to an Afghan leader who, during his days in the student movement, is believed to have ordered his followers to throw acid into the faces of those women students who refused to cover themselves with veils. See Rosalind P. Petchesky, "Phantom Towers: Feminist Reflections on the Battle between Global Capitalism and Fundamentalist Terrorism," *Ms.* 12.1 (December 2001/January 2002): 10. In a related context, see also Laura King, "After the War, Fearing the Future," *Los Angeles Times,* April 27, 2003, A1. King describes how the Iraqi invasion of 2003 unleashed fundamentalist forces opposed to women's rights to seek professional advancement, to drive, and to attend coeducational colleges, rights Iraqi women had enjoyed for decades.

4. Ibid., 8.

5. Ibid., 11.

6. Robert Kagan, "Power and Weakness," *Policy Review,* No. 113 (<www.policy review.org/JUN02/kagan_print.html>), 1.

7. Jennifer L. Pozner, "Missing in Action: Whatever Happened to the Gender Gap?" *Women's Review of Books* 19.5 (February 2002): 20.

8. Ibid., 20.

9. Ibid., 21.

10. Petchesky, "Phantom Towers," 13.

11. Barry Bearak, "Unreconstructed," *New York Times Magazine,* June 1, 2003, 47.

12. Carlotta Gall, "Afghan Motherhood in a Fight for Survival," *New York Times,* May 25, 2003, sec. 1, 3.

13. Hamilton quoted in Daphne Eviatar, "The Press and Private Lynch," *The Nation,* July 7, 2003, <*http://www.thenation.com/doc.mhtml?i=20030707&s=eviatar*>.

14. Dana Priest, William Booth, and Susan Schmidt, "A Broken Body, a Broken Story, Pieced Together," *Washington Post,* June 17, 2003, A1. See also Paul Krugman, "Standard Operating Procedures," *New York Times,* June 3, 2003, A31, and "Waggy Dog Stories," *New York Times,* May 30, 2003, A27. Lynch's loss of memory also recalls the recurring theme of memory loss in contemporary films, including *Memento* (Christopher Nolan, 2000), *Vanilla Sky* (Cameron Crowe, 2001), and *The Bourne Identity* (Doug Liman, 2002), with the significant difference that these films depict men who try both to remember and to forget their potential crimes against women and children. Also, unlike Lynch, none of them aspires to be a kindergarten teacher.

15. Mark Bowden, "War and Remembrance," *New York Times,* June 8, 2003, sec. 4, 14.

16. Dan Baum, "Nation Builders for Hire," *New York Times Magazine,* June 22, 2003, 35.

Anthony, Carl Sferrazza. *First Ladies,* Vol. II. New York: Morrow, 1991.

Auerbach, Erich. *Mimesis: The Representation of Reality in Western Literature.* Translated by Willard R. Trask. Princeton, N.J.: Princeton Univ. Press, 1953.

Baldwin, James. "The Devil Finds Work." In *James Baldwin: Collected Essays.* Selected by Toni Morrison. New York: Library of America, 1998.

Bataille, Georges. *Visions of Excess: Selected Writings, 1927–1939.* Translated and edited by Allan Stoekl. Minneapolis: Univ. of Minnesota Press, 1985.

Baum, Dan. "Nation Builders for Hire." *New York Times Magazine,* June 22, 2003, 32–37.

Bayliss, Sarah. "The Three Faces, All of Them Female, of Liberty." Review of "The Changing Face of Liberty: Female Allegories of America," an exhibit at the New York Historical Society. *New York Times,* July 2, 2000, sec. 2, 31.

Bearak, Barry. "Unreconstructed." *New York Times Magazine,* June 1, 2003.

Bell, David, and Barbara M. Kennedy, eds. *The Cybercultures Reader.* New York: Routledge, 2000.

Bhabha, Homi K. *The Location of Culture.* New York: Routledge, 1994.

Blaetz, Robin. "'You're going to live if I have to blow your brains out': War, Childbirth, and *The Big Red One,*" paper presented at a conference of the Society for Cinema Studies, Pittsburgh, 1992.

Boller, Jr., Paul F. *Presidential Wives.* New York: Oxford Univ. Press, 1988.

Boose, Lynda. "Techno-Muscularity and the 'Boy Eternal': From the Quagmire to the Gulf." In *Gendering War Talk,* edited by Miriam Cooke and Angela Woollacott, 67–106. Princeton, N.J.: Princeton Univ. Press, 1993.

Bordo, Susan. *Unbearable Weight: Feminism, Western Culture, and the Body.* Berkeley, Calif.: Univ. of California Press, 1993.

Bowden, Mark. "War and Remembrance." *New York Times,* June 8, 2003, sec. 4, 1, 14.

Braudy, Leo, and Marshall Cohen, eds. *Film Theory and Criticism.* 5th ed. New York: Oxford Univ. Press, 1999.

Brodie, Fawn M. *Richard Nixon: The Shaping of His Character.* New York: Norton, 1981.

Bronfen, Elisabeth. *Over Her Dead Body: Death, Femininity, and the Aesthetic.* New York: Routledge, 1992.

BIBLIOGRAPHY AND FILMOGRAPHY

Brooks, Peter. *The Melodramatic Imagination: Balzac, Henry James, Melodrama, and the Mode of Excess.* New Haven, Conn.: Yale Univ. Press, 1976.

Broyles, Jr., William. "Why Men Love War." *Esquire,* November 1984, 61.

Bukhari-Alston, Safiya. "On the Question of Sexism within the Black Panther Party." <http://www.hartford-hwp.com/archives/45a/014.html>. March 9, 1995.

Bulworth. Directed by Warren Beatty. Screenplay by Beatty and Jeremy Pikser. Produced by Beatty and Pieter Jan Brugge. Twentieth Century Fox, 1998.

Burgoyne, Robert. *Film Nation: Hollywood Looks at U.S. History.* Minneapolis: Univ. of Minnesota Press, 1997.

Burke, *A Philosophical Enquiry into the Origin of Our Ideas of the Sublime and Beautiful* (1757). Edited by James T. Boulton. South Bend, Ind.: Notre Dame Univ. Press, 1968.

Byers, Thomas. "History Re-Membered: *Forrest Gump,* Postfeminist Masculinity, and the Burial of the Counterculture." *Modern Fiction Studies* 42, no. 2 (Summer 1996): 419–444.

Byron, Stuart. "*The Searchers:* Cult Movie of the New Hollywood." *New York,* March 5, 1979, 45–48.

Capaccio, Tony. "The Kelly Flinn Spin Patrol," *American Journalism Review* 19, no. 7 (September 1997): 12–13.

Caroli, Betty Boyd. *First Ladies.* New York: Oxford Univ. Press, 1987.

Carson, Diane, Linda Dittmar, and Janice R. Welsch, eds. *Multiple Voices in Feminist Film Criticism.* Minneapolis: Univ. of Minnesota Press, 1994.

Casper, Kent. "All the President's Women." Unpublished conference paper for The American President on Film: A National Conference, Westlake Village, California, 2000.

Cixous, Hélène. "Fiction and Its Phantoms: A Reading of Freud's *Das Unheimliche* (The 'Uncanny')." Translated by Robert Dennomé. *New Literary History* 7, no. 3 (Spring 1976): 525–548.

Cobley, Paul, ed. *The Communication Theory Reader.* New York: Routledge, 1996.

Cohan, Steven. "Case Study: Interpreting *Singin' in the Rain.*" In *Reinventing Film Studies,* edited by Christine Gledhill and Linda Williams, 53–75. New York: Oxford Univ. Press/Arnold, 2000.

Cooke, Miriam, and Angela Woollacott, eds. *Gendering War Talk.* Princeton, N.J.: Princeton Univ. Press, 1993.

Corber, Richard J. *In the Name of National Security: Hitchcock, Homophobia, and the Political Construction of Gender in Postwar America.* Durham, N.C.: Duke Univ. Press, 1993.

Cotter, Holland. "Beyond Multiculturalism, Freedom?" *New York Times,* July 29, 2001, sec. 2, 1, 28.

Courage Under Fire. Directed by Edward Zwick. Screenplay by Patrick Sheane Duncan. Cinematography by Roger Deakins. Produced by Joseph M. Caracciolo et al. Fox 2000 Pictures, 1996.

David, Lester. *The Lonely Lady of San Clemente.* New York: Crowell, 1978.

Denby, David. "Good Guys," *New Yorker,* March 11, 2002, 92–93.

———. "Poor Richard." Review of *Nixon*. *New York*, January 8, 1996, 44.

Dent, Gina, ed. *Black Popular Culture*. Discussions in Contemporary Culture, no. 8. Seattle: Bay Press, 1993.

Derrida, Jacques. "Semiology and Grammatology: Interview with Julia Kristeva." In *The Communication Theory Reader*, edited by Paul Cobley, 209–224. New York: Routledge, 1996.

Dittmar, Linda, and Gene Michaud, eds. *From Hanoi to Hollywood: The Vietnam War in American Film*. New Brunswick, N.J.: Rutgers Univ. Press, 1990.

Doane, Mary Ann. *The Desire to Desire: The Woman's Film of the 1940s*. Bloomington: Indiana Univ. Press, 1987.

Doherty, Thomas. *Projections of War: Hollywood, American Culture, and World War II*, revised ed. New York: Columbia Univ. Press, 1999.

Dorment, Richard and Margaret F. MacDonald. *James McNeill Whistler*. New York: Harry N. Abrams, 1994.

Ebert, Roger. Review of *Bulworth*. <www.suntimes.com/ebert/ebert_reviews/1998/05/052202.html>.

———. Review of *Nixon*. <http://www.suntimes.com/ebert_reviews/1995/12/1012232.html>

———. Review of *Saving Private Ryan*. <http://www.suntimes.com/ebert/ebert_reviews/1998/07/072404.html>.

Ehrenhaus, Peter. "Why We Fought: Holocaust Memory in Spielberg's *Saving Private Ryan*." *Critical Studies in Media Communication* 18, no. 3 (September 2001): 321–337).

Enloe, Cynthia. "Sneak Attack: The Militarization of U.S. Culture." *Ms.* 12.1 (December 2001/January 2002): 15.

———. "The Gendered Gulf." In *Seeing Through the Media: The Persian Gulf War*, edited by Susan Jeffords and Lauren Rabinovitz, 211–228. New Brunswick, N.J.: Rutgers Univ. Press, 1994.

———. *Maneuvers: The International Politics of Militarizing Women's Lives*. Berkeley: Univ. of California Press, 2000.

Eviatar, Daphne. "The Press and Private Lynch." *The Nation*, July 7, 2003, <http://www.thenation.com/doc.mhtml?i=20030707&s=eviatar>.

Feminist Majority Press. "Women's Groups Urge Nike to Put Its Money Where Its Mouth Is." <www.feministorg/news/pr/pr102897.html>.

Fischer, Lucy. *Cinematernity: Film, Motherhood, Genre*. Princeton, N.J.: Princeton Univ. Press, 1996.

———. *Shot/Countershot: Film Tradition and Women's Cinema*. Princeton, N.J.: Princeton Univ. Press, 1986.

Fisher, Ian. "Blacks in the Military Wrestle with Issues of Race and Justice." *New York Times*, June 17, 1997, A1, A12.

Flinn, Kelly. *Proud to Be*. New York: Random House, 1997.

Forrest Gump. Directed by Robert Zemeckis. Screenplay by Eric Roth. Produced by Wendy Finerman, Charles Newirth, Steve Starkey, and Steve Tisch. Paramount Pictures, 1994.

Foucault, Michel. "On the Parrhesiastes." Talk given as part of the Humanities Lecture Series, Univ. of Colorado at Boulder, Boulder, Colorado, October 10, 1983.

Freud, Sigmund. "The Theme of the Three Caskets" (1913). Translated by Alix Strachey. In *On Creativity and the Unconscious: Papers on the Psychology of Art, Literature, Love, Religion*, edited by Benjamin Nelson, 63–75. New York: Harper and Row, 1958.

———. "The 'Uncanny'." Translated by Alix Strachey. In *On Creativity and the Unconscious: Papers on the Psychology of Art, Literature, Love, Religion*, edited by Benjamin Nelson, 122–161. New York: Harper and Row, 1958.

Gall, Carlotta. "Afghan Motherhood in a Fight for Survival." *New York Times*, May 25, 2003, sec. 1, 13.

Gardner, Helen. *Art Through the Ages*. 7th ed. Vol. 2. New York: Harcourt Brace Jovanovich, 1980.

Gelder, Ken. *Reading the Vampire*. New York: Routledge, 1994.

Gilligan, Carol. "Teaching Shakespeare's Sister: Notes from the Underground of Female Adolescence." Preface to *Making Connections: The Relational Worlds of Adolescent Girls at Emma Willard School*, edited by Gilligan, Nona P. Lyons, and Trudy J. Hanmer, 1–27. Cambridge, Mass.: Harvard Univ. Press, 1990.

Gilligan, Carol, Nona P. Lyons, and Trudy J. Hanmer, eds. *Making Connections: The Relational Worlds of Adolescent Girls at Emma Willard School*. Cambridge, Mass.: Harvard Univ. Press, 1990.

Gledhill, Christine, and Linda Williams, eds. *Reinventing Film Studies*. New York: Oxford Univ. Press/Arnold, 2000.

Goodwin, Sarah Webster, and Elisabeth Bronfen, eds. *Death and Representation*. Baltimore: John Hopkins Univ. Press, 1993.

Hamburg, Eric, ed. *Nixon: An Oliver Stone Film*. New York: Hyperion, 1995.

Harwood, Sarah. *Family Fictions: Representations of the Family in 1980s Hollywood Cinema*. New York: St. Martin's Press, 1997.

Hasian, Jr., Marouf. "Nostalgic Longings, Memories of the 'Good War,' and Cinematic Representations in *Saving Private Ryan*." *Critical Studies in Media Communication* 18, no. 3 (September 2001): 338–358.

Henderson, Brian. "*The Searchers*: An American Dilemma," in *Movies and Methods: An Anthology*, Vol. II, edited by Bill Nichols, 429–449. Berkeley: Univ. of California Press, 1985.

Hersch, Seymour M. *Cover-Up: The Army's Secret Investigation of the Massacre at My Lai 4*. New York: Random House, 1972.

———. *My Lai 4: A Report on the Massacre and Its Aftermath*. New York: Random House, 1970.

Hewitt, Andrew. *Political Inversions: Homosexuality, Fascism, and the Modernist Imaginary*. Stanford, Calif.: Stanford Univ. Press, 1996.

Hoffmann, E. T. A. "The Sand-Man," translated by J. T. Bealby. In *The Best Tales of Hoffmann*, edited by E. F. Bleiler, 183–214. New York: Dover, 1967.

Holden, Stephen. Review of *Wag the Dog*. *New York Times*, January 4, 1998, sec. 2, 11.

Huyssen, Andreas. *After the Great Divide: Modernism, Mass Culture, Postmodernism*. Bloomington, Ind.: Indiana Univ. Press, 1986.

Jaehne, Karen. Review of *Saving Private Ryan*. *Film Quarterly* 53, no. 1 (Fall 1999): 39–41.

Jameson, Fredric. "On Magic Realism in Film." *Critical Inquiry* 12 (Winter 1986): 301–325.

———. *The Political Unconscious: Narrative as a Socially Symbolic Act*. Ithaca, N.Y.: Cornell Univ. Press, 1981.

Jameson, Richard T. "History's Eyes," review of *Saving Private Ryan*. *Film Comment* 34, no. 5 (September/October 1998): 20–23.

Janes, Regina. "Beheadings." In *Death and Representation*, edited by Sarah Webster Goodwin and Elisabeth Bronfen, 242–262. Baltimore: Johns Hopkins Univ. Press, 1993.

Jeffords, Susan. *The Remasculinization of America: Gender and the Vietnam War*. Bloomington: Indiana Univ. Press, 1989.

Jeffords, Susan, and Lauren Rabinovitz, eds. *Seeing Through the Media: The Persian Gulf War*. New Brunswick, N.J.: Rutgers Univ. Press, 1994.

Johnson, Barbara. *The Feminist Difference: Literature, Psychoanalysis, Race, and Gender*. Cambridge, Mass.: Harvard Univ. Press, 1998.

Jones, Jacquie. "The Accusatory Space." In *Black Popular Culture*, Discussions in Contemporary Culture, no. 8, edited by Gina Dent, 94–98. Seattle: Bay Press, 1993.

Jones, James. *The Thin Red Line*. New York: Bantam, 1962.

Judt, Tony. "Counsels on Foreign Relations." Review of *A Tangled Web: The Making of Foreign Policy in the Nixon Presidency* by William Bundy. *New York Review of Books* 45, no. 13 (August 1998): 54–61.

Kagan, Norman. *The Cinema of Oliver Stone*. Expanded ed. New York: Continuum, 2000.

Kagan, Robert. "Power and Weakness." *Policy Review*, No. 113. <www.policyreview.org/JUN02/kagan_print.html>.

Kant, Immanuel. *Critique of Judgment*. Translated by J. H. Bernard. New York: Hafner Publishing Co., 1951.

Kaplan, E. Ann. *Motherhood and Representation: The Mother in Popular Culture and Melodrama*. New York: Routledge, 1992.

Kauffmann, Stanley. "Color Lines." Review of *Bulworth*, *The New Republic* Online. <www.tnr.com/archive/060898/kauffmann060898.html>.

King, Laura. "After the War, Fearing the Future." *Los Angeles Times*, April 27, 2003, A1.

Klein, Joe. "An American Marriage." *New Yorker*, February 9, 1998, 34–37.

Kracauer, Siegfried. *From Caligari to Hitler: A Psychological History of the German Film*. Princeton, N.J.: Princeton Univ. Press, 1947.

Kristeva, Julia. *Strangers to Ourselves*, translated by Leon S. Roudiez. New York: Columbia Univ. Press, 1991.

Krugman, Paul. "Standard Operating Procedures." *New York Times*, June 3, 2003, A31.

———. "Waggy Dog Stories." *New York Times*, May 30, 2003, A27.

Landsberg, Alison. "Prosthetic Memory: *Total Recall* and *Blade Runner*." In *The Cybercultures Reader*, edited by David Bell and Barbara M. Kennedy, 190–201. New York: Routlege, 2000.

Landy, Marcia, ed. *The Historical Film: History and Memory in Modern Media.* New Brunswick, N.J.: Rutgers Univ. Press, 2000.

Limbo. Directed by John Sayles. Screenplay by Sayles. Cinematography by Haskell Wexler. Produced by Sarah Connors and Maggie Renzi. Green/Renzi, 1999.

Lone Star. Directed by John Sayles. Screenplay by Sayles. Cinematography by Stuart Dryburgh. Produced by Maggie Renzi et al. Castle Rock et al., 1996.

López, Ana M. "Tears and Desire: Women and Melodrama in the 'Old' Mexican Cinema." In *Multiple Voices in Feminist Film Criticism,* edited by Diane Carson, Linda Dittmar, and Janice R. Welsch, 254–270. Minneapolis: Univ. of Minnesota Press, 1994.

Lyotard, Jean-François. "Can Thought Go on without a Body?" In *The Inhuman: Reflections on Time,* translated by Geoffrey Bennington and Rachel Bowlby. Stanford, Calif.: Stanford Univ. Press, 1991.

Maltin, Leonard, ed. *Leonard Maltin's Movie Encyclopedia.* New York: Plume-Penguin, 1995.

Marton, Kati. *Hidden Power: Presidential Marriages That Shaped Our Recent History.* New York: Pantheon, 2001.

Mayne, Judith. *Cinema and Spectatorship.* New York: Routledge, 1993.

Midnight Clear, A. Directed by Keith Gordon. Screenplay by Keith Gordon. Cinematography by Tom Richmond. Produced by Marc Abraham et al. A and M Films and Beacon Communications LLC, 1992.

Mitchell, Greg. *Tricky Dick and the Pink Lady: Richard Nixon vs. Helen Gahagan Douglas: Sexual Politics and the Red Scare, 1950.* New York: Random House, 1998.

Mitchell, W. J. T. *Iconology: Image, Text, Ideology.* Chicago: Univ. of Chicago Press, 1986.

Modleski, Tania. *Loving with a Vengeance: Mass-Produced Fantasies for Women.* New York: Methuen, 1982.

———. *Old Wives' Tales and Other Women's Stories.* New York: New York Univ. Press, 1998.

———. "The Terror of Pleasure: The Contemporary Horror Film and Postmodern Theory." In *Film Theory and Criticism,* 5th ed., edited by Leo Braudy and Marshall Cohen, 691–700. New York: Oxford Univ. Press, 1999.

———. *The Women Who Knew Too Much: Hitchcock and Feminist Theory.* New York: Methuen, 1988.

Molloy, Maureen. "Death and the Maiden: The Feminine and the Nation in Recent New Zealand Films." *Signs* 25, no. 1 (1999): 153–170.

Morgan, Robin, ed. *Sisterhood Is Powerful: An Anthology of Writings from the Women's Liberation Movement.* New York: Vintage, 1970.

Morrison, James. Review of *The Thin Red Line. Film Quarterly* 53, no. 1 (Fall 1999): 35–38.

Morrison, Toni. *Sula.* New York: Plume, 1973.

Morson, Gary Saul, and Caryl Emerson. *Mikhail Bakhtin: The Creation of a Prosaics.* Stanford, Calif.: Stanford Univ. Press, 1990.

Nelson, Benjamin, ed. *On Creativity and the Unconscious: Papers on the Psychology of Art, Literature, Love, Religion.* New York: Harper and Row, 1958.

Nichols, Bill, ed. *Movies and Methods: An Anthology.* Vol. II. Berkeley, Calif.: Univ. of California Press, 1985.

Nixon. Directed by Oliver Stone. Screenplay by Stephen J. Rivele et al. Cinematography by Robert Richardson. Produced by Dan Halsted, et al. Hollywood Pictures, 1995.

O'Brien, Tim. *The Things They Carried.* Boston: Houghton Mifflin, 1990.

Owen, A. Susan. "Memory, War and American Identity: *Saving Private Ryan* as Cinematic Jeremiad." *Critical Studies in Media Communication* 19, no. 3 (September 2002): 249–282.

Parker, Andrew, Mary Russo, Doris Sommer, and Patricia Yaeger, eds. Introduction to *Nationalisms and Sexualities.* New York: Routledge, 1992.

Pérez, Emma. *The Decolonial Imaginary: Writing Chicanas into History.* Bloomington, Ind.: Indiana Univ. Press, 1999.

Petchesky, Rosalind P. "Phantom Towers: Feminist Reflections on the Battle between Global Capitalism and Fundamentalist Terrorism." *Ms.* 12.1 (December 2001/January 2002): 6–14.

Petro, Patrice. *Joyless Streets: Women and Melodramatic Representation in Weimar Germany.* Princeton, N.J.: Princeton Univ. Press, 1989.

Pollitt, Katha. "No Sex, Please—We're Killers." *The Nation,* June 23, 1997, 9.

Pozner, Jennifer L. "Missing in Action: Whatever Happened to the Gender Gap?" *The Women's Review of Books* 19.5 (February 2002): 20–21.

Priest, Dana. "McKinney Accusers Tell of Hardships." *Washington Post,* March 16, 1998, A1, A6.

Priest, Dana, William Booth, and Susan Schmidt. "A Broken Body, a Broken Story, Pieced Together." *Washington Post,* June 17, 2003, A1.

Rabinow, Paul, ed. *The Foucault Reader.* New York: Pantheon, 1984.

Rayner, Richard. "The Warrior Besieged." *New York Times Magazine* June 22, 1997.

Reed, Julia. "Annie Gets Her Gun." *Vogue,* July 1997, 42.

Rifkin, Jeremy. *The Age of Access: The New Culture of Hypercapitalism Where All of Life Is a Paid-For Experience.* New York: Penguin Putnam Inc., 2000.

Rivele, Stephen J., Christopher Wilkinson, and Oliver Stone, "*Nixon:* The Original Annotated Screenplay." In Nixon: *An Oliver Stone Film,* edited by Eric Hamburg. New York: Hyperion, 1995.

Rosenstone, Robert A. *Visions of the Past: The Challenge of Film to Our Idea of History.* Cambridge, Mass.: Harvard Univ. Press, 1995.

Said, Edward. *Orientalism.* New York: Vintage Books, 1979.

Sandoval, Jr., Tomàs F. "The Burden of History and John Sayles's *Lone Star.*" In *Westerns: Films through History,* edited by Janet Walker, 71–85. New York: Routledge, 2001.

Saving Private Ryan. Directed by Steven Spielberg. Screenplay by Robert Rodat. Cinematography by Janasz Kaminski. Produced by Ian Bryce et al. Paramount et al., 1998.

Sayles, John. "Borders and Boundaries: An Interview with John Sayles." By Dennis West and Joan M. West. *Cinéaste* 22, no. 3 (1996): 14–17.

———. Interview by Gavin Smith. *Film Comment* 32, no. 3 (May–June 1996), 56–68.

Schickel, Richard. "Courage Underdone." Review of *Courage Under Fire. Time,* July 22, 1996, 94.

———. "Reel War," *Time,* July 27, 1998, 19.

Schlesinger, Jr., Arthur M. "On *JFK* and *Nixon,*" In *Oliver Stone's USA: Film, History, and Controversy,* edited by Robert Brent Toplin, 212–216. Lawrence, Kan.: Univ. of Kansas Press, 2000.

Schultz, Vicki. "Sex Is the Least of It: Let's Focus Harassment Law on Work, Not Sex." *The Nation,* May 25, 1998, 11.

Sconce, Jerry. *Haunted Media: Electronic Presence from Telegraphy to Television.* Durham, N.C.: Duke Univ. Press, 2000.

Searchers, The. Directed by John Ford. Screenplay by Frank S. Nugent. Produced by Merian C. Cooper, Patrick Ford, and C. V. Whitney. Warner Bros., 1956.

Sharrett, Christopher. "The Belly of the Beast: Oliver Stone's *Nixon* and the American Nightmare." *Cinéaste* 22, no. 1 (1996): 4–8.

Sherrow, Victoria. *Women and the Military: An Encyclopedia.* Santa Barbara: ABC-CLIO, Inc., 1996.

Shorter Oxford English Dictionary. Oxford: Oxford Univ. Press, 1973.

Sobchack, Vivian, ed. *The Persistence of History: Cinema, Television, and the Modern Event.* New York: Routledge, 1996.

Staples, Brent. "The Seminole Tribe, Running from History." *New York Times,* April 21, 2002, sec. 4, 12.

Thin Red Line, The. Directed by Terrence Malick. Screenplay by Terrence Malick. Cinematography by John Toll. Produced by Michael Geisler et al. Fox 2000 Pictures et al., 1998.

Tomasulo, Frank P. "Empire of the Gun: Steven Spielberg's *Saving Private Ryan* and American Values." Paper presented at a conference for the Society for Cinema Studies, Washington, D.C., 2001.

———. "The Politics of Ambivalence: *Apocalypse Now* as Prowar and Antiwar Film." In *From Hanoi to Hollywood: The Vietnam War in American Film,* edited by Linda Dittmar and Gene Michaud, 145–158. New Brunswick, N.J.: Rutgers Univ. Press, 1990.

Toplin, Robert Brent, ed. *Oliver Stone's USA: Film, History, and Controversy.* Lawrence, Kan.: Univ. of Kansas Press, 2000

Truman, Margaret. *First Ladies.* New York: Random House, 1995.

Vertigo. Directed by Alfred Hitchcock. Screenplay by Samuel A. Taylor and Alec Coppel. Produced by Herbert Coleman. Paramount Pictures, 1958.

Volkan, Vamik D., Norman Itskowitz, and Andrew W. Dod. *Richard Nixon: A Psychobiography.* New York: Columbia Univ. Press, 1997.

Waldman, Diane. "Architectural Metaphor in the Gothic Romance Film." *Iris: Cinema and Architecture,* no. 12 (1991): 55–69.

Walker, Janet. "Captive Images in the Traumatic Western." In *Westerns: Films through History,* edited by Janet Walker, 219–251. New York: Routledge, 2001.

———, ed. *Westerns: Films through History.* New York: Routledge, 2001.

"Warrior Women." Photographs by Dan Winters. *New York Times Magazine,* February 16, 2003, 23–34.

Weinstein, Allen and Alexander Vassilev. *Soviet Espionage in America: The Stalin Era.* New York: Random House, 1999.

Weisberg, Jacob. "Bombs and Blockbusters: World War II Nostalgia at the Movies Is Blurring the Picture of Kosovo." *New York Times Magazine,* April 11, 1999, 17–18.

White, Hayden. *The Content of the Form: Narrative Discourse and Historical Representation.* Baltimore: Johns Hopkins Univ. Press, 1987.

———. "The Modernist Event." In *The Persistence of History: Cinema, Television, and the Modern Event,* edited by Vivian Sobchack, 17–38. New York: Routledge, 1996.

Wiegman, Robyn. "Missiles and Melodrama (Masculinity and the Televisual War)." In *Seeing Through the Media: The Persian Gulf War,* edited by Susan Jeffords and Lauren Rabinovitz, 171–187. New Brunswick, N.J.: Rutgers Univ. Press, 1994.

Wigdahl, Matthew. "The Metaphysical Filmscapes of Hitchcock's *Vertigo.*" Master's thesis, Univ. of Colorado at Denver, 1997.

Williams, Linda. *Playing the Race Card: Melodramas of Black and White from Uncle Tom to O. J. Simpson.* Princeton, N.J.: Princeton Univ. Press, 2001.

Willis, Sharon. *High Contrast: Race and Gender in Contemporary Hollywood Film.* Durham, N.C.: Duke Univ. Press, 1997.

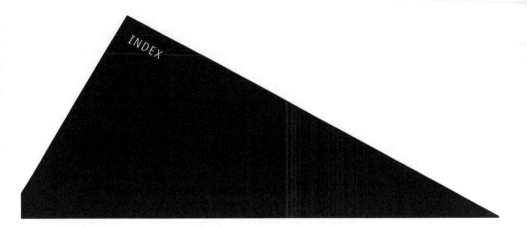

INDEX

Index   189

and national identity, 3, 14–15, 24, 31, 34, 75, 118–121; and problematic past, 4, 14–15; and repressed history, 3, 21, 32, 34–35, 125–126. *See also* feminine uncanny

feminine uncanny, 16–23, 115, 124–125, 142; as automata, 16, 19, 31, 64–65, 68–69, 84–85, 88; as doll, 13, 16, 21–22, 30–31, 69, 75; as mother, 3, 16, 27–29, 31–32, 64, 68, 70, 73, 76, 83, 113, 134–135; as vagina dentata, 25, 29; as womb/tomb, 27, 46, 55, 61–62, 112–113, 134–135

Fender, Freddie, 124, 173n17

firefighters, as compared to soldiers, 144–146

first lady, ambivalence toward, 31–32, 64–65, 68, 70, 79. *See also Nixon; Nixon, Pat*

Fischer, Lucy, 2, 16–17

Fisher, Ian, 94

Flinn, Kelly, 94–96, 98, 115, 168nn13–14

Foote, Shelby, 40

Ford, Betty, 88

Ford, Gerald, 87

Ford, John, 4, 39, 43

Forrest Gump, 4, 8–11, 15, 154nn11–12, 155n18

Foucault, Michel, 26–27

Franklin, Carl, 126

fratricide, 114, 165n44

French Revolution, 24–25, 54

Freud, Sigmund, 8, 40, 55, 62–63, 160n39, 163n19; and the uncanny, 15–23, 26–29, 56, 59, 68, 73, 86, 113, 157n55, 158n64

"friendly fire," 92, 103, 104–105

Fuller, Samuel, 42

Gabbeh, 172n4

Gall, Carlotta, 149

Galloway, Joseph, 144

Gallup poll, 148

Gardner, Helen, 7

gender identity. *See* combat films: and gender identity; female characters; masculinity

General, The, 105

genres of history film. *See* combat films; magic realism; national identity; presidential films; Western film genre

Gibson, Mel, 33

G. I. Jane, 96, 100

Gilliam, Seth, *102*

Gilligan, Carol, 1, 31, 153n1

Gladiator, 33

Glenn, Scott, 104

global capitalism, effects of, 12, 34, 143, 147, 155n20. *See also Limbo*

Gods and Monsters, 29

Goldberg, Adam, 46

Golden Bough, The, 87

Gordon, Keith, 31, 59–60, 63–64

Gothic, and women, 16–17

Grant, Cary, 38

Gray, John, 148

Grier, Pam, 127

Griffin, Rachel, 61

Griffith, D. W., 94

Grody, Kathryn, 132

Grune, Karl, 77, *79*

Guarding Tess, 88–89

guillotine, as uncanny image, 25

Gulf War, 91–98, 140, 148, 150, 167n1, 171n44; in film, 30, 32–33, 44, 92–93; and masculinity, 96–98, 113–115. *See also* combat film; *Courage Under Fire*

Gunfighter, The, 126

Haig, Alexander, 88

Haldeman, H. R., 71–73, 162n14, 165n44

Hanks, Tom, 8, 11, 37–38, 42, 44, 62

Hanlon, James, 143–145

Hartnett, Josh, 145

Hart's War, 144

Hasian, Marouf Jr., 50

haunting, as uncanny aesthetic motif, 8, 33, 121–130, 134–138, 157n55

Hawke, Ethan, 60, 62

Heavenly Creatures, 21, 118–119, 130

heimlich, 16, 27, 62

Hiss, Alger, 72–73, 163n16

history: aestheticization of, 3, 8, 39–40; "domestication" of, 25, 40, 45; "forgetting" of women's, 2–4, 6, 11, 13–15, 33–35, 45, 50, 143; as haunting, 8, 33, 121–130, 134–138; and "in between," 117–118, 127–128, 135; repressed, 3, 16, 21, 32, 34–35, 57, 63, 113–114, 124–126; traumatic, 2, 4, 19, 42, 104, 108, 113, 125. *See also* female characters; home: as site of trauma

history film genre, 1–4. *See also* combat films; magic realism; national identity; presidential film; Western

Hitchcock, Alfred, 4, 7, 11, 101, 161n43

Hoblit, Gregory, 144

Hoffman, E. T. A., 17, 19, 20, 69, 71, 88

Hollywood aesthetics, challenges to, 34. *See also* Sayles, John

home: as nation, 14–15, 43, 59, 61; as site of trauma, 62; as uncanny, 4–5, 20–21, 33; as unheimlich, 34, 59–62, 76; as unhomey, 3, 8–10, 14–18, 29, 63, 134–136, 141

home-front, in combat film, 43, 59–61

Homer, 97

home-sickness, 27–29

"homey" (homeboy), 13–14

Hoover, J. Edgar, 82

Hoover Institute, 148

Hopkins, Anthony, 67, *78,* 162n1

Horton, Willie, 98

House Un-American Activities Committee (HUAC), 76, 163n16

Hunt, Howard, 73

Hunter, Jeffrey, 4

Hunt for Red October, 33

Hussein, Saddam, 34, 91, 108–109, 115

Huyssen, Andreas, 113

Ice Storm, The, 75

identity: and borders, 4–8, 16–17, 34, 117, 130; and commercially constructed groups, 140–141, 174n37. *See also* combat film: and gender identity; melodrama: and male identity; national identity

Iliad, 97

Imitation of Life, 125

incest, as uncanny aesthetic motif, 121, 126, 128, 173nn19,23

Indian Princess (L'Amérique), 6

inside/outside dichotomy, 114, 118–119, 133, 135

interracial relationships, 12–14, 123–125, 139–140, 155nn21–22

Iraq: U.S. invasion of in 2003, 148–151, 174n3; women's resistance to, 148–149

Iraqi invasion of Kuwait, 93–94, 105

"I Want to Be a Cowboy's Sweetheart," 128

Jackson, Peter, 21

James, Clifton, 122

Jameson, Frederic, 2–3, 8, 18–19, 113, 126

Jameson, Richard T., 43–44

Janes, Regina, 25

Japanese "comfort women," 58, 94

Jeffords, Susan, 2, 44–45, 91

Jentsch, Ernst, 15–16

JFK, 49, 70, 151

John, Elton, 85, 166n50

Johnson, Barbara, 104

Johnson, Lyndon, 72

Jones, Jacquie, 12

Jones, James, 51–52, 54, 56

Jordan, Neil, 124

Judge, Father, 145

Judt, Tony, 86

Robinson, Eddie, 123
Romantic sublime, 25
Roosevelt, Eleanor, 76, 149
Rosenstone, Robert A., 2
Ross, Gary, 75
Rossi, Marie T., 168n4
Russell, David O., 114
Ryan, Meg, 38, 92, 99, 102

Said, Edward, 113
"Sand-Man, The," 17, 19–21, 26, 170n27
Saudi Arabia, 147–148
Save the Last Dance, 140
Saving Private Ryan, 31, 33, 37–39, 41–
    50, 61, 64, 98, 112, 128, 145, 158–
    159n11, 159nn19–20, 160n27
Sayles, John, 30, 34–35, 116–121, 125–
    127, 130–133, 138–142
Schiller, Friedrich von, 40
Schindler's List, 47
Schwarzenegger, Arnold, 63
Schwarzkopf, H. Norman, 91, 104
Sconce, Jeffrey, 141
Scott, Ridley, 33, 96, 144
Searchers, The, 4–6, 8, 11, 15, 29, 43, 45,
    120, 154n6
Secret Beyond the Door, 18
Secret of Roan Inish, The, 119
September 11, 2001 (9/11), 35, 143, 145–
    146, 170n34
sex tourism, 122, 172n13
"sexual esthetics," 53–54
Shakespeare, William, 1, 22, 29, 41, 67,
    126, 128, 131, 151
Sharrett, Christopher, 70, 75
Siege, The, 109
Simpson, O. J., 95
Sinese, Gary, 60
Singin' in the Rain, 4, 153n5
Sirk, Douglas, 125
Sisters, 17
Sizemore, Tom, 42
Sleepless in Seattle, 38
"smart bombs," 96. See also technology

Sobchack, Vivian, 2
Sofia, Zoe, 45, 55–56
Spectator, 69, 88
Spielberg, Steven, 31, 38, 41–43, 46–48,
    50–51, 59, 64, 126, 150, 160n27
Starship Troopers, 100
Statue of Liberty, 6, 9–10
Steenburgen, Mary, 68
"Stepford wife," 32, 75–76
Stewart, James, 6
Stockwell, John, 140
Stone, Oliver, 30, 49, 65, 67–70, 73–78,
    81–85, 87–89, 103, 151
Strand Magazine, 28
Strangers to Ourselves, 18
"stranger within," as uncanny aesthetic
    motif, 32, 64, 117, 137–138
Strathairn, David, 128
Street, The, 77, 79
Sturges, John, 115
sublime, aesthetics of, 23–26, 31, 39–42,
    46–47, 49–51, 54
Sula, 54, 157n62
Sweet Hereafter, The, 119–120, 172n4
Sycorax (Tempest), 3

Taggart, Rita, 132
Tailhook, 93, 114
Taliban, 35
Tamahori, Lee, 21
Taylor, Regina, 103
Technirama, 39
technology, effect of on combat, 32, 63,
    92, 96–97, 103, 112–113, 143
telenovela, 125–127
Tempest, The, 1–3, 112, 126, 132, 148,
    151
Terminator 2: Judgment Day, 63
terror, and aesthetics, 16, 41
Things They Carried, The, 39, 158n6
Thin Red Line, The, 31, 37–38, 41, 51–
    58, 160nn27,37
Thin Red Line, The (novel), 51–54, 63,
    160n37

Thomas, Helen, 88
Thoreau, Henry David, 111
III Henry VI, 67
Three Kings, 114
Thriller, 101
Tomasulo, Frank, 48–49
Tomb of the Unknown Soldier, 100
tourism industry, 128, 130–131, 137–138, 174n34
tragic mulatta, 125
traumatic Western, 120–121, 125–126, 142. *See also Searchers, The*
Treloar, Theresa Lynn, 168n4
Truman, Margaret, 68
Twin Towers, 144–145, 147–148
2001, 147

uncanny: as aesthetic mode, 2–3, 14–16, 26–29, 39–41; and ambivalence, 9, 16, 33, 64, 69–70, 124; and the concealed, 85–86, 95, 151, 158n64; as cultural critique, 3, 19, 30; as destabilizing, 17, 19, 23, 29, 41, 54, 63; feminine, 16–23, 115, 124–125, 142; national, 34–35, 86; and the repressed, 6, 16, 21, 26, 28, 119, 125–126; and the stranger/foreigner, 18, 56, 117, 173n19. *See also* automata; "buried alive"; cannibalism; castration; crocodile; death-in-life; déjà vu; dismemberment; doll; double; family, strange; Freud, Sigmund; guillotine; haunting; home; incest; mother; Oedipal conflict; religious ritual; "stranger within"; vagina dentata; womb/tomb
"Uncanny, The," 15–16, 26
unheimlich, 13–17, 19, 21, 27; aesthetics of, 41; in combat films, 45–49, 51–58, 59–64; home, 34, 59–62, 65; and the utopian yearning for change, 64. *See also* uncanny; unhomeliness; unhomey

unhomeliness, and national identity, 118–121, 130
unhomey: home, 3, 9, 14–18, 29, 134–136, 141; moment, 19–20
U.S. history, in film, 30, 32. *See also* combat films; *Lonestar;* national identity; *Nixon*

vagina dentata, as uncanny image, 25, 29
van Creveld, Martin, 110
Vertigo, 4, 6–8, 15, 17, 161n43
Vietnam War, 8, 11, 32, 39, 58, 72, 83–84, 87, 91, 97, 100, 103–106, 146, 170n30; as film genre, 33, 37, 57–58, 89; post-Vietnam War combat narrative, 44–45, 56, 92–93, 97–98, 103–106, 114, 154n11
violence, as gendered, 24–25
von Kleist, Heinrich, 26
von Trotta, Margarethe, 17

Wag the Dog, 115, 150, 171n44
Wahlberg, Mark, 115
Waldman, Diane, 18
Walker, Janet, 6, 120, 125
Walker, Mary Edward, 168n4
Wallace, Randall, 144
Walsh, Raoul, 29
war: and the maternal, 28–29, 55, 59–63; and the uncanny, 26–31, 46–50, 52–54, 64, 151. *See also* combat films; *Courage Under Fire;* Gulf War; *Midnight Clear, A; Saving Private Ryan; Thin Red Line, The;* Vietnam War; World War II
war film genre. *See* combat films; *Courage Under Fire;* Gulf War; *Midnight Clear, A; Saving Private Ryan; Thin Red Line, The;* Vietnam War; World War II
"war on terror," 35, 49, 147–151, 174n3
Washington, Denzel, 92, 107
Washington Post, 148, 150
Watergate, 33, 72, 92, 150, 166n50

Milton Keynes UK
Ingram Content Group UK Ltd.
UKHW030658220824
447225UK00001B/13